The Reformation

The Reformation

Its Roots and Its Legacy

Edited by
PIERRE BERTHOUD
& PIETER J. LALLEMAN

Foreword by Herman J. Selderhuis

☙PICKWICK *Publications* • Eugene, Oregon

THE REFORMATION
Its Roots and Its Legacy

Copyright © 2017 Wipf and Stock Publishers. All rights reserved. Except for brief quotations in critical publications or reviews, no part of this book may be reproduced in any manner without prior written permission from the publisher. Write: Permissions, Wipf and Stock Publishers, 199 W. 8th Ave., Suite 3, Eugene, OR 97401.

Pickwick Publications
An Imprint of Wipf and Stock Publishers
199 W. 8th Ave., Suite 3
Eugene, OR 97401

www.wipfandstock.com

PAPERBACK ISBN: 978-1-4982-3569-3
HARDCOVER ISBN: 978-1-4982-3571-6
EBOOK ISBN: 978-1-4982-3570-9

Cataloguing-in-Publication data:

Names: Berthoud, Pierre. | Lalleman, Pieter J. | Selderhuis, H. J. (Herman J.), 1961–, foreword writer

Title: The Reformation : its roots and its legacy / Pierre Berthoud and Pieter J. Lalleman.

Description: Eugene, OR: Pickwick Publications, 2017 | Includes bibliographical references.

Identifiers: ISBN 978-1-4982-3569-3 (paperback) | ISBN 978-1-4982-3571-6 (hardcover) | ISBN 978-1-4982-3570-9 (ebook)

Subjects: LCSH: Reformation | Theology—16th Century

Classification: BR305.3 B277 2017 (paperback) | BR305.3 (ebook)

Manufactured in the U.S.A.   09/06/17

Contents

Contributors | vii

Illustrations | ix

Foreword by Herman J. Selderhuis | xi

Introduction | xv
  —PIERRE BERTHOUD

1   The Reformation, Denominationalism, and the Unity of the Church: Why Is the Church So Divided? | 1
    —GERALD BRAY

2   Reformation and Education: Jan Amos Comenius's "Becoming Truly Human" and His Reformation of Human Affairs | 19
    —JAN HÁBL

3   The Artistic Legacy of the Reformation and Protestant Artists Today | 33
    —MARLEEN HENGELAAR-ROOKMAAKER

4   "With Psalms and Hymns": The Reformation, Music, and Liturgy | 55
    —WALTER HILBRANDS

5   The Reformation and Historical-Critical Research in Biblical Interpretation | 74
    —GERT KWAKKEL

6   Justification by Faith: Are Protestants and Catholics Irreconcilably Divided? | 88
    —A. N. S. (TONY) LANE

7   The Reformation and the Questions of Authority and Truth | 102
    —ANDREW T. B. MCGOWAN

8 Guilt, Shame, and Forgiveness: Crucial Questions of Life in the Perspective of Reformation Theology | 121
—Christoph Raedel

9 The Reformation and the Jews | 140
—Jean-Paul Rempp

10 The Reformation and the Challenge of Islam | 158
—Thomas Schirrmacher

11 *Theologia Crucis* and the Persecuted Church | 16
—Frank-Ole Thoresen

12 Freedom of Conscience, Reformation, and the Advent of Secularism | 191
—Paul Wells

Contributors

Pierre Berthoud is professor emeritus of Old Testament and Apologetics at the Faculté Jean Calvin, Aix-en-Provence, France, and chair of the Fellowship of European Evangelical Theologians.

Gerald Bray is research professor of Divinity at Beeson Divinity School, Samford University, Birmingham, Alabama, USA, and director of research for the Latimer Trust, London.

Jan Hábl is professor of Pedagogy at the universities of Ústí nad Labem and Hradec Králové, Czech Republic. He has taught Systematic Theology and Ethics at the Evangelical Theological Seminary in Prague.

Marleen Hengelaar-Rookmaaker is the editor-in-chief of ArtWay, www.artway.eu, an online service and resource about the visual arts. She worked as an editor, translator, and writer, and she edited the *Complete Works* of her father, the art historian Hans Rookmaaker. She lives in Zwolle, Netherlands.

Walter Hilbrands is dean and tutor of Old Testament at the Freie Theologische Hochschule in Gießen, Germany.

Gert Kwakkel is professor of Old Testament at the Theologische Universteit in Kampen, Netherlands, and at the Faculté Jean Calvin, Aix-en-Provence, France.

Pieter J. Lalleman is tutor in Biblical Studies at Spurgeon's College, London.

A. N. S. (Tony) Lane is professor of Historical Theology at the London School of Theology.

Contributors

Andrew McGowan is the minister of Inverness East Church and professor of Theology at the University of the Highlands & Islands, Scotland.

Christoph Raedel is professor of Systematic Theology at the Freie Theologische Hochschule in Gießen, Germany.

Jean-Paul Rempp is the pastor of *La Bonne Nouvelle* evangelical church in Lyon, the national representative of Christian Witness to Israel (CWI) in France, and the former European Coordinator of the Lausanne Committee for Jewish Evangelism.

Thomas Schirrmacher is the rector of the Martin Bucer Seminary and Research Institutes in Bonn, Germany, chair of the Theological Commission of the World Evangelical Alliance, and the director of the International Institute for Religious Freedom.

Herman J. Selderhuis is professor of church history at the Theological University of the Christian Reformed Churches in Apeldoorn, Netherlands, and the director of Refo500.

Frank-Ole Thoresen is the rector of the Fjellhaug International University College in Oslo.

Paul Wells is professor emeritus of Systematic Theology at the Faculté Jean Calvin, Aix-en-Provence, France, extraordinary professor at North-West University, South Africa, and editor in chief of *Unio cum Christo*.

Illustrations

In the book:

1. Rembrandt: *Annunciation*, c. 1635.
2. Caspar David Friedrich: *Firs in the Snow*, 1828.
3. Zak Benjamin: *Christ and Consumerism*, 1999.
4. Willem Zijlstra: *Agnus Dei*, 2005.

On the website http://www.paternosterperiodicals.co.uk/european-journal-of-theology/rookmaaker:

1. Lucas Cranach: *Christ and the Adulteress*, c. 1545–50.
2. Gillis van Coninxloo: *Elijah Fed by the Ravens*, end of sixteenth century.
3. Rembrandt: *Annunciation*, c. 1635.
4. Gerard Dou: *Portrait of a Reading Old Woman*, 1630.
5. Jan Davidsz. de Heem and N. van Veerendael: *Bouquet with Crucifix and Shell*, 1640s.
6. Jacob van Ruisdael: *View of Haarlem from the Dunes at Overveen*, c. 1670.
7. Eugène Burnand: *Peter and John Running to the Tomb*, 1898.
8. Caspar David Friedrich: *Firs in the Snow*, 1828.
9. Vincent van Gogh: *Starry Night*, 1889.
10. Marlene Dumas: *Jesus is Angry*, 1983.
11. Henk Helmantel: *Still Life with Red Onions and Garlic*, 2011.
12. Catherine Prescott: *Daphne Holding her Neck*, 2015.
13. Zak Benjamin: *Christ and Consumerism*, 1999.
14. Georg Meistermann: *Pentecost Window*, Marburg, 1963.
15. Willem Zijlstra: *Agnus Dei*, 2005.
16. Madeleine Dietz: *Cross*, 2003.
17. Liviu Mocan: *Invitation/Decalogue*, 2008–09.
18. Jake Lever: *Soul Boats*, 2015.

Foreword

It is not so hard to organize events around the commemoration of the 500th anniversary of the Reformation and yet it is surprising to see the multitude of exhibitions, tours, conferences, and books—to mention only some of the many kinds of events—that are already taking place or will take place in 2017, not only in Germany, not only in Europe, but literally worldwide. Many of these activities are of a purely historical nature in the sense that they tell or show the story of Martin Luther, the world in which he lived, and the changes he brought about. This is the 'not so hard' part of the commemoration, although it is impressive to see how innovative and attractive many of the exhibitions are.

It is much harder to organize events which deal with the relevance of Luther's action, for to describe or show what his rediscovery of the gospel of grace means for the church and the world now, and for the individual Christian as well as for the non-Christian living 500 years later, is quite a challenge. These efforts are certainly being undertaken and thus the question is raised as to what Luther has to say to present issues in theology, culture, politics, and social life. It is fascinating to see what answers come out of these efforts.

The papers in this volume are in fact not so much a commemoration of the Reformation, since the conference at which they were presented focused on the question what to do with the message of the Reformation in the era after 2017. Thus a very important and often forgotten aspect is highlighted, namely that what is commemorated in 2017 is not the Reformation as such, but the *beginning* of the Reformation. Luther's action was not a one-day event and the result was not a one-year program. It was the dynamics of his new theology that caused a radical change with global effects and it is this theology that has demonstrated to be so dynamic that it has kept inspiring, correcting, and guiding church, theology, and—mainly but not exclusively—protestant Christians. Reformation is not just an historical event but an ongoing movement of renewal and change. The message of the Reformation constantly challenges us to think through positions, actions, attitudes, and programs for anyone wishing to start from the same principles as Luther.

This last point is essential as there are also conferences and books that adopt a hermeneutical theory which changes Luther's message into a gospel of individual freedom and religious tolerance that hides the key ideas for which Luther stood, viz. the normativity of Scripture and the justification of the sinner through reconciliation. That is of course an option and this option does take into account that there are 500 years between the man from Wittenberg and us today, that the world in which he lived is fundamentally different from ours, and that his views on some issues are simply unacceptable and must be rejected.

This book presents us with experts who do take all of this into account and who are certainly aware of the limitations of Luther and of the fact that we cannot just ignore the fact that between 1517 and 2017 scientific discoveries and philosophical and theological developments occurred which have to be considered if Luther's relevance for today and tomorrow is to be demonstrated. All authors are aware of this and yet they deal with their various topics in the conviction that the essence of Luther's theology does not need to be adapted to make it relevant. It is up to the reader to decide if the authors have succeeded, but let every reader do so not only after reading, but also after having thought through all that is to be found here.

There is no doubt that what Luther did in 1517 was a courageous enterprise, for which in 2017 friends praise him and as even his foes recognize. But will today's friends of Luther also have the courage to appreciate that other friends of Luther are also courageous in challenging old and dear points of view? There certainly is quite some material in this book that goes against or—to put it more accurately—that goes beyond what the reformed tradition has always thought. Ideas on the unity of the church, on ecumenical relations, and on liturgy for example as they are presented here will cause discussion, and that is just what Luther wanted, as long as it was discussion based on the solid ground of Scripture and not on the weak ground of tradition.

And that is a lesson for reformed Christians. We can celebrate Luther, we can commemorate the Reformation, we can praise the man who is seen on nearly every statue with a Bible in the one hand and pointing to the Bible with the other hand, but reformed Christians must ask themselves if they do not do the opposite and value tradition nearly as much as Scripture—and sometimes maybe even more.

All of this means that the present book is not one of the "not so hard to do"-2017 activities. For this reason the book will survive when the celebrations of the 500th anniversary of Luther's action are over. These papers will keep taking us back to what Luther really stood for and wanted in order to decide what is the calling of reformed churches and reformed people for the next 500 years.

Herman J. Selderhuis
Professor of Church History,
Theological University of the Christian Reformed Churches,
Apeldoorn, Netherlands

Introduction

Pierre Berthoud

The present monograph contains the proceedings of the conference of the Fellowship of European Evangelical Theologians which took place in Wittenberg in August 2016. Since conferences of the Fellowship are biennial, it seemed appropriate to commemorate and celebrate early the 500th anniversary of the Reformation as it began with Martin Luther nailing his 95 theses on the doors of the Castle Church in Wittenberg in 1517. The aim of the conference was to study and reflect on aspects of the theological heritage and legacy of the Reformation. Themes such as the sovereignty of God's grace and justification by faith, the proclamation of the Word, and the unity of the church as well as the unique authority of Scripture and its cultural impact are cherished by evangelical Christians and theologians, but how do they relate to the Reformation and what relevance do they have for the contemporary world?

There is no golden age . . . at least in the present order of things, on this side of the return of Jesus Christ. Nevertheless, we should not despise the heritage which we have received. History and tradition are important. They help us understand where we come from and how previous generations have coped with the issues they met both in the church and in the civil society. Thus we can face the major private and public challenges that are before us in Europe at the beginning of the twenty-first century. In this introduction, I reflect briefly on the development of the Reformation in France, and how it can help us understand better where we come from and how it is possible to work within our European cultures towards the reformation and renaissance of the Christian Faith as we anticipate the return of Christ.

SOME HISTORICAL AND PHILOSOPHICAL MARKERS

France has a rich historical and cultural heritage that has contributed significantly to its national contemporary identity. It is heir to both the Greco-Roman and the Judeo-Christian legacies. Up until the sixteenth century, Christianity in its Roman Catholic version was dominant. But with the rise of humanism during late-medieval times, the Renaissance, and especially the Enlightenment, a struggle gradually arose between those who strove for the emancipation that autonomous reason was expected to offer to the individual and civil society and those who considered that only the church could contribute significantly to the salvation and peace of both. In other words, the modern era is characterized by recurring conflicts between two forms of authority, that of reason and that of the church. Historically and culturally speaking Protestantism, with its emphasis on Scripture as the ultimate norm, was caught between these two dominant currents in French society, between these two forms of authority, the authority of the Roman Catholic Church and the authority of autonomous reason which sought to emancipate itself from the religious and political dominance of the church.

In the sixteenth century, the Reformation had a significant impact on the French people. Historians suggest that a least ten percent (and probably more) of the population joined the Protestant movement. The Reformed faith had a significant impact on culture, society, and politics. If the Protestants had not lost the wars of religion, which should in fact be considered as civil wars, the face of France would be quite different. This is what a former French President, François Mitterrand, suggested in a speech in 1983 in La Rochelle, one of the sixteenth-century fortified Protestant cities of France. Speaking about the tragic siege of La Rochelle, instigated by king Louis XIII and cardinal Richelieu (1627–28), he said: "I think the history of France hesitated on that day. It was even somewhat broken."[1]

The Reformation in the sixteenth century changed the face of Europe and was one of the most significant spiritual, theological, and cultural renewals in the history of Christianity, which impacted church and society alike, so much so that it still has a hearing and significant influence in many parts of the world, such as South Korea, Indonesia, Brazil, and North America. The uniqueness of the Reformation, with its world and life view deeply rooted in the Word of God, is well illustrated by John Calvin. In the Introduction to his Commentary on the Psalms, Calvin gives an account of his conversion. As he rarely refers to himself in his writings, this account is important. He identifies his conversion with a radical change of mind

---

1. Mitterrand, "Allocution," lines 44–45.

involving a break with both the Roman Catholic mindset and superstitions and the humanist philosophy of the Renaissance.[2]

No doubt the Renaissance was a significant movement with its emphasis on the humanities and the rediscovery of the Greek and Roman heritage. With discernment, Calvin and the other reformers appreciated and integrated these achievements into their system of education. But philosophically it was the first major break from the existing Christian world and life view. We should not forget that Calvin's first publication was a commentary on Seneca's *De Clementia* (1532). This publication reveals that he was then a humanist in the tradition of Erasmus and that he had fully mastered his classics.

While he was breaking with these two major currents, the writings of Luther (and others) made the reformer of Geneva understand that the ultimate fountain of wisdom was in God and his Word, both written and incarnate, and in the living Christian tradition that remained faithful to the truth and beauty of this glorious heritage. We can understand why already during his lifetime Calvin was involved in a fierce spiritual warfare, underwent incessant criticism, and experienced strong opposition which continues through the centuries until today.

As Europe entered a new era, the modern era, the triune God was at work opening up new perspectives that would bring about changes in all spheres of life and culture. The Reformation and the revival it inspired spread like fire to the four corners of Europe and with time far beyond. The unique contribution of the main Reformation current in its early stages was its break with both the Roman Catholic system and the humanist Renaissance philosophy, without relinquishing the positive aspects of both. The Reformers shared fifteen centuries of history and Christian thought with the Roman Catholics and supported the renewed interest in the Greek and Roman heritage as well as the humanities. The Academy in Geneva taught—in addition to Hebrew—Classical Greek and Latin. Its students were well versed not only in the theology of the ecumenical councils, the Early Church Fathers and the Middle Ages, but also in the classics, which they studied from a Christian perspective.

In France the clear stand of the Reformers was maintained until about the middle of the eighteenth century,[3] although already during the previous century Cartesian rationalism had made significant inroads. The persecutions and the civil wars between Protestants and Catholics that lasted some thirty years represented a major disaster for the Kingdom of France as well

---

2. Calvin, *Commentaire*, v–xii.
3. *La Saine Doctrine*, iv–xii.

as for the Protestant churches. In spite of the Edict of Nantes (1598), the Protestants eventually experienced harassment, second rate citizenship, persecution, and exile. In fact, in this kingdom, an absolute state with emphasis on one faith, one law, and one king, there was no place for religious plurality and specifically for the descendants of the Reformation. Thus by the end of the seventeenth century, the Protestants had been all but eradicated. Such was the aim of the Edict of Fontainebleau, signed by Louis XIV in 1685, which revoked the Edict of Nantes. Numerous Huguenots left their homeland. As a consequence France was impoverished while many Protestant nations in Europe and beyond were enriched by the arrival of many well-trained and reliable migrants.

During that period humanism, with its emphasis on the autonomy of reason, was gaining ground. Thus the Classicism of the seventeenth century gave way to the Enlightenment of the eighteenth century. The aim of this movement, which was rooted in the Renaissance, was to emancipate itself from the tyranny of the absolute state and the all-embracing Roman Catholic Church. In a way, both Protestants and humanist philosophers were facing the same obstacles, resisting and fighting the same opponents. It is precisely at this moment in history that many Protestants made a fatal mistake with lasting effects. Not only were they cobelligerent with the humanists, but they actually became their allies. In other words, they thought they could adopt some tenets of humanism while upholding the Christian faith. Considering their plight, their struggle for survival and recognition, we can understand their move, but as a result the French heirs of the Reformation were tempted to practice a modern version of the syncretism that continually threatened both the people of Israel and the church since their very beginnings.

In fact, this alliance was the root, the beginning of the doctrinal, ethical, and spiritual confusion and decline we are witnessing in many historical churches, Christian universities and theological institutions today. To seek such a synthesis, such a compromise, is to seek to conform to the cultural climate of the age. Such a move is suicidal, for a God-centered world and life view and a human-centered philosophy are incompatible. Of course, there are points of contact and there are profound insights in human wisdom; the truth is welcome from wherever it comes. However, the basic outlook and presuppositions of Christianity and humanism cannot be brought together, just like water and oil cannot be mixed. When theologians and church leaders give in to this seduction, it is usually the Christian faith that is eroded. Having been emptied of its content and power, all that is left is a bright but superficial and ineffective varnish (2 Tim 3:4–5)!

Unfortunately, this tendency was confirmed during the following periods and right into the twenty-first century. It is illustrated by the decision of the United Protestant Church of France, which includes both Reformed and Lutheran communities, at its National Synod in May 2015, to allow same-gender couples who have been married civilly to receive the blessing of the local church. Pluralism in world and life views and doctrine sooner or later leads to pluralism in vital ethical issues. Truth matters, the unity and diversity of truth matters, for it is rooted in the very character and the revealed Word of the triune God. He is the ultimate authority before whom both reason and church councils are called to bow!

ADVANCED MODERNITY AND RADICAL ISLAM

In the last two years we in France have experienced some disastrous events: in 2015 Paris suffered two major series of terrorist attacks which killed 149 persons and wounded many more; in 2016 three more terrorist acts took place, causing the death of 88 people and the injury of many others. For all these attacks, ISIS claimed responsibility. These dramatic events have left the French population utterly shocked and stunned. The state of emergency declared by the president, François Hollande, contributed significantly to the disruption of various cultural and public events. One sensed within French society a degree of tension, hostility, and anger, as well as some friction and potential conflict between different factions of society.

It is interesting to note that all the places that were attacked had symbolic overtones as they represented significant aspects of French culture, life, and values: freedom of speech and conscience; a life-style involving human relations, leisure, and entertainment; the Jewish community; the law-enforcement institution; Independence Day; and Christianity embodied by the Roman Catholic Church. In this light it is difficult not to think in terms of a clash of cultural values. But are we equipped to respond to the transcendent religious challenge of radical Islam, when the mindset and action of the majority of our contemporaries are based on the horizontal world and life view which they inherited from the Enlightenment?

Whatever one's stance and outlook on these issues, such evil and disastrous events are an invitation to reflection. As Ecclesiastes says: "When times are good be happy, but when times are bad, consider" ("look," Eccl 7:14a). When times are evil, it is time to observe, to consider, to ponder, and to reflect on what is actually happening and on its meaning as well as on the dignity, the fragility, and wickedness of heart found in every human being. We are in the midst of a major cultural crisis related to the rapid secularization of France and the rest of Europe, not to mention the West, to the breakdown of modernity, and the unexpected challenge of the Islamic faith with its coherent political and religious world and life view. As Os Guinness says, "after the West has beaten back the totalitarian pretensions of both Hitler's would-be master race in Germany and Stalin's would-be master class in the Soviet Union, . . . it [the West] as a whole is in crisis, for the present moment has falsified the utopian Enlightenment hope that secular progressives placed in history."[4] Guinness understands the present moment of history as a time of transition toward a post-Christian world (West) qualified as "advanced modernity," which better captures the "entire spirit, systems, and structures of modernity viewed as the child of the forces of the industrial revolution and globalization."[5]

To be sure, the French are aware of the cultural crisis they are experiencing and the political challenge that the radical Islamic movements represent, but the political and intellectual elites are divided as to how to meet such a challenge. Before the tragic events took place the French government was far too lenient, but after the bloodshed of November 2015 it took a stronger political stand: military action against ISIS and crucial measures to combat the terrorists within France and to protect its population. It also emphasized the importance of both education and social care, especially in the neglected neighborhoods of large cities. But unfortunately these measures did not prevent the more recent terrorist acts near Paris, in Nice and St Etienne du Rouvray. The real problem lies in the fact that the French totally underestimate the impact that religions have on the mindset and the fabric of societies. In fact this is not surprising, for humanism—in considering religious faith, including Christianity, as unreal, as a mere speech event, and as fiction—neglects an important aspect of reality, the supernatural invisible world. Humanism is thus ill-equipped to handle the present crisis of modernity or to understand Islam and to respond to it appropriately.

The present cultural challenge has religious and spiritual dimensions. That is why it is of paramount importance for Christians to get involved in this spiritual warfare which includes the question of truth, of personal divine truth, and how it enlightens and bears on all aspects of life in society, but in a way that is significantly different from the Islamic faith. While Christianity maintains a clear distinction between church and state (cf. Luke 20:20–26), Islam does not. As the Lebanese Maronite patriarch, Bechara Raï, says, "Muslims don't separate Religion and State."[6]

---

4. Guinness, *Renaissance*, 18–19.

5. Ibid., 26.

6. Raï, *Entretiens*, 49, 65.

RENAISSANCE

The chancellor of Germany, Angela Merkel, showed that she understands this issue well when giving a lecture at the University of Bern, Switzerland, in September 2015. To a "middle-aged woman who rose from the audience to ask what the Chancellor intended to do to prevent the 'Islamization' process with so many Muslims entering the country," Merkel's response was most interesting. She rightly emphasized that "fear has never been a good advisor, neither in our personal lives nor in our societies." She went a step further by saying that "cultures and societies that are shaped by fear will without doubt not get a grip on the future." She also added, and this was both unexpected and amazing, that the answer really is in our "courage to be Christians, to be able to create dialogue (with Muslims), to return to church, and to read and study the Bible." Thus the arrival of many refugees in Europe and the debates this provokes are an opportunity "to reconsider our own roots." If we want to dialogue and speak of ourselves, this requires that we know and understand ourselves.[7]

The best answer to the challenge of "Islamization" is indeed the renaissance of the Christian faith both in France and in the rest of Europe, without which there will be no significant and lasting revival and reformation. While avoiding speculation about the future, Guinness does mention three factors that will shape the coming world:

- Globalization with its trends, interactions, and challenges the Christians cannot ignore.
- "Whether (or not) the worldwide Christian Church recovers its integrity and effectiveness and demonstrates a faith that can escape cultural captivity and prevail under the conditions of advanced modernity."[8]
- God is "sovereign over the course of history and the rise and fall of powers." This, of course, remains unknown to us, but we can be sure that the future "lies in God's good and strong hands,"[9] in his faithfulness, justice and love.

Because of these last two factors, Guinness is able to avoid the pitfalls of nostalgia and of despair, and to lay hold of a Christ-centered hope. He then goes on to specify the challenge Christians are to meet in the advanced modern world:

---

7. Merkel, "Courageous," lines 1–27.
8. Guinness, *Renaissance*, 25–26.
9. Ibid., 26–27.

It is, I believe, that we trust in God and his Gospel and move out confidently into the world, living and working for a new Christian renaissance, and thus challenge the darkness with the hope of the Christian faith, believing in an outcome that lies beyond the horizon of all we can see and accomplish today.[10]

G. K. Chesterton made a significant and witty point when he wrote: "At least five times the Faith has to all appearances gone to the dogs. In each of these five cases, it was the dog that died."[11] One can think of two of these instances: the Augustinian moment and the Reformation. With regards to the latter, Lucien Carrive, in a study on classic English Protestantism, shows us the way forward:

> The break that matters to us is not a break in the future and in the imagination, it is not the break between this world and the world to come; it is the break hic et nunc between sin and obedience. As of now, we must use all our gifts, be they of our body, mind, fortune, our social status, our spiritual gifts, such as they are. As of now, we must know how to recognize "the sight of a new and better world in this olde bad one."[12]

CONCLUSION

As we look to the future with hope, Ezekiel's image of the valley of dry bones comes to mind. The dry bones gradually come back to life: first they come together and then sinews, flesh, and skin come on them and cover them. But in order to stand up, they need the breath of life to come into them. It is by the prophetic word that these bones come back to life and stand up (37:4, 7, 10). The emphasis is on the unique intervention of the LORD who "brings up" his people from the grave, "puts his Spirit in them" and "brings them back to the land of Israel." Thus they will know and confess that he is indeed the living and faithful God (11–14). Our hope is in the truth and power of the Word of the living God, even Jesus Christ!

May this collection of essays contribute in a small but significant way to the renewal and renaissance, within our generation, of the Christian faith which sheds light on every aspect of reality and life, on thought, on culture, and on the city. Let us remember the exhortation of Paul, "I urge, then, first

---

10. Ibid., 28.

11. Chesterton, *The Everlasting Man*, 260–61, quoted by Guinness, *Renaissance*, 14.

12. Carrive, "Royaume de Dieu," 42. The last phrase of the quotation is in Old English. Translation mine.

of all, that requests, prayers, intercessions, and thanksgiving be made for everyone—for kings and all those in authority, that we may live peaceful and quiet lives in all godliness and holiness. This is good, and pleases God our Savior, who wants all people to be saved and to come to the knowledge of the truth." (1 Tim 2:1–4)

BIBLIOGRAPHY

Calvin, Jean. *Commentaire sur le livre des Psaumes*, Volume 1. Paris: Meyrueis, 1859.

Carrive, Lucien. «Le Royaume de Dieu, l'Apocalypse et le Millénium dans le Protestantisme anglais classique.» In *Age d'Or et Apocalypse*, edited by Robert Ellrodt and Bernard Brugère, 31–46. Paris: Publications de la Sorbonne, 1986.

Chesterton, Gilbert K. *The Everlasting Man*. Garden City: Image Books, 1955.

Guinness, Os. *Renaissance, the Power of the Gospel However Dark the Times*. Downers Grove: Inter-Varsity Press, 2014.

La Saine Doctrine tirée des écrits des plus célèbres Docteurs de l'Eglise réformée. Neuchâtel: Louis Fauché-Borel, 1804 (Bâle, 1769). [Editor's name not given.]

Merkel, Angela. "The threat of Islamization." Speech on September 3, 2015, at the University of Bern, Switzerland. Gatesofvienna.net/2015/. . ./angela-merkel-lectures-germans-about- [Accessed December 21, 2016].

Mitterrand, François. «Allocution à la Maison de la Culture de la Rochelle (Charente-Maritime), 4 novembre 1983.» http://discours.vie-publique.fr/notices/837192000.html [accessed December 21, 2016].

Raï, Patriarche Bechara. *Entretiens avec Isabelle Dillmann*. Au coeur du chaos, La résistance d'un Chrétien en Orient. Paris: Albin Michel, 2016.

1

The Reformation, Denominationalism, and the Unity of the Church

Why is the Church so Divided?

GERALD BRAY

ONE MOVEMENT OR MANY?

It is now customary to date the beginning of the Protestant Reformation to 31 October 1517, the day on which Martin Luther nailed his Ninety-five Theses to the church door in Wittenberg, thereby challenging the authority of the pope and the legitimacy of his claim to exercise jurisdiction over souls in purgatory by the grant of indulgences. What effect Luther's action actually had is the stuff of legend, but it is safe to say that virtually all Protestants look back to it as the dramatic gesture that signaled the birth of a new and distinct form of Christianity. There is no doubt that Luther ignited a fire that spread across Europe and could not be put out, but he was not the first person to attack the power of the pope over the church. Protest movements against the papacy and its claims had been in the air for a long time and had nothing to do with Luther or with his theological agenda. In England, John Wycliffe (1328–84) and his followers, known as Lollards, had stirred up revolt in the late fourteenth century, promoting the doctrine of

Scripture alone as the source of doctrinal authority, and objecting to the idea of transubstantiation in the Eucharist.[1] Jan Hus (1370?–1415) and the so-called Utraquists in Bohemia had also objected to what was then the relatively new practice of communion in one kind only, rightly claiming that it had no scriptural justification. Wycliffe and Hus were not connected to each other, but their followers made common cause and created a kind of proto-Protestantism a century before Luther's Reformation. Earlier still, Peter Waldo (1140?–1205?) had done something similar and attracted followers in Provence (France) and parts of northern Italy. In spite of persecution, they had managed to survive in the Alpine valleys, and their descendants still worship there today. None of these "reform" movements was successful to the degree that the Lutherans would later be, but they all left their mark and remnants of them were still active in the sixteenth century. When Luther's protest against Rome got going, they mostly identified with it, even though their origins were quite different. The Lollards, who by then were few in number and lacking any organization of their own, merged without trace into the reformed Church of England. The Waldensians survived as an independent church, though they eventually aligned themselves theologically with Calvin and the Reformed tradition, while the Czech Brethren remained a distinct group that has maintained its separate existence to the present time.

At almost exactly the same time as Luther made his initial protest against what he saw as an overbearing papacy, Huldrych Zwingli did much the same thing in Zürich. Whether Luther inspired Zwingli to speak out is debated, but even if he did, the Swiss protest took a different form from its north German counterpart.[2] Zwingli focused his attention on the sacraments, which he believed had been corrupted by a false theology, and he developed an understanding of them that was alien to Luther's mind. Luther's primary concern was justification by faith alone, which he regarded as the foundation of a true church. When asked to rethink the so-called "real presence" of Christ in the Eucharist, he was willing to reject the Roman doctrine of transubstantiation, which in any case had been a medieval concoction, but he would not adopt the subjective, "receptionist" position advocated by the Zwinglians. Whatever happened in the consecration of the elements of bread and wine, Luther was convinced that Christ was objectively present in the Lord's Supper, and he regarded Zwingli's position on

---

1. The popular view that Wycliffe was the "morning star" of the Reformation has been contested in recent years and modern scholars generally emphasize how *unlike* Luther and his contemporaries he really was. See for example Rex, *Lollards*; Evans, *Wyclif*; Lahey, *Wyclif*.

2. See Gäbler, *Huldrych Zwingli*; Stephens, *Zwingli*.

this point as deeply unsatisfactory. Their contrasting personalities and different doctrinal concerns also played a role in preventing them from making common cause, but as the joint statement from the Colloquy of Marburg (1529) testifies, they were not as far apart as modern observers like to think. There was still a reasonable hope that, with the right amount of discussion and reflection, a solution could be found that would permit them to unite with one another. But before that possibility could be properly explored, the emperor demanded that Luther and his followers should compose a confession of faith, which was then ratified at the Diet of Augsburg in 1530. This confession ignored the Zwinglians and defined what would henceforth be known as Protestantism according to Luther's theological criteria. For the next hundred years and more, a Protestant would be someone who adhered to the Augsburg Confession, and anyone who did not accept it would not be recognized as belonging to what had become an alternative church. Later controversies would reveal differences of detail between the Reformers of Zürich and those of Geneva, which were eventually patched up, and there would be a schism among the followers of Luther as well, with some of them inclining more towards the Swiss and others leaning in the opposite direction. By the 1560s the Swiss of both Zürich and Geneva, along with Germans who were sympathetic to them, united under one broadly Reformed label, while the bulk of Luther's followers declared themselves to be the "genuine" Lutherans, claiming the title by which we know their descendants today.[3]

But even before the Augsburg Confession was written, some of Zwingli's followers were pushing the logic of his principles further than he himself was willing or able to go, and they renounced the practice of infant baptism. The Anabaptists, as these people were called, inspired similar movements elsewhere, and before long there were several groups that were loosely included under the Anabaptist label, though their connections with one another were few or non-existent. Some of these radicals revolted against the civil authorities, on whom both Luther and Zwingli depended for support, provoking serious unrest. Soon they were being persecuted by secular rulers, often with the consent of the mainline Reformers, and in the end only remnants of their movements survived. In some cases these survivors joined together with others of like mind, but others rejected any form of compromise and went their separate ways, creating a number of small sects that all wore the Anabaptist label.[4]

Of course, neither Luther nor Zwingli had any desire to split the church and both men initially hoped that their protest would lead to a

---

3. For a good overview, see Arand, Kolb, and Nestingen, *Lutheran Confessions*.
4. See Lumpkin and Leonard, *Baptist Confessions*.

general reformation of Western Christendom. They might have accepted the papacy in some kind of figurehead role if the popes had been prepared to support their theological positions, but they wanted a much more conciliar and decentralized approach to church government than the one they knew. Unfortunately neither Rome nor the Holy Roman emperor, whose co-operation would have been needed if any long-term solution was to be found, was willing to accede to the Reformers' demands, even in principle. As time went on, the papacy recovered from the initial shock of Luther's revolt and did what it could to restore the unity of the church by overcoming it as best it could. On the theological and diplomatic front the pope summoned what was to become the great reform Council of Trent (1545–63), and initially the Protestants were invited to attend. When they refused, the secular authorities resorted to force of arms, which was more successful in crushing their resistance that many people now realize. Eventually a truce was agreed and the German rulers were allowed to determine whether their states would be Protestant (in the Lutheran sense) or Catholic (*cuius regio, eius religio*). This was a political decision, not a theological one, and subjects who dissented from their rulers' verdict were expected to move to a more congenial jurisdiction, thereby aligning church divisions even more closely to the pattern of secular government.[5]

This solution was unstable because it ignored the growing difference between Lutherans and the so-called "Reformed," who either had to sign the Augsburg Confession or be excluded from the settlement. Despite some initial prevarication, most of them held their ground and as time went on their numbers increased, with the result that it was not always possible for the secular authorities to enforce a strictly Lutheran interpretation of Protestantism in their territories. It would not be until 1648 that the Reformed would achieve formal recognition, both in the United Provinces of the Netherlands and the Swiss Confederation, which were then effectively detached from the Holy Roman Empire, and also in a number of German states that remained under a revamped imperial jurisdiction which acknowledged their distinct identity for the first time. By then, of course, animosity between the two (or if we include the Anabaptists, three) main branches of Protestantism was almost as great as that between the Protestants and the Roman Catholics, making any form of pan-Protestant unity seem more utopian than ever.[6]

---

5. See Olin, *Catholic Reform*. On the political aspect, the best recent study is Whaley, *Germany*; the Reformation and the religious settlement are covered in vol. 1: *Maximilian I to the Peace of Westphalia, 1493–1648*.

6. See Busch et al., *Reformierte Bekenntnisschriften*; Dennison, *Reformed Confessions*. For the historical narrative, see Benedict, *Christ's Churches*.

Politics versus Theology

It might be thought that the danger of persecution from Rome would drive the different Protestant groups together, and to some extent it did, but that outside pressure was never enough to counteract the internal forces that were pulling them in the opposite direction. One factor that must be borne in mind was largely cultural in origin. In its earliest phase the Reformation was almost entirely a "German" affair. Despite their theological differences, Luther and Zwingli spoke the same language and the Zwinglians generally adopted Luther's German Bible without protest. The Czech Brethren, however, were Slavs, and anti-German feeling had played a part in the Hussite movement from the beginning. On the western side of the Holy Roman Empire, Geneva and Lausanne were French-speaking, and the Netherlands was a world of its own, a collection of seventeen autonomous provinces that spoke a Low German dialect sufficiently different from Luther's High German to constitute a different language with its own translation of the Scriptures. As the Bible was translated into the vernaculars of Europe and church services were conducted in the local languages rather than in Latin, differences of this kind played an important role in the construction of what became independent national churches that had little desire to submerge their newly formed identities into a wider, international whole.

The Holy Roman Empire was also very loosely structured and ill-equipped to promote church unity of any kind. There were a large number of semi-independent principalities, free cities and other territories, some of which had been under the direct rule of the Roman church. Their autonomy had long been considerable, and the Reformation was used by many local rulers to increase it still further. Church unity beyond their frontiers was not in their interest, and one of the ways their political independence could be enhanced was by recognizing a form of Protestantism that was not like that found in surrounding regions. In addition to this, many of the principalities stayed loyal to Rome, creating blocks of loyal Catholics that hindered the consolidation of Protestant territories and made Germany resemble a patchwork quilt in religious terms. This arrangement should not be confused with denominational pluralism, however. Within any given jurisdiction there was only one recognized church, to which everyone was expected to belong. As time went on the system became unwieldy because some rulers converted from Protestantism to Catholicism or from Lutheranism to the Reformed faith, but they found it impossible to take their people with them. Occasionally they inherited or conquered territories of another confession, which they could not fully incorporate into their existing domains.

But for all the awkwardness that these anomalies created, the system itself endured into the nineteenth century, and traces of it can still be seen today.

The rift between Lutherans and Reformed in the Protestant world went deep and proved to be enduring. Even when the rising tide of secularism that accompanied the French Revolution persuaded the king of Prussia that the time had come to unite the Lutheran and Reformed confessions in a single church, resistance to this among the more conservative Lutherans was such that many of them emigrated to America rather than conform. Today their descendants make up the Lutheran Church Missouri Synod, as well as the small and even more conservative Wisconsin Synod, perpetuating a division among more "open" and "closed" Lutherans that persists to this day.[7]

Regions

The Reformed churches meanwhile tended to coalesce around the teaching of John Calvin (1509–64) but differences of opinion about what that actually meant soon produced divisions of a different kind. These were especially noticeable in the Netherlands, where a conflict arose between those who saw themselves as strict Calvinists and the so-called Remonstrants. The latter claimed to be the followers of the Dutch theologian Jacob Arminius (1560–1609) and promoted what their opponents saw as a semi-Pelagian form of salvation by freewill, if not exactly by works. The conflict was only partially resolved at the Synod of Dort (1618–19) in favor of the stricter Calvinists. The Reformed churches split along these lines, but although the Arminians were much the smaller and weaker group, the decentralized, tolerant atmosphere of the Netherlands made it difficult for the victorious Calvinists to impose any kind of unity, let alone uniformity, by suppressing them or others who dissented from the official church's theological position. Instead, the Low Countries became a relative haven of religious toleration and religious dissidents of all kinds flocked there. The United Provinces of the (northern) Netherlands thus became the most religiously tolerant and diverse state in Europe, a status that made it unique at that time but that was to be the harbinger of things to come elsewhere.[8]

In other countries, Protestantism was much less varied. The kingdom of Denmark, which at that time included Norway and Iceland, became solidly Lutheran, as did Sweden and its Baltic possessions—Finland, Estonia and Latvia. On the whole these countries have remained that way ever since,

---

7. See Clark, *Iron Kingdom*.
8. The best account is Israel, *Dutch Republic*.

though the two kingdoms were not in full communion with one another, and Sweden in particular has seen the growth of independent churches that were born out of periodic revivals. But it is fair to say that in the other Nordic countries, non-Lutheran forms of Protestantism have remained marginal at best.[9]

French Protestants, by contrast, became solidly Reformed in the Calvinist mode, and remained so until 1685, when they were forcibly suppressed or expelled from the country. The modern French Protestant churches have relatively little in common with the Reformed church of the sixteenth century, but the Calvinist influence is still noticeable in them, despite the presence of a considerable body of Lutherans (almost all from formerly German Alsace) and Evangelical groups, who often owe their existence to foreign missionary work in more recent times.[10]

In eastern Europe, the configuration of the Protestant churches reflects both the decisions taken by local rulers in the sixteenth and seventeenth centuries, and the policies of later times, which either promoted or hindered religious toleration in specific areas. Because of this, Transylvania (now in Romania but before 1918 in Hungary) has a degree of religious pluralism similar to that of the Netherlands, whereas Lutherans are the main Protestant body in Slovakia and Poland, and the Reformed church is dominant among Protestants in Hungary. Other Protestant groups exist in those places but, as in France, they are mostly the products of more recent missionary activity and are marginal in wider society.[11]

England

The denominational pluralism that now exists in parts of continental Europe is largely the work of missionaries who have gone there from the English-speaking world. Indeed, denominationalism can be regarded as an Anglo-Saxon export, and owes its unique character to the particular history of the British Isles in the sixteenth and seventeenth centuries.[12] The Reformation in Great Britain and Ireland was different from its counterparts in Germany, the Netherlands, and France, in that it was begun and continued as an act of state, not as a popular movement. When king Henry VIII of England broke with the papacy in 1534 it was over his desire to

9. See Derry, *History of Scandinavia*.

10. The best recent study is Cabanel, *Histoire des protestants*.

11. There is no general study that covers the whole of eastern Europe, but see Jobert, *De Luther à Mohila*; and the relevant chapters in Prestwich, *International Calvinism*.

12. The best overview is Heal, *Reformation in Britain*. See also Bray, *Documents*.

annul his marriage for purely dynastic reasons—he wanted a son to succeed him and his queen was unable to provide one. In the circumstances of the time, Henry had to reject the authority of the pope, who would not annul his marriage, and his power was such that he was able to take his kingdom with him. England thus became a Protestant country, but one that had no Protestants in it! That anomaly was eventually put right, but not without a considerable amount of compromise, back-pedaling, and confusion. At one level, the institutional and judicial structures of the Church of England hardly changed at all. Its doctrine evolved along Protestant lines, but the Anglican church always tried to keep confessional statements to a minimum in order to make it possible for the greatest number of Christians, including the so-called "papists," to come to terms with it, and no Englishman ever signed the Augsburg Confession. Its worship was fixed in a liturgy that was imposed on everyone, whether they liked it or not, and reflected this desire to compromise—it was, in effect, Protestant doctrine in Catholic dress, and so it has remained ever since.[13]

In some ways, this compromise English Reformation was a great success. At a time when France and later Germany were wracked by religious warfare, England was an oasis of calm where the entire nation was united behind a single form of worship—or so it appeared. Those who did not like this state of affairs could protest in Parliament (if they were Protestants) or plot to restore a Catholic sovereign (if they were "papists"), but for the most part both extremes were generally quiescent and serious opposition to the establishment was kept at bay.[14] The English inclined more to the Reformed churches of Europe than to the Lutheran ones, but they did their best to avoid entanglements that might commit them to intervene in continental affairs that were of no real interest to them. Queen Elizabeth I managed to provoke a reformation in Scotland, which took on a more consistently Reformed flavor than it had in England, but at the time nobody seemed to mind this very much.[15] Protestants in England knew that when the queen died she would probably be succeeded by James VI, the Calvinist king of Scotland, and many of them hoped that he would then introduce a Scottish style of reformation in the southern kingdom.

In this expectation they were to be disappointed. When James VI ascended the English throne as James I in 1603, he made some gestures towards the more ardent reformers in England, of which the most notable

13. Of the many studies of this subject, perhaps the fairest, and certainly one of the most readable, is Neill, *Anglicanism*.

14. See Collinson, *Elizabethan Puritan Movement*.

15. See Dawson, *John Knox*, for an interesting appraisal of English influence on the Scottish reformation.

was his acquiescence in authorizing a new translation of the Bible, but on the whole he perpetuated the compromise settlement of his predecessors, despite the fact that this had come under increasing pressure in the closing years of Elizabeth's reign.[16] Gradually, those who wanted a more thoroughgoing Reformed church were alienated from the state. Some of them left the country altogether, whereas others refused to conform to the sometimes petty rules laid down in the official Prayer Book. By the time James died in 1625, there were even new colonies in North America that proclaimed religious freedom, by which they meant the freedom to impose their own system of church government and worship independent of the established Church of England.[17]

The reign of Charles I (1625–49) saw the pressures and tendencies that were bubbling under the surface of English Protestantism finally come to a head. Charles lacked the diplomatic touch of his father and was unable to contain the growing desire for change among the more ardent Protestants. His attempts to impose a conservative order on the Church eventually led to civil war and the victory of his enemies, who in reaction to his dictatorial tendencies, somewhat rashly declared freedom of religion for all. Unfortunately, that led to chaos because the different groups that emerged could not agree on a common form of church order that would hold things together and in the end, the old régime was brought back. In 1662, those who could not accept the rule of bishops (appointed by the king) were forced to leave the established church and set up independent congregations of their own or else migrate to America.[18] After a further generation of attempted repression, a Dutch-style form of toleration was introduced by a Dutch king, William III of Orange (1689–1702). Protestant dissenters from the state church were allowed to register themselves as corporate bodies, and what we now call "denominationalism" was enshrined in the law of the land.[19] There have been changes to this original settlement, in that the English Presbyterians mostly became Unitarians in the early eighteenth century, and the subsequent Evangelical revival produced the Methodists under the reluctant leadership of John and Charles Wesley, neither of whom ever left the established church and did not want their followers to do so, but the basic pattern remained. To this day, England is a country that has an established Anglican church and a number of non-conformist Protestants, who are usually

16. On James's wider ecumenical interests, see Patterson, *King James*.
17. There is no really comprehensive study of this period, but see Milton, *Catholic and Reformed*.
18. See Spurr, *Restoration Church*.
19. See Claydon, *William III*.

lumped together in the popular mind as the "free churches." Scotland has an established Presbyterian church with a number of free churches alongside it, but many of them are also Presbyterian—the result of internal political divisions rather than of different theological beliefs. Ireland has remained largely Catholic, but its Protestants are divided more or less equally into Anglicans, with a special connection to England, and Presbyterians, who are mostly of Scottish descent. Other denominations also exist, but they are small and relatively less important than they are in England or Scotland.

The United States

Almost from the beginning, British overseas expansion provided an outlet for religious dissenters, who often became extremely influential, especially in North America. When the United States was formed, the country was too diverse for a state church to be established, and the prevailing intellectual mood at that time was secular. The result was a formal separation of church and state, the first of its kind in the traditionally Christian world, which gave different religious bodies the freedom to develop independently and to compete in what was effectively an open market in religion. Thus it is that the United States is the true and lasting home of denominationalism, where Protestant pluralism is accepted as the social norm in a way that has never really been the case in Europe.

DENOMINATIONAL CHURCH UNITY

The religious freedom that produced this denominationalism has worked as well as it has at least partly because the divisions it caused have never been primarily theological in nature. Of course, most of the different denominations have their own confessions of faith, but these have seldom been a barrier to mutual co-operation and lay people, in particular, have gone from one denomination to another with relative ease. Interdenominational societies, and even missionary organizations, are common and they encourage their members to attend the church of their choice, making it clear that as far as they are concerned, denominational differences are secondary. This claim is plausible because so many of those differences originated in political struggles that have now passed into history, and only a few dedicated historians are aware of them or think that they matter very much. More often than not, denominations are defined by the system of church government they have adopted, and (to a lesser extent) by their pattern of worship.

This is clear from their names—Episcopal, Presbyterian, Congregationalist, even Methodist, and Baptist.

The Baptists stand out from the rest because of their rejection of infant baptism, but although this sometimes causes difficulties in individual cases, it is not often a barrier to interdenominational co-operation. The many other "denominations" that exist are mostly either subsets of these main ones (that is to say, there are different kinds of Episcopalians, Presbyterians, and Methodists) or offshoots from one or more of them that have become distinct over time, like the Pentecostals. There are also imported denominations like the Dutch Reformed or the Scandinavian Lutherans, who reflect inherited national differences and seek to preserve them as part of their heritage. In more recent times, liberal and conservative theological tendencies have emerged that cross traditional denominational lines, often producing new splits—and thus new denominations. This variety can appear bewildering to outsiders, and of course, it is frequently held up by Roman Catholics as evidence that Protestantism cannot be true. In recent years, many American Protestants, and especially Evangelicals, have been persuaded by this argument and have converted either to Rome or to one of the Eastern Orthodox Churches, a development that puzzles Protestants in other countries and is almost unthinkable for those who are minorities in traditionally Catholic or Orthodox countries. It is probably not too much to say that such conversions are possible because the traditionally non-Reformed churches have themselves taken on the character of "denominations" in the American context, and market themselves to others just as the Baptists or Presbyterians do. What can we say about this? Have these converts found the one true church and exposed their former Protestantism as an inadequate expression of Christianity?

Doctrine of the Church

To answer these questions, we must first understand what has happened to the doctrine of the church in the Protestant world. To do this, we must recognize that at its heart, the Protestant Reformation was a dispute about the nature of the work of the Holy Spirit. In traditional Catholic thinking, the Holy Spirit acted primarily through outward signs, of which the sacraments were by far the most important. In the Catholic world, a baptized person was considered to be a Christian by virtue of that fact. In the Eucharist, communicants received the real body and blood of Christ, transubstantiated by the consecration of an ordained priest, who had been given—by virtue of the hands laid upon him—the power to perform what was known as "the miracle of the altar." To be cut off from the sacraments was to be excluded from the fellowship of grace, because outside the church there was no salvation. Religious experience was not ignored or disparaged but it was channeled into religious orders and controlled, in so far as it could be, by the traditions that had been enshrined in canon law. Outbreaks of enthusiasm were either suppressed or else converted into new forms of the religious life—hence the emergence of the different monastic orders, and later on, of the friars. In the fifteenth century the church was even able to absorb the growing desire for what we might now call "family spirituality" by tolerating the so-called "new devotion," a kind of communal organization in which married couples and their children lived together under a rule of spiritual discipline adapted to their needs and circumstances.[20]

Protestantism overturned all this by proclaiming a different understanding of the work of the Holy Spirit. For Protestants, a true Christian was not someone who was baptized in the authorized way, but someone who had a personal experience of Christ in their heart and life. The true church was not the social institution that embraced the whole of society, whether its members were believers or not, but a gathering of the elect who were born again by the Spirit of God. In most European countries, the structure and worship of Protestant churches were reformed in ways that reflected those beliefs to a greater or lesser degree. It was the failure of the English Church to follow through on these principles that produced the Puritan movement, whose adherents wanted a "pure" spiritual Christianity to supplant the visible imposition of religious uniformity by the state. The Puritans were relatively unconcerned with the visible structures of the church, as long as it could discipline its members effectively, something which the Church of England appeared to be incapable of doing. Church government became a matter of great importance to the Puritans, because they wanted an effective form of spiritual discipline and argued among themselves as to the best way of achieving this.[21] Their failure to agree on this led to the divisions which created modern denominationalism, but because they were not doctrinally motivated, the different bodies which emerged from this controversy remained open to one another in a way that was not true between them and the Roman Catholics.

---

20. For this movement and its ambiguous relationship to later Protestantism, see Post, *Modern Devotion*.

21. See Murray, *Reformation of the Church*.

"Higher Unity"

It is true that at the time of the Reformation, not all Protestant churches were prepared to accept the primacy of the invisible over the visible church, and barriers to inter-communion often remained. In some cases, they are still there, especially among conservative Lutherans. But on the whole, successive Evangelical revivals and the experience of working together in missionary and other situations have created a willingness to set aside inter-Protestant differences in the interest of a higher unity in the Gospel. This does not normally involve institutional merger, which often takes place only when particular denominations are dying or in serious danger from hostile forces around them. In countries where Christians have suffered persecution, denominations have often come together to help one another and their differences have been set aside, but whether that form of co-operation can survive the end of persecution and the restoration of "normality" is hard to say—it may well be that the old divisions will resurface once the danger has passed. But even if that happens, the experience of working together under duress will not be quickly forgotten, and it is probably not an exaggeration to say that denominational differences will remain a matter that concerns the clergy far more than the lay members of the respective churches. The spiritual unity of the church is often very real at the grassroots level, even if the institutional framework in which that might (or ought to) be expressed is weak or lacking.

At the same time, this spiritual unity often cuts across denominational lines and divides those who otherwise belong to the same church. In the more established, mixed Protestant churches that trace their origins back to the sixteenth century, it has long been known that many of their members find it easier to have fellowship with people from other denominations who share their spiritual outlook than with those who wear the same confessional label but whose actual beliefs are very different. Thus we find that "liberal" Methodists, Presbyterians, Baptists, Lutherans, and Anglicans (Episcopalians) will unite in a body like the World Council of Churches and get along quite well with one another, devising common lectionaries and forms of worship that they can share. It is not unusual today for a Methodist to go to a Presbyterian or Lutheran church and find that the service is virtually identical to the one he or she is used to, including the Scripture readings set for that particular day. Parallelism of this kind creates a form of unity that respects institutional differences but does what it can to transcend them at the practical level, even if the average worshipper is scarcely aware of this.

At the other end of the theological spectrum, conservative Evangelicals from different denominations can easily come together and often do, because their beliefs are clear and their informal style of worship is more flexible than that of the established denominations. In these circles, great attention may be paid to the theological soundness of the preaching and teaching, including the accuracy of the translation of the Bible being used, but nobody would think to ask what the denominational origin of those taking part might be, and traditional denominational "distinctives" are unlikely to be emphasized, even in congregations that officially belong to one. Sacramental practices might continue to differ to some extent, but as the sacraments are not central to the worshipping life of most conservative Evangelical churches, this is unlikely to cause much of a problem most of the time. Apart from occasional friction over whether a person baptized in infancy ought to be baptized again after conversion and the occasional practice of "closed" communion by conservative Lutherans, such differences are usually not allowed to interfere with the spirit of fellowship in the congregation as a whole.

What is true of individual churches is even more true of seminaries, conferences, and other interdenominational and parachurch activities. Some denominations continue to maintain their own patterns of training and to insist that their clergy be subjected to them, but this is not always the case and even in a denominational seminary it would be unthinkable for the program of study to include nothing except what its members have written and approved. Academic theology is now completely interdenominational and anything else would seem bizarre and unacceptable to practically everybody. Much the same is true of conferences and evangelistic campaigns. Some people will be inclined to opt out of them for theological reasons, perhaps, but they are few in number and unrepresentative of conservative Evangelicals generally. For the most part, people are prepared to subordinate their particular preferences to the wider whole and object only if a theological principle is at stake. Even then, there is a hierarchy of theological differences, some of which are more tolerable than others. Arguments about the nature and extent of election, for example, or about the real presence of Christ in the Eucharist, may attract some controversy among theological specialists, but most people are liable to see such things as a distraction from the main point and avoid them accordingly. This does not mean that these people are theologically indifferent, however. They would not show the same tolerance to those who deny penal substitutionary atonement, for example, because that is central to the Gospel. On a subject like that there can be no compromise among Evangelicals, although it should be said that "liberals," even those in the same denomination as Evangelicals, often find it an abhorrent doctrine and regard it as a barrier to church unity rather than as central to it.

Here we have a classic example of a divide that cuts across denominations and is far more important today than anything that caused those divisions centuries ago. Baptists, for example, are unlikely to regard their sacramental practice as more fundamental than their doctrine of the atonement, and the conservative Evangelicals among them will certainly not do so, even if they continue to insist that their own church members must submit to their form of baptism. A similar approach is usually the norm on other Protestant churches as well—fellowship in the Gospel is wider than membership of a particular church, where traditional denominational criteria may still be regarded as important.

EVALUATION

It would be foolish to pretend that this kind of Protestant unity is perfect, but it should not be dismissed out of hand in the way that many Catholics and Orthodox are inclined to do. It is an attempt to overcome divisions that often have deep political and cultural causes as well as theological ones which will not easily be overcome. Denominationalism recognizes that human beings are sinful and that the schisms in the church reflect that sad reality. Some people are temperamentally divisive and will never accept any form of unity with those with whom they disagree, even on minor points of detail. Others are set in their ways and find it difficult to budge from what they are accustomed to. Still others are wary of large organizations and think that it is better to take decisions at the local level, making institutional connections with other congregations problematic, if not impossible. The weight of history lies heavily upon us, and those who have tried to achieve visible unity in the form of denominational mergers have seldom been successful. All too often, when two denominations get together they end up creating a third, because remnants of their previous church bodies refuse to join in the union. Denominationalism is not ideal, but in the present context it is often able to accommodate differences of opinion on matters of secondary importance without preventing wider co-operation on the main question of preaching the Gospel. This does not mean that there is no room for improvement—there clearly is. But it should make us wary of condemning superficial divisions when it is clear that beneath them there is a spiritual unity that for most people, most of the time, is far more important.

Those who hanker after visible, institutional union need to consider the situation of those churches that have achieved it and ask themselves what the result has been. Both the Roman Catholic and the Eastern Orthodox churches appear to be united, at least at the visible, institutional level, but the cost of this must be weighed very carefully by those who are impressed by what they see on the outside. For one thing, both of these great communions contain large numbers of nominal members who inflate the membership statistics but who cannot be regarded as true believers. They belong to their church for family, cultural, or political reasons rather than because they have a living faith of their own. Catholics and Orthodox who have a real faith are often exasperated by this large fringe membership, which they regard as a hindrance to the church's true witness.

Secondly, history has also shown that when revival movements break out in such churches, they are often persecuted by the authorities and find it very difficult to establish themselves. In that respect, Francis of Assisi and Martin Luther had more in common than we might think. Rome eventually came to terms with the former, and the Franciscans were absorbed into the structures of the church, but it failed with the latter. Yet as anyone involved in a renewal movement within the Catholic Church today will know, the difference between these two cases is more apparent than real, and the end result may have been more influenced by political and other non-theological factors than by any sort of faith commitment. Within the Protestant world, on the other hand, spiritual renewal movements can either find a place within an existing denomination or, if that proves to be impossible, they can leave it and start one of their own. They may not be popular for doing so, but in most cases they will not be formally condemned or excommunicated by the body they are leaving, as happens with the Catholics and the Orthodox as a matter of course. Their way of proceeding is not only different from that of most Protestants, but it may easily be worse, especially in places where the institutional church is in a position to penalize those who dissent from it.

CONCLUSION

The church is a spiritual body of believers, called into being by the work of the Holy Spirit. The visible form which that work takes will be imperfect, because that is the nature of the world in which we live. No institutional church is exactly what God wants it to be, and human sinfulness ensures that such an ideal will never be attained in this life. As Christians we must strive for unity with one another and do what we can to prevent differences of opinion from provoking unnecessary divisions. We must also be ready to co-operate with our fellow believers, even if that means setting secondary questions aside for the sake of the Gospel. Above all, we cannot remain indifferent to the corruptions we see in the visible churches, and we must do all that we can to remove them. But try as we must to achieve this, we also have to remember that perfection will elude our grasp. Outward rites and institutions, however good and useful they may be for the life of the church, are not the heart of the matter. The church lives in the presence and power of the Holy Spirit, and if he departs from it, then all the outward forms of visible unity count for nothing and we shall be left with no more than the outward shell of an institution that has lost the reason for its being.

BIBLIOGRAPHY

Arand, Charles P., R. Kolb, and J. A. Nestingen, eds. *The Lutheran Confessions: History and Theology of the Book of Concord*. Minneapolis: Fortress, 2012.

Benedict, Philip. *Christ's Churches Purely Reformed*. New Haven: Yale University Press, 2002.

Bray, Gerald L, ed. *Documents of the English Reformation*. 2nd ed. Cambridge: Clarke, 2004.

Busch, Eberhard, et al. *Reformierte Bekenntnisschriften*. 3 vols. Neukirchen-Vluyn: Neukirchener, 2002–.

Cabanel, Patrick. *Histoire des protestants en France*. Paris: Fayard, 2012.

Clark, Christopher. *Iron Kingdom: The Rise and Downfall of Prussia 1600–1947*. London: Lane, 2006.

Claydon, Tony. *William III and the Godly Revolution*. Cambridge: Cambridge University Press, 1996.

Collinson, Patrick. *The Elizabethan Puritan Movement*. Oxford: Clarendon, 1967.

Dawson, Jane. *John Knox*. New Haven: Yale University Press, 2015.

Dennison, James T., Jr. *Reformed Confessions of the 16th and 17th Centuries in English Translation*. 4 vols. Grand Rapids: Reformation Heritage, 2008–14.

Derry, T. K. *A History of Scandinavia*. London: George, Allen and Unwin, 1979.

Evans, Gillian R. *John Wyclif: Myth and Reality*. Oxford: Lion Hudson, 2005.

Gäbler, Ulrich. *Huldrych Zwingli: Leben und Werk*. Munich: Beck, 1983; English: *Huldrych Zwingli: His Life and Work*. Edinburgh: T. & T. Clark, 1986.

Heal, Felicity. *Reformation in Britain and Ireland*. Oxford: Oxford University Press, 2003.

Israel, Jonathan I. *The Dutch Republic: Its Rise, Greatness and Fall, 1477–1806*. Oxford: Oxford University Press, 1995.

Jobert, Ambroise. *De Luther à Mohila: La Pologne dans la crise de la chrétienté 1517–1648*. Paris: Institut d'Etudes Slaves, 1974.

Lahey, Stephen E. *John Wyclif*. Oxford: Oxford University Press, 2009.

Lumpkin, William L., and B. J. Leonard. *Baptist Confessions of Faith*. 2nd ed. Valley Forge, PA: Judson, 2011.

Milton, Anthony. *Catholic and Reformed: The Roman and Protestant churches in English Protestant thought 1600–1640*. Cambridge: Cambridge University Press, 1995.

Murray, Iain. *The Reformation of the Church: A Collection of Reformed and Puritan Documents on Church Issues*. Edinburgh: Banner of Truth Trust, 1987.

Neill, Stephen. *Anglicanism*. 2nd ed. London: Mowbray, 1977.

Olin, John C. *Catholic Reform. From Cardinal Ximenes to the Council of Trent, 1495–1563*. New York: Fordham University Press, 1990.

Patterson, W. B. *King James VI and I and the Reunion of Christendom*. Cambridge: Cambridge University Press, 1997.

Post, Regnerus R. *The Modern Devotion. Confrontation with Reformation and humanism*. Leiden: Brill, 1968.

Prestwich, Menna. ed. *International Calvinism 1541–1715*. Oxford: Clarendon, 1985.

Rex, Richard. *The Lollards*. Basingstoke, UK: Palgrave, 2002.

Spurr, John. *The Restoration Church of England 1646–1689*. New Haven: Yale University Press, 1991.

Stephens, William P. *Zwingli: An Introduction to His Thought*. Oxford: Clarendon, 1992.

Whaley, Joachim. *Germany and the Holy Roman Empire*. 2 vols. Oxford: Oxford University Press, 2012.

2

Reformation and Education
Jan Amos Comenius's "Becoming Truly Human" and his Reformation of Human Affairs

Jan Hábl

INTRODUCTION

Jan Amos Komenský, internationally known as Comenius (1592–1670), was a Czech (or more precisely Moravian) seventeenth-century Brethren pastor, philosopher, and educator who is celebrated especially for his timeless educational ideas and international irenic efforts. These efforts earned him the epithet "the teacher of nations." In this chapter I want to focus on the relationship between his anthropology and education; in particular I will enquire into his views of the ontological and moral character of human beings, in relation to so-called educational humanization.

Comenius's understanding of human nature changed during the course of his life. The classification and interpretation of Comenius's thoughts to which I adhere are closely linked to the so-called "major" discoveries of the 1930s. In that period certain Comeniologists were able to track down some extremely important manuscripts of his, which had been assumed to have been lost. Before these discoveries, the periodization of the development of Comenius's thought and work was usually determined by external and accidental factors, such as where he was living, historic events, and so on. The discoveries in the 1930s enabled the contemporary Comeniologists to classify his work according to internal factors, that is, factors which Comenius himself considered to be important and which significantly shifted his thinking.[1] In light of these discoveries it is now possible to distinguish four or five main stages in Comenius's thought: 1) encyclopedic or preparatory; 2) comforting–with an emphasis on resignation; 3) narrative allegory; 4) educational pansophy; 5) emendation or reformation. The last two periods somewhat overlap.[2] Each of these stages is characterized by a specific understanding of the human being; of course, the definitions are only relative. Some transitions between them are comparatively abrupt; others were slower and more gradual. I will limit this study to the final period of Comenius's work, because it provides the climax of his thinking about reformation and restoration.

"OMNES, OMNIA, OMNENO": THE PEDAGOGY OF EMENDATION

The final stage of Comenius's thought (after 1640) is usually referred to as his pansophic, emendational, or universal remedy stage. The shift toward pansophy came about as soon as he realized the universal dimension of education. It is true that the universal element was already present in his Czech *Great Didactic* (1633–38), which was built on the idea of the harmonization of various levels of the universe, but at that time its actual application was limited to the reformation of schools. It took Comenius some time to fully realize the universal potential of his method.[3] In fact, we can observe an

---

1. The most important discoveries were basically three. The first were Souček's so-called "Leningrad Discoveries" in 1931, which consist of six important manuscripts that include, among other works, *Prima Philosophia, Geometrie,* and *Cosmographiae Compendium*. The second discovery was made by G. H. Turnbull in 1933; some of these papers were originals of previously known works by Comenius, but Turnbull also found a series of completely new documents and letters. The greatest findings came with the third discovery: on Christmas Eve 1934, after long focused research, D. Čižévskyj discovered a large manuscript of 2,000 pages in the archives of the Francky orphanage in Halle. These turned out to be four parts (of seven) of Comenius's pivotal work *De rerum humanarum emendatione consultatio catholica* (*General Consultation Concerning the Restoration of Human Affairs*). For details, see Patočka, *Komeniologické studie* 2: 7–63.

2. Compare Floss, *Od divadla,* or Patočka, *Komeniologické studie,* 1:175.

3. Perhaps one of the stimuli was a devastating critique of the *Great Didactic* by Joachim Hübner (1611–1663), who belonged to the intellectual circle of Samuel Hartlib. His criticism was aimed at two main concerns: first, Comenius limited teaching

overlap of the educational and pansophic phases in his thinking. It is clear that the purpose of his didactic writings was to correct the disorders of society, but originally this was only the Czech society. Yet during the 1630s—because of external political changes and the internal maturing of Comenius's pansophic ideas—the addressee of his writings gradually changed: it was no longer only the Czech society but society in general. This shift is apparent in the fact that in 1633 Comenius began to translate (and slightly rework) his *Czech Didactic* of 1630 (and other writings) into Latin. In the words of Jan Patočka, Comenius's didactic works from this period gradually "yielded to the process of pansophization," which ended in a clear awareness of the "necessity to restore the order of the world."[4] In a letter to Samuel Hartlib in 1638, Comenius indicated he now understood education as "an instrument for the pansophic method."[5] Thus the concept of the universal restoration of human affairs was born in Comenius's mind.[6] It was a shift from a latent educational universalism in the *Didactic* to an explicit and fully elaborated didactic universalism in his magnum opus *General Consultation* (1666), on which Comenius worked (with several interruptions) almost until the end of his life. It consist of seven parts: 1) Panegersia—universal awakening, 2) Panaugia—universal enlightenment, 3) Pansophia—universal wisdom, 4) Pampaedia—universal education, 5) Panglottia—universal language, 6) Panorthosia—universal reform, 7) Pannuthesia—universal warning.

The key idea of the *Consultation* is that the true restoration or reformation of humanity cannot come from any individual nation, but that all nations have to unite and participate in it. This reformation includes a fundamental reform of the scientific, religious, educational, political, and other realities. Comenius considered upbringing to be the essential element of this reformation.

The focus on universal harmony, expressed in the systematic use of the *pan-* prefixes (meaning "all"), did not mean, however, that Comenius put education aside in this new phase. On the contrary, education lies in

---

solely to schools, as if outside of school it was of no use; second, since the didactic principles are self-evident, it is unnecessary to derive them from nature. Because of this criticism, Comenius postponed the publication of the edited Latin version of the *Great Didactic* for more than twenty years.

4. Patočka, *Komeniologické studie*, 1:405. Translations from the Czech are mine unless otherwise indicated.

5. Ryba, *Sto listů*, 32.

6. It seems that his stay in England was of great importance to Comenius's development. He met with acceptance and encouragement from his friends. As a result, he wrote *Via lucis* (*The Way of Light*) in 1641 and *Consultationis brevissima delineatio* (*A Very Brief Description of the Consultation*) in 1642, in which he first outlined his pansophic plans.

the center of the *Consultation*; it is even visualized in the way Comenius structured the contents of the work; it has seven parts, with the *Pampaedia* as the center of a triad, opened and closed in turn by a threefold introduction and a threefold conclusion; this can be seen clearly in Comenius's own synopsis.[7]

PRACTICAL CONSEQUENCES

A practical result of this method based on the requirement of universal harmony was the development of the art (*ars*) of handling things in accordance with their natural character; this means that human activities should not undermine their basic natural function and designation. Comenius's basic didactic motto expressed this principle well: *Omnia sponte fluant, absit violentia rebus* (let everything flow spontaneously, without violence).[8] Patočka saw in this notion of *ars* the creative (synergetic) role of human beings, a concept which had not been developed by anyone before Comenius. He did not separate the human being from the whole of the universe. The starting point of his concept was not an isolated human individual, or even the human mind, as it was with Descartes, but universal harmony. If Comenius was cutting-edge in anything it was precisely in this, Patočka argues, because on the threshold of the modern age Comenius proved almost prophetic in seeing the danger of the subject-object division of reality; he warned against "fragmentation, self-centeredness, undervaluation of service and overvaluation of control and power, a lack of harmony."[9]

The subject of the *Consultation* is *mundus sub specie educationis* (the world from the educational point of view).[10] Comenius developed the idea of the *world as school* (which had been typical for his didactic period) one step further: nature is endowed with educative keys not merely for the reformation of the school system but for the whole of society. The foundational idea of education as outlined in Comenius's earlier didactic writings remains, but in the *General Consultation* education has become pan-education and emendation pan-emendation. The remedy must be universal in every aspect and every area of human endeavor:

---

7. The Latin version of the book is available online: https://archive.org/details/bub_gb_e2dTAAAAcAAJ [accessed August 13, 2016]. See, e.g., Comenius, *Obecná porada o nápravě věcí lidských*, 69.

8. This motto is written on the first page of Comenius's *Opera Didactica Omnia*. See also *Didaktika analytická*, 42.

9. Patočka, *Komeniologické studie* 2:133.

10. Ibid., 199.

> If the human classes are to be restored, the individual people that constitute the classes must be restored; if the individual people are to be restored, the workshops of humanity, the schools, must be first restored; to restore the schools, books, which are to be the appropriate tools of formation, must be first restored; to restore books, it is necessary to restore the method of writing and handling of the books; and finally, if the method is to be fully restored, it is needed to take heed of the order of things themselves.... Thus the foundation of all hope for true restoration of human disorders is the order of things.... For in accordance with the laws of things (I repeat), the method of learning things must be reformed, so that books might be reformed through method, school through books, people through schools, human societies through people, so that the whole human generation might be reformed. And thus light and peace with abundance of God's blessing will return to schools, churches, and states.[11]

One of the interesting pedagogical results of the pansophic shift was the fusion of two of Comenius's concepts: the idea of *world as a school* and the idea of *life as a school*. In his *Didactic* Comenius had outlined four stages of education, ending at age 24, but in the *Pampaedia* he added and quite thoroughly elaborated four more schools: the school of youth, the school of adulthood, the school of old age, and the school of death. The description of the complementary school phases sounds entirely consistent with previous ones:

> The whole of life is a school, as we have seen in the preceding chapters. Thus also is its middle period, which is characterized by full strength. In fact, this period is the most important part, for the previous ones were but steps on the way to this point. Not moving ahead would mean to decline, especially when there remains so much to be learned, and not only through some preliminary games but through serious behavior. Much might have been received from the schools, but no school could give what this one can, that real touch with things and people throughout the whole life. Certainly they spoke the truth who said: I have learned much from my teachers; more from my schoolfellows, but most from my pupils. For through forming we form ourselves, and only through work do we become masters of work.[12]

In the same way Comenius considered old age to be truly educative. At any previous moment in their life, "people might die, but here they have

11. Comenius, *Panorthosia or Universal Reform*, 307.
12. Comenius, *Pampaedia, or, Universal Education*, 95.

to," which fact gives them the opportunity to turn away from the vanishing things, to give thanks, and to prepare for "embracing death and entering into a new, everlasting life." Comenius recognized that of all fearful things, death is the most fearful, but in faith and full reliance on God, there is no need to fear: "You had no fear when being born; why should you have any fear of dying? In neither of the cases does the decision lie in your hand but in God's."[13] The whole of our earthly life is a preparation for "the eternal academy."[14]

The changes which are observable in Comenius's system during this final period were of "a peculiar kind," writes Patočka:

> There is not a complete replacement of older concepts in Comenius's restoration project, but we rather see that old schemes are placed into a new context, a context that is to be in principle holistic, general, and unifying.[15]

The universal shift had some interesting practical implications,[16] but Comenius's anthropological views did not change much in comparison to the previous stage. Human beings were still teleologically rooted in God, that is, he saw their ultimate purpose as lying in God; men and women were learners in the school of the world (and life) which was given by God with an educative purpose. What had "merely" changed was the scope of human activity or engagement within the world. The ultimate goal of all education was still the restoration of fallen human nature, but what was now added was a regard to the whole, because Comenius had realized that all human affairs are mutually interdependent. The harmony of an individual cannot be attained without the harmony of the whole—as Comenius often expressed in an apropos motto: *Homines omnes sumus, eiusdem mundi cives* (We are all citizens of one world).

---

13. Ibid., 135.
14. Ibid., 141.
15. Patočka, *Komeniologické studie* 3:30.
16. One such implication was the proposal to organize the so-called *Collegium Lucis*, which was to be a kind of international ministry for education, for the purpose of overseeing the implementation of the restorative plans for the world.

COMENIUS: AHEAD OF TIME OR BEHIND?

How relevant are Comenius's anthropological and educational concepts for our time? Our view of any given historical era changes over time. What was pertinent in the recent past is not necessarily pertinent today.[17] František X. Šalda captured the situation well when he said that Comenius was "a great man who was strangely ahead of his time, and yet also behind it."[18] The question is: In what ways was Comenius ahead and in what ways behind? Was he so ahead of his own time as to approach ours? What in his work is relevant for us and what is not? Jaroslava Pešková answers succinctly: Comenius "isn't great for his answers to the questions of the time, he is important for raising the right questions, by which he was able to express the key issues of his day."[19]

It is clear that Comenius's anthropology was built on the foundations of a broader philosophical and theological system. As a theologian he saw nature and the entire natural world as a creation, as the work of the Creator who had created everything effectively and meaningfully. As a philosopher he explored nature "under the guise of education,"[20] in order to discover in its essence, that is, in its nature, the educational potential. In the introductory part of the *Didactics* (both the Czech *Didactic* of 1630 and the later Latin *Great Didactic*) it says that "whatever exists, exists for some end."[21] The natural world is not a random occurrence of things or the result of events which took place haphazardly, coming out of nowhere and going nowhere, but a purposeful existence capable of meaning. Everything has some purpose. Every thing, every being is characterized by its teleological nature. This means that it has a goal which lies outside of itself, beyond itself; there exists a "coming out" of oneself, because that is what each person was intended and created for. As Comenius put it, nothing exists for itself. On this deposit rests the pedagogical bent of the natural world. The world is imbued with an educational spirit. From birth a person enters the school of the world, which by its very nature aims to educate them towards the true essence of humanity.

---

17. The period of the national revival, for example, regarded different aspects of Comenius's work as relevant than the post-modern period. We can make a similar distinction between the modern and postmodern periods. For further information about which periods of Comenius's work were valued and considered relevant, see, e.g., Hábl, *Lessons in Humanity*.

18. Šalda, "O literárním baroku," in *Z období zápisníku*, 302.

19. Pešková, "Aktuální aspekty," 5.

20. Cf. Patočka, *Komeniologické studie* 2:133.

21. Comenius, *Great Didactic*, 41.

That a person needs such an education was evident to Comenius. In all of creation there is only one being which is able to make itself the final goal of its existence, to make itself *homo mensura* (humankind as the measure of all things). Unlike scholars in both antiquity and modernity, Comenius did not view this state of affairs as something positive, but as the core of the human tragedy, the source of all human confusion and bewilderment. Those for whom the meaning of life is to be found within themselves stand out from the order of creation and from the universal harmony of all creation in an annoying way, for their purpose is unnatural, non-native, and out of order. The separation of human beings from God, from whom flows all "breath and life itself," also separates them from each other, because it "forces man to make himself the goal of his existence, that is, to love himself, to pay attention to himself, and care for himself first."[22]

BIBLICAL ANTHROPOLOGY?

Comenius's explanation of the origin of the ambivalent nature of human beings comes from the biblical narrative of the creation of humankind as in the *imago Dei*. Humans are ontologically clothed so that their character mirrors God's character and their essential being is a reflection of the greatest conceivable good (*summum bonum*). All of the unique capacities of a person, such as thinking, choosing, experiencing beauty, feeling, and self-knowledge, have their ontological basis in the creative act of God. Yet as a result of the fall of humanity, which was caused by their desire for equality with God, human beings have lost the so-called *nexus hypostaticus*, the deep, personal relationship with their Creator. As equal with God, humans have lost or "bent" themselves, which alienates them from their natural preordained authority that was to enable them to transcend their own selves. As a result of this moral distortion, all of humanity's ontological capacity for true humanism is also affected, so that we are not able to fulfill our human calling, but require help and salvation. Given the miserable state of humanity, such help is supremely desirable, and thanks to the salvific action of Jesus Christ it is possible. All inhumanity needs to be done away with, guilt can and must be confessed and forgiven. This is the key spiritual principle, through which comes the important "rest for humanity," that is the reconciliation of humankind with God, with others, and with themselves. Only then a person becomes "truly human" (*Pampaedia*, 2:8).

---

22. The citation is given in Kožmín and Kožmínová, *Zvětšeniny*, 60.

Such a theology of reality was by no means unusual in Comenius's time,[23] but out of Comenius's creative synthesis of various philosophical sources arose a unique system of thought. His distinction between the ontological and moral nature of the human being realistically captured the complexity and ambivalence of humanity. Humans are endowed with both positive and negative potential. The ontological value of a person (humanity) is firmly anchored in God but their moral nature (humaneness) is open. It is not pre-determined as, for example, the earthworm-ness of the earthworm or the triangle-ness of a triangle. A triangle cannot do anything about its triangle-ness; it cannot become more or less triangular, but a person can. A person is capable of both humanity and inhumanity. Every human potential, each piece of knowledge or skill (including what is acquired at school), can have a positive or negative realization. They can be used for good or for evil. *Usus* and *abusus*, Comenius called these possibilities. In the end the greater the potential, the greater the danger, because *corruptio optimi pessima* (the corruption of the best thing is the worst thing). Humanity is not okay; but it is not lost.

Therefore, according to Comenius, a "workshop" or a "forging-place" of humanity is necessary: there must be schools and education whose primary task is the correction of the negative human tendencies. All education consists in combatting the tendency to live life only for ourselves, that is, in coming out (*e-ducatio*) away from our twisted self-centeredness and isolation. Thus conceived, pedagogy by its very nature implies the ascendancy of humanity, or an upward movement which is desirable because it leads one to the sought-after transcendent relationship to God. In practice this reaching out means that people learn to act, decide, and be responsible not only for themselves. Learners are led to the recognition that within the order of being there is an authority which fundamentally transcends them and to which they are subordinated. Here we can see the basis for Comenius's treasured didactic universalism or holism, which has significant social and ethical consequences.[24] Comenius did not intend the cultivation and reparation of humanity only for individuals, but holistically, globally, as is indicated by his use of the prefix *pan-*, which at the height of his work was prefixed to every human effort. The reason for this conviction is that a proper relationship (reconciling) to the final authority implies a proper relationship to others, and thus to the whole of creation. Comenius's burden was not merely partial existence, but the whole human being. His school

---

23. See for example the anthropological insights in Pascal, *Pensées*, fragments 613, 206.

24. See for example Patočka, *Komeniologické studie* 3:30.

system was not just intended to humanize individuals but it envisaged "the restoration of human affairs," because Comenius knew that the welfare of the individual could not be achieved without the welfare of the whole: "We all stand on the one great stage of the world, and whatever happens here happens to everyone."

CONCLUSION

From what was said it follows that Comenius's anthropological assumptions determine his concept of pedagogical humanization. His anthropology leads to an entirely different kind of humanization than the one we encounter in the modern conception. For Comenius, educational resources are not adapted to the demands and needs of the individual, because an individual is neither autonomous nor the final word on humanity. The individual and the didactic means by which that individual is to be cultivated are submitted to requirements which transcend them.

I believe that here lies the core problem of the modern concept of humanization. Human nature is in reality not as unproblematic or positive as modernity used to imagine. If human nature itself is problematic, as Comenius proposed, that is, if it is endowed with both positive and negative potential, then simply complying with the demands of the individual does not guarantee humanization, because an individual can have needs and demands which not only do not lead to the development of humanity but can even go in the opposite direction, towards inhumanity. Simply heeding the demands of individuals can lead towards indolence, superficiality, malice, greed, dishonesty, and other evils. Therefore humanization which operates from the romantic model of human beings as basically good does not work. It is essentially a tautology, as Karel Rýdl correctly notes, because to humanize what is already human makes no sense; it would be like naturalizing nature.[25] However well-meaning the modern pursuit of educational humanization may be, its non-functionality has long ago exposed it as an empty "slogan" or "cloak"[26] under which it is possible to "promote virtually anything" that is in some way non-traditional, innovative, alternative, or fun.[27] But it does not bring about the humanization of humanity.

Jean-Jacques Rousseau's conception of humanity can serve as a good example. Unlike Comenius, Rousseau believed that human beings

---

25. Rýdl, "Didaktické perspektivy," 351.
26. Rýdl's concept, ibid.
27. Ibid.

are basically good, both ontologically and morally;[28] and on this belief he based his romantic (non-)education. His representative boy, Emil, was only watched and accompanied by the teacher, who in fact was no longer a teacher, but merely an assistant. Rousseau believed that education should simply allow the good that dwells within a person to blossom on its own. All liberalizing approaches to minimal education likewise stand on this premise.

The reverse assumption, however, which is at the opposite end of the anthropological spectrum, also results in a problematic pedagogy. If we assume that human beings are both ontologically and morally "nothing but"—the typical phrase of modern reductionism—for example, nothing but an animal, a machine or even just matter, we will treat them accordingly. We will teach, form, tame, indoctrinate, or condition them, but never humanize them.[29] All totalitarian and authoritarian approaches tend to this type of pedagogy.[30]

I am convinced that it is exactly here that the relevance of Comenius's anthropology, as well as of his entire system of thought, can be seen most clearly. His main contribution lies not so much in his didactic principles and propositions, fascinating as they are,[31] but in his ontological and moral presumptions, which have proven to be realistic and functional, and which were based on his Reformed faith. His teaching on humanity as *imago Dei* provides for the essential dignity of humanity while at the same time it functions as a refined anthropological teleology. The teaching about the violation of humanity that is included in Comenius's system, on the other hand, works as a precaution against any over-romanticizing of human nature. This realistic anthropological conception creates the space for a meaningful cul-

28. Wolfgang Röd was right when he said that "Rousseau's thinking constantly circles around the concept of nature and the concept of human nature in particular, without ever defining those concepts or at least describing them clearly enough" (Röd, *Novověká filosofie*, 488). But the attentive reader cannot miss Rousseau's anthropological presumption in Röd's work—human nature is fine, "sinless," the only thing that corrupts a person is the world, society, and "culture." Where the corruption of society came from if every individual was born good, Rousseau never explains. See also primarily Rousseau, *Emil*.

29. Human nature (not only that of children) needs the kind of education envisaged in these concepts, and not only in pathological cases. Pedagogy knows the "regime methodology," authoritarian approaches, directives, and so on, but if it knows nothing more than these, it is no longer pedagogy.

30. Cf. Thiessen, *Teaching for Commitment*.

31. Patočka subtly uncovers that the typical modernist Comeniology, which strives to derive from Comenius some pseudo-modern psychological, pedagogical, linguistic, etc., doctrines, is merely a cover for its own self-admiration. What is the point of constantly—through Comenius—applauding what is already well known from modern empirical science?

tivation of all human potential—which is neither over- nor under-valued, but truly taught. The dimension of responsibility towards the transcendent creates the functional moral framework which is so important for the proper handling of the school-acquired arsenal. Knowledge and virtue are in close association here, because Comenius knew that knowledge alone does not guarantee humanity. An educated but immoral person is a threat, a "burden," to himself and others. Comenius's metaphysics, the anchor of his anthropology, is clearly non-modern or pre-modern, and it is based on Reformed principles. I believe that this is its greatest value. If we take into account the fact that the modern paradigm is currently in crisis, Comenius's "old-fashionedness" no longer appears as a weakness but rather as an advantage.[32] Moreover, together with his "old-fashioned" anthropology it has proven to be fruitful and effective not only in pedagogy but also in everyday life. That is why in this chapter I have allowed Comenius to speak in his own words, witness to his intellectual integrity. To the modern or postmodern[33] ear his words can sound foreign, but if it is the modern paradigm that has alienated human beings from their humanity, then Comenius can best serve us by his very foreignness, because it shows us the limits of our spiritual universe.[34]

A key conclusion and contribution of this essay is that Comenius's anthropological position includes the ambivalence of ontological nobility and moral depravity. At the height of his intellectual development Comenius understood humanity as a being which is essentially excellent because of having been created in the *imago Dei*. Yet that same humanity has a dubious morality as a result of falling into sin, and it now seeks its ultimate goal and purpose only in itself. For this Comenius used the specific term *samosvojnost*, which refers to the typical human tendency to seek one's ultimate goal and purpose only within oneself.

---

32. Stephen Toulmin illustrated the crisis of modernity with the help of a picture. He suggests that the trajectory of modern philosophy is like the shape of the Greek letter, omega, Ω. This means that despite achievements in experimental and technical areas, the philosophical questions about the meaning of the final order of things are still unresolved. About 300 years later we are once again at the beginning; we did not get very far. See Toulmin, *Cosmopolis*, 167.

33. I have not dealt with the problem of modern and postmodern philosophy and culture per se. Others have already discussed it thoroughly and well. See for example Eagleton, *Illusions of Postmodernism*; Erickson, *Truth or Consequences*; Harvey, *The Condition of Postmodernity*; Lyotard, *The Postmodern Condition*; Murphy, *Beyond Liberalism*; Murphy and McClendon, "Distinguishing Modern and Postmodern"; Murphy, *Theology*; Wright, *Religion*.

34. Compare Patočka, *Komeniologické studie* 1:21.

All of Comenius's emendational and humanizing efforts arose from this basic anthropological assumption. The need for the pedagogical "workshop of humanity" flows from the fact that human affairs are corrupted in terms of its morals, but not completely lost because its ontology is unchanged. The goal, content, and method of his project of humanization flow out of this assumption about human nature.

BIBLIOGRAPHY

Comenius, J. A. *Comenius's Panegersia, or, Universal Awakening*. Translated from the Latin by A. M. O. Dobbie. Shipston-on-Stour, UK: Drinkwater, 1990.

———. *The Great Didactic (Didactica Magna)*. Translated by M. W. Keatinge. New York: Russell & Russell, 1967.

———. *Orbis Sensualium Pictus*. Translated by Charles Hoole. Menston, UK: Scholar, 1970. Facsimile reprint of the 1st English ed., London: J. Kirton, 1659.

———. *Pampaedia, or, Universal Education*. Translated from the Latin by A. M. O. Dobbie. Dover, UK: Buckland, 1986.

———. *Panaugia, or, Universal Light*. Translated from the Latin by A. M. O. Dobbie. Shipston-on-Stour, UK: Drinkwater, 1987.

———. *Panglottia, or, Universal Language*. Translated from the Latin by A. M. O. Dobbie. Shipton-on-Stour, UK: Drinkwater, 1989.

———. *Panorthosia or Universal Reform*. Translated from the Latin by A. M. O. Dobbie. Sheffield: Sheffield Academic, 1995.

———. *Porta linguarum trilinguis reserata*. (Latin, English, and French in parallel columns. Facsimile reprint of the first edition London, George Miller, 1631). Menston, UK: Scholar 1970.

———. *The School of Infancy*. Chapel Hill: University of North Carolina Press, 1956.

———. *The Way of Light*. Translated by E. T. Campagnac. Liverpool: Liverpool University Press, 1938.

Comenius, John *The Labyrinth of the World and The Paradise of the Heart*. Translated by H. Louthan and A. Sterk. Mahwah, NJ: Paulist, 1997.

Eagleton, Terry. *The Illusions of Postmodernism*. Oxford: Blackwell, 1996.

Erickson, Millard J. *Truth or Consequences: The Promise and Perils of Postmodernism*. Downers Grove, IL: InterVarsity, 2001.

Floss, Pavel. *Od divadla věcí k dramatu člověka [From the Theater of Things to the Drama of Man]*. Ostrava, Czech Republic: Profil, 1970.

Greer, Thomas H., and Gavin Lewis. *A Brief History of the Western World*. Vol. 1: *To 1715*. 7th ed. Fort Worth: Harcourt Brace, 1997.

Hábl, Jan. *Lessons in Humanity from the Life and Works of Jan Amos Komenský*. Bonn: Verlag für Kultur und Wissenschaft, 2011.

Harvey, David. *The Condition of Postmodernity: An Enquiry into the Conditions of Cultural Change*. Oxford: Blackwell, 1991.

Kožmín, Zdeněk, and Drahomíra Kožmínová. *Zvětšeniny z Komenského*. Brno, Czech Republic: Host, 2007.

Lyotard, Jean-François. *The Postmodern Condition: A Report on Knowledge.* Translated by Geoff Bennington and Brian Massumi. Minneapolis: University of Minnesota Press, 1984.

Murphy, Nancey. *Beyond Liberalism and Fundamentalism: How Modern and Postmodern Philosophy Set the Theological Agenda.* Valley Forge, PA: Trinity, 1996.

———. *Theology in a Postmodern Age.* Prague: IBTS, 2003.

Murphy, Nancey, and James Wm. McClendon Jr. "Distinguishing Modern and Postmodern Theologies." *Modern Theology* 5, no. 3 (1989) 191–214.

Pascal, Blaise. *Pensées.* Translated by A. J. Krailsheimer. New York: Penguin, 1995.

Patočka, Jan. *Komeniologické studie* 3 vols. Prague: Oikoymenh, 1997, 1998, 2003.

Pešková, Jaroslava. "Aktuální aspekty filosofické argumentace v Komenského 'Konsultaci'" [Current Aspects of the Philosophical Arguments in Comenius's *Consultations*]. *Filosofický časopis* 40, no. 1 (1992) 5.

Pospíšil, Jiří. "Náboženská pedagogika a cíle výchovy v Obecné poradě o nápravě věcí lidských J. A. Komenského" ["Religious Pedagogy and the Goal of Education in Comenius's General Consultation on Human Affairs"]. *Paidagogos* 16, no. 4 (2004). http://old.paidagogos.net/.

Röd, Wolfgang. *Novověká filosofie* [*New Age of Philosophy*]. Prague: Oikoymenh, 2004.

Rousseau, Jean-Jacques. *Emil, čili o vychování* [*Emil, or on Education*]. Translated by J. Novák and M. Svoboda. Prague: Dědictví Komenského, 1911.

Ryba, Bohumil, ed. *Sto listů Jana Amosa Komenského* [*One Hundred Letters of Jan Amos Comenius*]. Prague: Laichter, 1945.

Rýdl, Karel. "Didaktické perspektivy inovujících procesů v rámci humanizace výchovy a vzdělávání" ["Didactic Perspectives on Innovative Processes within the Framework of the Humanization of Education"]. In *Historie a perspektivy didaktického myšlení*, edited by A. Vališová, 350–57. Prague: Karolinum, 2004.

Šalda, František X. *Z období zápisníku* Vol. 1. Prague: Odeon, 1987.

Thiessen, E. J. *Teaching for Commitment: Liberal Education, Indoctrination, and Christian Nurture.* Montreal: McGill-Queen's University Press, 1993.

Toulmin, Stephen. *Cosmopolis: The Hidden Agenda of Modernity.* Chicago: University of Chicago Press, 1990.

Wright, Andrew. *Religion, Education and Postmodernity.* London: Routledge, 2004.

3

The Artistic Legacy of the Reformation and Protestant Artists Today

MARLEEN HENGELAAR-ROOKMAAKER

INTRODUCTION

The Reformation did not only impact the faith and theology of its followers, but it also had its consequences for how they viewed the visual arts. As the various Protestant traditions all had and to some extent still have their own relationship to art, it is impossible to do justice to all of them in just one essay.[1] Hence our main focus will be on Calvinistic art, first of all tracing its development in the Netherlands. However, at appropriate points Dutch Calvinistic visual artists and developments will be paralleled and contrasted with those in other Reformed traditions and other western countries. The resulting picture will highlight the characteristics of Calvinistic art from the time of the Reformation until today and the common features of Protestant art in general. The latter part of this essay will be devoted to contemporary Protestant visual art in its rich variety of media and approaches.

    1. This text was originally presented as a workshop, during which many slides were shown. Some of the images discussed here can be found online at http://www.paternosterperiodicals.co.uk/european-journal-of-theology/rookmaaker, which also has color versions of the four illustrations in this chapter. See the list at the end of the chapter.

LUTHER

Let me begin with a brief note on Luther's view of the visual arts. Luther's primary rule for church art was to reject only what went against biblical teaching, which meant that he rejected images of Mary and the saints. He also opposed the veneration of images, but otherwise Luther was positive about images and open to them in worship and private devotion. He said: "If it is not a sin but good to have an image of Christ in my heart, why should it be a sin to have it in my eyes?"[2]

During his lifetime a number of artists were among his followers, of whom Albrecht Dürer and Lucas Cranach the Elder are the best known. Lucas Cranach the Elder, who lived in Wittenberg just like Luther, was a good friend of Luther and they were godfathers to each other's children. They were well aware that images were an important tool for spreading Luther's new ideas. In the light of Reformation theology, several themes came to the fore and were given a new meaning, such as Nature and Grace, Christ and the Adulteress, Jesus Welcoming the Children, the Ten Commandments, and the Prodigal Son. Luther and Cranach also made extensive use of cartoons, which mocked the ideas of the various other religious groups. Thus the theological differences of the time were not only emphasized in word but also in image.

CALVIN AND HIS FOLLOWERS

In his *Institutes*, Calvin writes this about art: "I am not gripped by the superstition of thinking absolutely no images permissible, but because sculpture and painting are gifts of God, I seek a *pure and legitimate use* of each."[3] This statement deals a square blow to all, many Calvinists included, who think that there is no place for visual art in the Reformed tradition. It makes clear that Calvin was not against the arts in general, but that he was against works of art that were *impure* or *used in an improper way*. He gave the following guidelines for what he considered "pure" art: submission to the Word of God, humility, sobriety and simplicity, faithfulness to the nature of things, skill, harmony, and moderation. That Calvin was positive about art in general should actually not surprise us, as his theology embraces all of creation as a good gift of God, including the gift of art.

What did Calvin consider to be an improper use of art? He was critical of the devotional practices of his time and he was wary of the danger of

---

2. Luther, *Against the Heavenly Prophets*, 100.
3. Calvin, *Institutes* I.11.12.i.

idolatry. He rejected the veneration of images of Mary and the saints and the custom of praying before and through them. In order to prevent this practice, he not only advocated the removal of these images from the churches but he also ordered the doors of the churches to be closed during weekdays. This is in line with his emphasis on the direct relationship we can have with God. God is always with us; we can always communicate with him. We do not need to go to a church or stand before a statue in order to pray to him. We can and we should, according to Calvin, live our life of faith at home and in the world.

As to worship services, his emphasis was on the preaching of the Word. He saw the presence of images as a distraction from the inward focus on the Word of God read, preached, and sung. Calvin's theology placed great emphasis on the Holy Spirit and his work in us, including during the church service. Five centuries later we may ask if images cannot actually also help us inwardly to focus on God, but for Calvin images in churches came in the category of improper use. It is not true, however, that he ordered the iconoclasm of his day; he rather wanted the magistrates to remove the paintings and sculptures in an orderly fashion.

Calvin also objected to images of God and Jesus. This sprung first of all from a fear of idolatry, but also from a concern that images of God and Jesus are bound to fall short of their majesty. Calvin said: "Surely there is nothing less fitting than to wish to reduce God who is immeasurable and incomprehensible to a five-foot measure!"[4]

To sum up Calvin's position: he was cautious that art should be used in the right way and that the art produced should be wholesome and pure, but—granted this—he affirms and embraces the visual arts of his day that consisted of painting, sculpture, woodcuts, etchings, drawings, stained-glass windows, wood and stone reliefs, and scenes on tapestries.

How did Calvin's followers deal with this legacy? The history of Calvinistic art has its ups and downs. On the one hand there is the growing and rich production of visual art in the sixteenth and seventeenth centuries, especially in the Dutch Golden Age. On the other hand, the dualistic approach to life with its division of life into high and low, nature and grace, or sacred and secular, returned in Pietism, and in Puritanism in England. This approach dominated until well into the twentieth century and is still with us today. I use the word "returned" because this dualism had been part of the medieval Catholic view of life and especially of the rather mystical movement *devotio moderna* or Brothers of the Common Life, which had been strong in a number of northern European countries. In fact, the

---

4. Ibid., I.11. 4.

Reformation owed much to this movement with its emphasis on personal piety and devotion, and it can partly be seen as its continuation. The dualistic division of life never fully disappeared but surfaced time and again, for a great deal determining the developments in Protestant art from the late seventeenth century onwards. Pietism meant a shunning and a negative view of all that is not part of a life of devotion, hence of so-called secular art. Because art in the church was not an option for Calvinists either, Pietism led to a slow decline of most forms of art.[5]

THE SIXTEENTH CENTURY

Returning to the sixteenth century, let us—as an example of the expanding Calvinistic art production—briefly consider a work by Gillis van Coninxloo, who was born in Antwerp and, after this city was reconquered by Spain in 1585, fled to Frankenthal, a small Calvinistic town near Heidelberg in Germany. This safe haven for many a Calvinistic artist became known for its tapestries and paintings of landscapes and to a lesser extent of biblical subjects. The Frankenthal School, as this group of painters came to be called, made an important contribution to the development of landscape painting, and Gillis van Coninxloo was the first main painter of forest landscapes.[6] Thus it comes as no surprise that in his painting *Elijah Fed by the Ravens* we see a combination of a large forest landscape and a small Elijah. Van Coninxloo moved to Amsterdam in 1595, as did many Calvinist painters who originally came from Flanders and France around this time. They were a major influence in the flourishing of cultural life in seventeenth-century Holland.

THE SEVENTEENTH CENTURY

The best known Calvinistic painter of the Dutch Golden Age was Rembrandt van Rijn, who is especially known for his portraits, mythological works, and biblical paintings. The biblical works were not made for churches, but for the homes of citizens. Rembrandt stands out because of the craftsmanship, originality, and psychological depth of his work.

---

5. Hengelaar-Rookmaaker, *Complete Works of Hans Rookmaaker*, 6:270–71.
6. Ibid., 269–70.

His drawing of the Annunciation (c. 1635) is hugely different from the pious Annunciation scenes that we usually see, in which Mary and Gabriel reverently bow towards each other. In Rembrandt's rendering of the event Mary actually faints and slides from her chair, when the impressive angel suddenly fills the room where she was quietly reading her Bible. Mary is portrayed as a woman of real flesh and blood. She seems flushed, perhaps ashamed about the intimacy of what is happening to her, while her shaded face may also allude to the angel who "overshadowed" her. The angel appears full of concern for her, extending his wings over her in a protective and blessing gesture.

Biblical scenes did not make up the main part of the work that was produced by Calvinists in seventeenth-century Holland, even though the genre of biblical history painting scored highest in their regard. Various other genres gained prominence, as for instance the portrait. The Reformers saw humans as the image of God, which meant that the individual gained in importance. Portraits furthermore told the story of God's grace and care for people, while they also functioned as examples of virtue.

Another genre that had slowly come to the fore in the sixteenth century and blossomed in the seventeenth century was the still life, in which the various objects also tended to have symbolic meanings. By way of this symbolism the artists addressed the vanity of life, the danger of temptation, and the reality of sin, while first of all speaking about the beauty and richness of creation. In the painting entitled, *Bouquet with Crucifix and Shell*, (1640s) by Jan Davidszoon de Heem (and in N. van Veerendael, for instance), we see different flowers, various fruits, and a beautiful shell. They speak of the beauty of nature. But some flowers have almost withered. We also see some dry leaves, a fallen leaf, and thistles. In this way the picture speaks of vanity, of the passing away and shortness of life. The clock makes this even more distinct. Included in the picture are also a pen with a feather (a symbol of frivolity) and a piece of paper on which is written: "But people neglect the most beautiful flower" (*Maer naer d'Allerschoonste Blom / daer en siet men niet naer om*). This flower, on the left, is Christ on the cross (the crucifix), who came to redeem nature and life from vanity. Thus this painting is like a sermon that speaks about creation, fall, and redemption in one simple picture.

There are also the genre paintings that portray domestic scenes and other aspects of human life. While they depict the folly of human life, they usually have a satirical undertone and a moral message. This genre, going as far back as Jheronimus Bosch (c. 1450–1516), was further developed by Pieter Bruegel (c. 1525–69) and his contemporaries, and was continued by artists of the seventeenth century as a good way to speak about the pitfalls of human behavior. These works were meant "for education and entertainment" and were very popular.

Another important seventeenth-century genre was landscape painting. In these works nature is the main subject, which according to Calvin can be seen as God's second book of revelation and as a theater for the glory of God. These landscape paintings were not simple *en plein air* snapshots of actual places, but all the elements in these works were chosen and interwoven with an eye to their meaning—a method which John Walford calls "selective naturalism."[7] In Jacob van Ruisdael's *View of Haarlem from the Dunes at Overveen* (c. 1670) we look down from the dunes over the fields towards the city of Haarlem with its churches in the distance. The land in the foreground was reclaimed from the sea after flooding, thus pointing at damage and danger. However, we see restoration in the human commercial activity of the bleaching of linen now taking place on this land. The sky makes up two thirds of the painting, with the spire of the Saint Bavo Church

---

7. Walford, *Jacob Van Ruisdael*, 18, 29.

connecting earth and heaven. Some of the sky is blue, some parts of it are filled with clouds, but Haarlem itself—which adopted Calvinism around 1580—is gently flooded with heavenly light. In this way the painting speaks about God's presence and providence.[8]

From what we have seen so far of the artistic Calvinistic production in the seventeenth century, we conclude that it reflects a very rich and broad world and life view that embraces all of life. It deals with the common daily life of ordinary people and it paints reality from a biblical perspective including a moral dimension. The goodness of creation, the brokenness of life, our responsibility to live godly lives, and God's grace and providence are recurring underlying themes.

As the seventeenth century draws to an end, so does its lavish art production. The rise of Pietism brings a narrowing of what is considered important in life. Faith becomes "spiritual" and regard for the material side of life becomes sinful and worldly. As a result, the domain of the visual arts is increasingly shunned and the number of artists drops dramatically.

THE EIGHTEENTH AND NINETEENTH CENTURIES

However, this change of perspective did not mean that there was no appreciation whatsoever of beauty among Calvinists of this time. Recent research has shown that Dutch church interiors were not as plain and empty as commonly thought.[9] Our view of Calvinistic churches tends to be influenced by the austere representation the Dutch painter Pieter Saenredam offered in his paintings, but in reality they were often anything but sober. Memorial boards hung against columns, decorated tombs, pulpits, and benches were common, the organ panels had paintings of biblical scenes, and coats of arms of magistrates as well as portraits of pastors adorned the walls. There were large illustrated Bibles on lecterns, and stained-glass windows, sometimes even with biblical subjects. It was not unusual to find wooden boards with beautiful calligraphy of, for instance, the Ten Commandments, which were commonly read during the morning services. This is true not only for the Netherlands, but also for Switzerland. Swiss Reformed churches are beautiful, and more often than not one or more works of art (both old and new) are on display—even in Calvin's own church in Geneva, *La cathédrale de Saint-Pierre*.

The developments in the broader art world, however, fell outside the attention of the common Calvinistic—and more widely—Protestant

---

8. Romaine, "Introduction," 23–38.
9. Tolsma and Van Wijngaarden, *Prachtig Protestant*.

believer. Yet, the nineteenth century was not without some important Protestant artists. The first of these is Eugène Burnand, a Swiss Calvinistic artist who lived in Moudon close to Lausanne. He painted Swiss domestic scenes and landscapes, but he also depicted biblical subjects such as his famous work, *Peter and John Running to the Tomb* (1898), which hangs in the *Musée d'Orsay* in Paris. It powerfully portrays the emotions of these two disciples: Peter, aware of his guilt, of his recent betrayal of Jesus, and afraid to face him; John, full of expectations but also so afraid that the tale of Jesus' resurrection might not be true after all.[10]

Another Protestant artist, a major figure in German romantic art, was Caspar David Friedrich (1774–1840). Friedrich's theology owed much to the Lutheran theologian, pastor, and poet Ludwig Gotthard Kosegarten, who preached a theology of the heart influenced by Moravian theology, which emphasized the personal experience of God. Kosegarten held regular services on the shores of Rügen in the very north of Germany. He saw all of creation as the temple of God, who sustains his world and shines through all things.[11]

When we look at Friedrich's paintings we can see how this theology shaped his work. In comparison with Ruisdael, his landscapes are more grandiose and sublime; they contain more mist, more yearning, and fewer people, though they often include one or two persons who are present in nature in a contemplative way. We usually see these characters from the back and in the foreground of the paintings, so that we look at the world with them and also with them experience the grandeur of creation and of God's presence in it.

---

10. Edgar, "Come, Hurry and Run," lines 14–28.
11. Holmes, *Kosegarten's Cultural Legacy*, chap. 8.

Another major influence on Friedrich was seventeenth-century Dutch landscape painting and the subtle ways in which it suggests the transcendent. In an unusually small painting by Friedrich, *Firs in the Snow* (1828), we see him doing the same by depicting a cluster of firs—evergreens, hence symbols of eternity—pointing upwards, covered with pure-white snow, and arched by a sunny blue sky. Would it be justified to see the Trinity in the three main trees? Friedrich similarly has a preference for the verticality of church steeples and boat masts, the latter adorning boats on their dangerous journeys towards distant ports or just about to arrive in safe havens. Crosses are also a recurring feature in Friedrich's works, which makes clear that they are not only about the experience of God in nature, but also about Christ and his work of redemption.

The last Protestant artist of major importance in the nineteenth century was Vincent van Gogh. His father was a pastor in the Dutch Reformed Church and belonged to a group of theologians called the Groninger School, which was considered liberal at the time because it sought to avoid all forms of dogmatism, yet it also emphasized an inner surrender to Christ and a life of service to others. Thomas à Kempis and John Bunyan were widely read in this circle, and especially *The Imitation of Christ* by Thomas à Kempis and the radically committed lifestyle it advocates had a great influence on Van Gogh with his intense personality, even though his behavior was sometimes unorthodox.

Van Gogh painted landscapes, portraits, still-life paintings, domestic scenes, and biblical subjects, all of which we can understand as closely connected with his Calvinistic faith. He struggled to find ways to depict the world as God's creation and show God's presence in all of reality. The naturalism and impressionism of his time with their surface rendering of reality made it necessary to look for new ways to represent deeper and higher meaning. In a letter to his brother Theo he says:

> I would like to paint men or women with that indefinable something (*je ne sais quoi*) of the eternal, of which the halo used to be the symbol, and which we try to achieve through the radiance itself, through the vibrancy of our colorations.[12]

Elsewhere he writes about "*quelque chose là-haut*" ("something up there") that enlivens all things with its presence and meaning.[13] In order to capture this presence and meaning Van Gogh's work became increasingly expressionistic and vibrant.

THE TWENTIETH CENTURY

In the twentieth century the gap between the world of art and the Christian community became even wider, as it saw the rise of various art movements that were further and further removed in spirit from a Christian view of life. Yet, there were also various theologians, philosophers, and art historians who emphasized once again the importance of art within a Christian framework.

In the Netherlands, the first since Calvin to point to the importance of art was Abraham Kuyper (1837–1920), who was a theologian and pastor, a minister of state, the founder of a Christian University, as well as the founder and editor-in-chief of a Christian newspaper. His impact on the Dutch Calvinist world was immense. He called himself a Neo-Calvinist, as he went back to Calvin and his unified view of life, thinking it through for his own time. Many know his famous words that "There is not a square inch in the whole domain of our human existence over which Christ, who is Sovereign over all, does not cry, Mine!"[14] This means that instead of the Pietistic division of life into sacred and secular, Kuyper recovered the view that art is a good creational gift of God and that sin runs through all of life, whether so-called sacred or so-called secular, because all of it is affected by

---

12. Bakker et al., *Vincent van Gogh*, letter 673, to Theo, 3 September 1888.
13. Ibid., letter 294, to Theo, between 13 and 18 December 1882.
14. Bratt, *Abraham Kuyper*, 488.

the Fall and in need of redemption. Needless to say, this rediscovery also had consequences for how he approached and appreciated art. One of his famous *Lectures on Calvinism* dealt with the visual arts and he also wrote a book about liturgy. He said that "The church is not hostile towards visual art, provided that it does not act as ruler [instead of servant, MHR] and the outward beauty does not drive back the inner beauty."[15] Kuyper was a champion of good Christian art in all its breadth and even allowed murals, stained-glass windows, and painted organ panels in churches.

Kuyper's ideas were elaborated into a philosophical system by Herman Dooyeweerd, in which art and aesthetics were included as one of the fourteen main spheres of the created order.[16] Hans Rookmaaker, a pupil of Dooyeweerd, became an art historian, while another pupil, Calvin Seerveld, specialized in the field of aesthetics. Both of them had pupils of their own: Graham Birtwistle, John Walford, and James Romaine for instance followed in the footsteps of Rookmaaker, while Lambert Zuidervaart and Adrienne Dengerink Chaplin are building on Seerveld's work. It would take up too much space to account for the thinking of any of these scholars in this essay, yet they did and do provide the conceptual framework for a tenaciously slow opening up of the orthodox Protestant and evangelical world to the visual arts.[17] Indeed, this process, far from being completed, is definitely taking place. These days there are thousands of Protestant artists across the world making art for our homes and schools, for the public buildings and squares of our cities, for local galleries or—when they are given the opportunity—for the more prestigious galleries, art fairs, and museums in the major cities of the western world. In addition to this, many Protestant churches and to a lesser extent evangelical congregations have opened their doors to the visual arts and are developing an eye for the importance of beauty in the places where Christians gather.

The Neo-Calvinist line of reflection on the arts is only half of the story of art in the Protestant world in the twentieth century. I also need to mention the Dutch Reformed theologian Gerardus van der Leeuw and the German Lutheran theologian Paul Tillich, who each developed their own view of the visual arts, mainly impacting the more liberal Protestant churches. Especially Tillich's influence is evident until today in various European countries and the United States, while Van der Leeuw's influence was limited to the Netherlands and in the course of time incorporated Tillich's ideas.

15. Kuyper, *Onze Eeredienst*, 77.
16. Hengelaar-Rookmaaker, *Complete Works of Hans Rookmaaker*, 6:179–82.
17. A book about these scholars, edited by Ida Slump, Roger Henderson, and Marleen Hengelaar-Rookmaaker, will be published by Square Halo Books in 2018.

Paul Tillich (1886–1965) contended that religion is not about a higher reality, but deals with the meaning dimension of our own reality. Religion is not about God as object besides or above other objects, but about manifestations of the divine in and through all things. Hence religious art is not art that deals with a supernatural reality, but art that deals with the search for and the experience of a deeper dimension of meaning in life. According to Tillich, art should deal with existential questions and when it does so, art and religion are closely linked.[18]

Gerardus van der Leeuw's (1890–1950) main undertaking was to clarify the relationship between art and religion. For him, art and religion are not the same: religion deals with the holy, art with the beautiful—and, as he said, "what is holy is more than what is beautiful."[19] He was concerned that the autonomous art of his time no longer had a need for religious subjects and that because of this art and religion had come to stand opposite each other as two hostile forces. It was this gap that he sought to bridge. He argued that art should not be totally autonomous, but that real art should serve God and a higher reality.[20]

Both of these theologians were trying to formulate a response to an increasingly secular and autonomous art world. Van der Leeuw's work and the Van der Leeuw Foundation which his pupils founded in 1954 did much to introduce art into the mainline Protestant churches during the period of reconstruction with its many new churches after World War II. This new church art (murals, windows, sculptures, liturgical tapestries, etc.) was mildly modern, we would say, but in its time this type of art was revolutionary. Indeed, I would call this period, which introduced art into mainline Calvinistic churches, a quiet revolution, as what happened here was totally new and unheard of in the history of Dutch Calvinism. Most of this art in the 1950s and 1960s was made by believing artists, while increasingly non-Christian artists were involved in these projects.[21]

The followers of Paul Tillich had an even greater preference for the work of non-believing artists, as they stressed that art should ask questions and shock people out of their traditional beliefs.[22] In the Netherlands these ideas were propagated by the theologian Regnerus Steensma. It led to the incorporation in church services of works like *Jesus is Angry* by Marlene

---

18. Dyrness, *Visual Faith*, 62–64.

19. Noordmans, *Verzamelde werken*, 6:171; and Oosterhof, *Niet door stomme beelden*, 91.

20. Oosterhof, *Niet door stomme beelden*, 89–92

21. Ibid., 94–98.

22. Steensma, *In de spiegel van het beeld*.

Dumas. I am not saying that there should never be a place for this kind of work in churches, and that it cannot lead to interesting and deep discussions, but I do have difficulty with the partiality of the Tillich followers to works that debunk faith rather than build it up—although this doubting kind of faith probably *is* the one they really do want to build up.

PROTESTANT ARTISTS TODAY

Figurative Art

From the 1960s up until the 1980s the art that was made by a dozen or so of orthodox Reformed artists in the Netherlands was all figurative; it consisted of landscapes, portraits, still-life paintings, and church interiors. It was figurative art in a time when abstract art was fiercely dominant. Against the tide of the art world these artists persisted in making reality- and creation-affirming art. Henk Helmantel became the best known of these artists.[23] He makes mainly still-life paintings and church interiors. Over the years he has become one of Holland's best-selling artists and in 2008 he was even elected artist of the year in the Netherlands. Even though his technique leans heavily on that of his seventeenth-century predecessors, his work definitely has a contemporary feel to it. What also differs from his old examples is the lack of symbolism. His paintings are serene and very beautiful, but lack perhaps in additional depth.

Increasing Diversity

Around the 1990s the art world became increasingly pluralistic and diverse. As in other areas of western culture the big stories of the various isms—such as abstract expressionism and minimalism—lost their credibility and a much more relativistic and tolerant art climate emerged. Figurative art was accepted again as one possible style among others. I would like to mention two (among many) Protestant artists who make outstanding work in this area today.

The American artist Catherine Prescott, who came to faith through L'Abri and attends an orthodox Presbyterian church, specializes in portraits and depictions of people. She does not merely emphasize resemblance in her paintings, but uses the tools of her craft with great purposefulness to bring out the character and emotional state of her subjects. She does not

---

23. Kraaijpoel and van Seventer, *Henk Helmantel*.

idealize the people she paints; indeed, she makes their portraits intensely human and shows their struggles and vulnerability, but in a loving way. Her husband Theodore Prescott, also an artist, says about her work:

> The result is the uncanny sense that she has not only recorded how someone looks, but that she seems to know who they really are. In these paintings she separates portraiture from the common accusation that it necessarily flatters its subject and obscures true character.[24]

Another development in the 1990s was that orthodox Protestant or evangelical artists started to open themselves to religious subjects. This happened in the Netherlands and the United States, but probably in other countries as well. Previously their output had by and large limited itself to landscapes, portraits, and still-life paintings. This was probably due to the Calvinistic emphasis on the importance of all of life, the absence of church art, and the huge challenge of presenting religious and biblical subjects in a contemporary way without becoming cliché or sentimental.

An artist whose work covers a broad array of themes (from landscapes and still-life paintings to social, religious, and biblical themes) is

---

24. Prescott, "Likeness and Presence," paragraph 5, lines 6–8.

the South-African artist Zak Benjamin, who came to faith through reading *Modern Art and the Death of a Culture* by Hans Rookmaaker. His painting *Christ and Consumerism* shows his originality in tackling religious themes. In it we see something that is a cross between an opened box of blocks and a computer. The blocks represent the building blocks of our lives or the keys that we hit again and again on our life's computer: a nice car, a big house, food, drink, relaxation, entertainment, travel, television, etc. They denote longings. The two burning candles besides the box stand for the religious and idolatrous quality of these building blocks. Yet, whatever key we hit, Jesus keeps on showing up on our screen, as he is the real fulfillment of all our longings. The screen cannot even contain him; he is much bigger than what we think we need.

Abstract Art

Today many styles, media, materials, and worldviews exist side by side. Contemporary art consists of installations, performance art, multimedia art, photography, video art, and computer art besides old media like painting and sculpture. Works can be figurative, abstract, or conceptual. For many people figurative art is not a problem, but abstract and conceptual art are often considered to be less accessible. So, let us take a closer look at these.

Just like abstract thinking, abstract art takes a few steps back when looking at reality, so that it gets a better overview. It wants to get at the essence of things and leave out the particulars. It wants to get at the basic processes and experiences that are applicable to various concrete situations. Not a painting of one happy child, but a painting of the dynamics of happiness in general. Not a portrayal of Jesus' resurrection, but of that which is characteristic of resurrection and new life. Through the use of color, contrast, light, and dark, recognizable forms, and the title of the work we as viewers can make all kinds of associations with various areas of reality.

The Pentecost window (1963) by the German artist Georg Meistermann in the Elisabeth Church in Marburg, for instance, does not show us the twelve disciples with tongues of fire on their heads, but instead portrays by abstract means what the Spirit is like and the effect his descending has on us. In the window we see six vertical pillars with small circles at their tops which look like people, a fierce wind blowing through their inner beings. This is depicted through a wild conglomeration of dynamic grey forms in the lower half of the window. Thus the Spirit of God is rendered as an agent of movement, blowing us free from places in which we are stuck and imprisoned, helping us to take little steps in new directions, come alive again, and grow and blossom. This is portrayed by the patches of warm and bright colors that have been placed besides and above the grey area. These colors can also be an image for the purifying and sanctifying flame-and-fire aspect of the Holy Spirit which sets us ablaze with new warmth and love. Figurative art cannot bring out these kinds of inner processes, but abstraction does make this possible.[25]

However, not all abstract art is out to portray something, be it in its own manner. Sometimes it just wants to bring some color and beauty to a place while being mostly decorative, or create an atmosphere of rest and peace—which the absence of a subject or a story can help achieve. This often is the case in churches.

Conceptual Art

Conceptual art started around 1960. Conceptual artists begin with an idea or concept for which they seek to find an adequate visual representation. In order to do so, they move beyond the traditional borders of art and incorporate all conceivable materials, media, and objects: from found and made objects, paintings, photos, sculptures, texts, and textile to sound, performance, and video. The resulting so-called installations come in many shapes and forms, from grandiose and spectacular to small and intimate. Installations address all kinds of themes: from social criticism and ideas about our time, humanity, art, nature, and reality to religious themes. Often they let us experience something. They do, for instance, create spaces in which we can move around or lie down. They can also have an interactive aspect, offering the viewer the opportunity to perform certain acts. They intend to be thought-provoking and to renew our thinking. They *can* be plainly obscure, but there are also many examples of installations that have been able to appeal to a broad audience.

Protestant artists have also embraced this form of art. I am enthusiastic about what installations have to offer. Artists can bring the reflective, critical, meditative, interactive, and socially-minded sides of conceptual art into play in a way that is meaningful and enriching.

---

25. Hengelaar-Rookmaaker, "Images for the Spirit," paragraph 10.

The Dutch evangelical artist Willem Zijlstra writes the following about the making of his installation entitled *Agnus Dei* (2005):

> During a church service in which we sang about "the Lamb of God slain for us" I thought: "Do we still know what this is all about?" Then I bought a lamb. I filmed it during its birth, life, and while it was being slaughtered. I stood face to face with the essence of this biblical theme: an innocent animal, barely half a year old, is brought to the slaughter without offering any resistance, yet without having done anything wrong. Next I had the lamb stuffed. I built an altar of newspapers, piling up the inability of human beings to live in peace. Unfolding the papers I found this title: "Man is capable of anything." It was an article about the Holocaust. The moment the lamb put its head next to this title and to the photo of Auschwitz it became for me a touching icon of Jesus himself, who voluntarily gave his life as a blameless and everlasting sacrifice.[26]

The installation project entitled *Cross* (2003) by the German Lutheran artist Madeleine Dietz consists of a steel frame in the form of a cross filled with earth. The steel frame makes clear that the cross proclaims an enduring

---

26. Zijlstra, "Behold the Lamb of God."

message, firm and unchanging like steel. Its content, the earth within the cross, reminds us of our human fleetingness: "You are dust, and to dust you shall return." The dryness of the earth speaks of our lack of life and infertility. Yet the soil also has an enormous potential for fertility. It looks dead and lifeless, but a little water is enough to awaken hidden seeds and bring them to life. Hence this cross speaks of the possibility of new life through the death of Christ, indeed of death and resurrection.[27]

The artwork, *Invitation/Decalogue* (2008–09), by the Romanian evangelical sculptor Liviu Mocan is an interactive work. It invites us to do something, so that we may experience something that can make us aware of new things. The work's title makes clear that the large vertical pillar-like structures stand for the Ten Commandments. They look like fingers, fingers of God standing in a circle with an open space in the middle; two hands of God forming a space of safety and well-being like the Ten Commandments do. The fingers are sharp and rough on the outside, keeping out temptations and sins. The title invites us to come into the circle, to sit down, and to meet with others who have strayed into it. Before we know it, we may end up reflecting on God's commandments and discussing them with others.[28]

CONCLUSION

Artistic Breadth

We have seen that Protestant, more specifically Calvinistic, art has had a history with ups and downs. It began with a period of great flowering, followed by a time of artistic poverty and shunning of art, followed by a slow re-acceptance of the visual arts, which is now developing into what looks like a new flourishing period. We are certainly justified to say this when looking at the many professional artists involved.

We have seen that a strength of Calvinistic art is its breadth: it deals with all of reality, not just with the religious aspect of life. With the resurgence of religious themes, we need to be careful not to lose this breadth. The threat of Pietistic dualism is not over yet. It does not only make itself felt in the area of subject matter, but also in its equation of art and mission. This can easily lead to one-dimensional art (as the message should not be misunderstood) and hence to a lack of depth and quality.

Another development we have witnessed is the reintroduction of art in Calvinistic churches. To me this is a justified correction of Calvin's view

---

27. Scherrer, "A Cross of Steel and Dust."
28. Tame, "Laws of Life and Love."

of art in the church. There is no reason why images could not be as beneficial to worshippers as words. Word and image each have their own way of speaking to us and therefore can be used in complimentary ways. We should, however, be careful that art for the church does not become the only or main focus of Protestant artists. That would mean another retreat into a subculture of our own. There are many possible vocations for Christian artists today as to style, subject matter, places, and people for whom one can choose to make art. Such a breadth of choice and possibilities is one of the strengths of art today.

The Artist as Servant

The present-day art world is not without its problems and it is not easy, especially for young artists, to find their way. Yet it is much easier than fifty years ago, because there is so much more freedom in the pluralistic art world. Artists can look for their own voice and be accepted. If the quality and appeal of their work are high enough, they will even be appreciated by the art world, as the favorable reception of artists of faith in various countries shows: Henk Helmantel and Marc Mulders in the Netherlands, Hans Thomann in Switzerland, Roger Wagner in the UK, David Robinson in Canada, Makoto Fujimura in the USA, etc.

Artists can join hands with what is good in the present art world and try to avoid its darker sides. To my mind its greatest problem remains that art is generally still put on a pedestal and that the world of art is still quite esoteric to most people. Hence the great challenge for Christian artists is to bridge various gaps: between the art world and the public, between the Christian art world and the Christian public, and between the Christian culture and our culture at large.

This task above all requires a different mindset. We should stop regarding the artist as some kind of prophet who is considered as totally autonomous in all that he or she does. It would be much more helpful if artists were to see themselves as servants: servants of their communities, churches, and culture at large. Autonomy is not a biblical word; servanthood is. Makoto Fujimura recently introduced the term "Culture Care," which wants to correct the old paradigm of hostility between Christians and the surrounding culture. Instead, he says, we should start to care for our culture with acts of generosity, care for our culture's soul, and offer it our bouquet of flowers.[29]

This can be done in all sorts of creative ways. Here I want to highlight just one installation project, done in England by Jake Lever, called

---

29. Fujimura, *Culture Care*, 1–6.

Soul Boats. A few years ago Lever was commissioned to make a work to celebrate the 300th anniversary of Birmingham Cathedral. Working with as many people as possible in schools, hospitals, day centers, homes for older people, hospices, churches, and at festivals across Birmingham and beyond, he encouraged each person to fashion a similar small boat. The outside of each boat was golden and inside they could write their own thoughts, ideas, experiences, or prayers. Lever says,

> The depth of engagement by participants of all ages in making their boats was incredible. Some for example made boats in memory of loved ones who'd died, some ranted about their difficulty in finding work and others celebrated the high points of long lives lived well. These moving reflections are on the inside of the boats, hidden from public view.[30]

He then created the installation with these boats, honoring each participant and aiming to create a "cluster of souls," all on a journey, unknown to each other yet brought together across the vast space of the cathedral roof. His hope was that the experience of gazing up would be one of beauty and mystery—an encounter with two thousand souls making one cloud of prayer.

LIST OF IMAGES TO BE FOUND ON THE WEBSITE HTTP://WWW.PATERNOSTERPERIODICALS.CO.UK/ EUROPEAN-JOURNAL-OF-THEOLOGY/ROOKMAAKER

1. Lucas Cranach: *Christ and the Adulteress*, c. 1545–50.
2. Gillis van Coninxloo: *Elijah Fed by the Ravens*, end of sixteenth century.
3. Rembrandt: *Annunciation*, c. 1635.
4. Gerard Dou: *Portrait of a Reading Old Woman*, 1630.
5. Jan Davidszoon de Heem and N. van Veerendael: *Bouquet with Crucifix and Shell*, 1640s.
6. Jacob van Ruisdael: *View of Haarlem from the Dunes at Overveen*, c. 1670.
7. Eugène Burnand: *Peter and John Running to the Tomb*, 1898.
8. Caspar David Friedrich: *Firs in the Snow*, 1828.
9. Vincent van Gogh: *Starry Night*, 1889.
10. Marlene Dumas: *Jesus is Angry*, 1983.

30. Doney, "A Copious Cloud," paragraph 4.

11. Henk Helmantel: *Still Life with Red Onions and Garlic*, 2011.

12. Catherine Prescott: *Daphne Holding her Neck*, 2015.

13. Zak Benjamin: *Christ and Consumerism*, 1999.

14. Georg Meistermann: *Pentecost Window*, Marburg, 1963.

15. Willem Zijlstra: *Agnus Dei*, 2005.

16. Madeleine Dietz: *Cross*, 2003.

17. Liviu Mocan: *Invitation/Decalogue*, 2008–09.

18. Jake Lever: *Soul Boats*, 2015.

BIBLIOGRAPHY

Bakker, Nienke, Leo Jansen, and Hans Luijten, eds. *Vincent van Gogh—The Letters. The Complete Illustrated and Annotated Edition*. New York: Thames & Hudson, 2009.

Boonstra, Harry, ed. *Abraham Kuyper: Our Worship*. Grand Rapids: Eerdmans, 2009.

Bratt, James D., ed. *Abraham Kuyper: A Centennial Reader*. Grand Rapids: Eerdmans, 1998.

Brigstocke, Hugh, ed. *The Oxford Companion to Western Art*. Oxford: Oxford University Press, 2001.

Calvin, John, *Institutes of the Christian Religion*. London: Westminster, 1960.

Doney, Meryl. "A Copious Cloud." http://www.artway.eu/content.php?id=2173&action=show&lang=en.

Dyrness, William A. *Visual Faith. Art, Theology, and Worship in Dialogue*. Grand Rapids: Baker Academic, 2001.

Edgar, William. "Come, Hurry and Run!" http://www.artway.eu/content.php?id=1340&action=show&lang=en.

Fujimura, Makoto. *Culture Care*. New York: Fujimura Institute, 2014.

Hengelaar-Rookmaaker, Marleen, ed. *The Complete Works of Hans Rookmaaker*. 6 vols. Carlisle, UK: Piquant, 2003.

———. "Images for the Spirit." http://www.artway.eu/content.php?id=1037&action=show&lang=en.

Holmes, Lewis M. *Kosegarten's Cultural Legacy: Aesthetics, Religion, Literature, Art, and Music*. New York: Lang, 2005.

Kraaijpoel, Diederik, and Hans van Seventer. *Henk Helmantel*. Aduard, Netherlands: Art Revisited, 2000.

Kuyper, Abraham. *Onze Eeredienst*. Kampen, Netherlands: Kok, 1911.

Leeuw, Gerardus van der. *Sacred and Profane Beauty: The Holy in Art*. 1957. Repr., Oxford, New York: Oxford University Press, 2006.

Luther, Martin. *Against the Heavenly Prophets in the Matter of Images and Sacraments*. In *Luther's Works*, edited by Helmut Lehmann, 40/2:79–223. Philadelphia: Muhlenberg, 1958.

Noordmans, O. *Verzamelde werken*. Vol. 6. Kampen, Netherlands: Kok, 1978.

Oosterhof, Wout. *Niet door stomme beelden. Het beeldenverbod in de hervormde traditie*. Gorinchem, Netherlands: Narratio, 1991.

Prescott, Theodore. "Likeness and Presence: Catherine Prescott's Portraits." http://www.artway.eu/content.php?id=1973&action=show&lang=en.

Romaine, James. "Introduction: You Will See Greater Things than These: John Walford's Content-oriented Method of Art History." In *Art as Spiritual Perception. Essays in Honor of E. John Walford,* edited by James Romaine, 23–40. Wheaton, IL: Crossway, 2012.

Scherrer, Patrik. "A Cross of Steel and Dust." http://www.artway.eu/content.php?id=1609&action=show&lang=en.

Steensma, Regnerus. *In de Spiegel van het beeld. Kerk en moderne kunst.* Baarn, Netherlands: Ten Have, 1987.

Tame, Jonathan. "Laws of Life and Love." http://www.artway.eu/content.php?id=757&action=show&lang=en.

Tolsma, Marijke and Wijngaarden, Martin L. van, ed. *Prachtig Protestant.* Zwolle, Netherlands: Waanders, 2008.

Walford, E. John. *Jacob Van Ruisdael and the Perception of Landscape.* New Haven: Yale University Press, 1992.

Zijlstra, Willem. "Behold the Lamb of God." http://www.artway.eu/content.php?id=1122&action=show&lang=en.

4

"With Psalms and Hymns"
The Reformation, Music, and Liturgy

Walter Hilbrands

THE ROLE OF HYMNS IN THE REFORMATION

Without the Protestant hymns, the Reformation would have likely taken an altogether different course. Some have argued that these new songs played an important role in the spreading of the ideas of the Reformation, possibly even a larger role than the sermons and the many writings of the Reformers. Eugen Eckert expressed this aptly, "The Reformation was ultimately spread through song, not through preaching or writing."[1]

According to historical tradition, the church in Schweinfurt sang Reformation hymns before and after the sermon:

> At the very least they sang in the chapel of the Carmelite monastery (for this was not allowed in the main church) German Psalms, always before the sermon, if one was held, and afterward, every time a song: "A Mighty Fortress is our God." This could not be forbidden by the Provincial of the Carmelite order,

---

1 Eckert, "Reformatorische Risiken," 9. Translations from the German are mine, unless otherwise indicated.

who had been present a few times, and even the children sang German Psalms at night in the streets, without even the slightest thing being done to put an end to it by the local authorities. The impact was such that one simply had no more taste for the previous flavor- and spiritless ceremonies, and as a consequence the Reformation became a self-propagating movement.[2]

Regardless of the fact that we are here dealing with a document from the sixteenth century, the immense influence of hymns in the spread of the Reformation is clear. In other places we find similar reports that Catholic masses, funerals, and processions were often significantly disturbed through the singing of Luther's hymns. These new hymns became protest songs, and the authorities quickly recognized their power. Protestant hymns were even banned completely in the city of Hildesheim in 1524 and 1531.[3]

During the Middle Ages music was generally included in the liturgy. Priests, soloists, and the *Schola cantorum* were, however, increasingly responsible for singing, so that the role of the congregation in singing was progressively suppressed. The Reformers took over some of these ancient and medieval songs, but also created their own texts with completely new melodies for congregational singing. During the Reformation, the Lutheran hymn was the unaccompanied, unisonous "chorale," which in many ways had the character of a folk song. Every line was sung in one breath, leading to a very fast tempo. For this reason, it is not surprising that, in some situations, secular songs were "spiritualized" using the method of *contrafactum*. Luther describes this practice as follows:

> Therefore we have divested and stripped such idolatrous, dead, and senseless texts of their noble music and with it clothed the living, Holy Word of God to sing, praise, and glorify Him and thereby confirm and strengthen our faith.[4]

Luther's "From Heaven Above to Earth I Come" (1534) was actually a *contrafactum* of the well-known song "Ich komm aus fremden Landen her":[5]

---

2 Sixt, *Reformationsgeschichte*, 90.

3 Dürr and Killy, *Protestantische Kirchenlied*, 29.

4 Luther's foreword to the funeral songs (*Begräbniß-Gesänge*, 1542), in WA 35:479–80.

5 Hahn and Henkys, *Liederkunde*, 18.

Ich komm aus fremden Landen her	I come from foreign lands
und bring euch viel der neuen Mär;	and bring you many tidings
der neuen Mär bring ich so viel,	I bring so many tidings,
mehr dann ich euch hier sagen will.	more than I want to tell you now.
Vom Himmel hoch, da komm ich her.	From heaven above to earth I come
Ich bring' euch gute neue Mär,	to bear good news to every home;
Der guten Mär bring ich so viel,	Glad tidings of great joy I bring
Davon ich singen und sagen will.	Whereof I now will say and sing.[A]

A. The translations of the songs are not my own.

This "children's song" is based on the passage Luke 2:8–18, in which the angels bring good news to the shepherds in the fields. The setting becomes *viva vox evangelii* (living voice of the Gospel). However, in 1539 Luther composed a new melody for this popular text.[6]

At the time of the Reformation a third major genre appeared alongside the psalm and the hymn, viz. the chorale. This was a new, independent, and revolutionary element in the liturgy in comparison to the practice of the Middle Ages. It was easy for both individual believers and the whole community to identify with the Reformation chorale. This element therefore corresponded perfectly with the notion of the priesthood of all believers.

LUTHERAN HYMNALS

In the sixteenth century around 500 different hymnals were published. The first vernacular hymnal with 88 songs in Czech was published in 1501 by Lukas van Prag for the Bohemian Brethren, the *Unitas Fratrum* in Bohemia and Moravia, a group which goes back to Jan Hus (c. 1370–1415). Michael Weisse's hymnal of 1531 for the German-speaking Bohemian churches already consisted of 157 songs, including some children's songs.[7]

Due to the Reformation's focus on the local church and the new possibilities of the printing press, the first Protestant hymnals were quickly published (some polyphonic). The "Achtliederbuch" (Nuremberg, 1523/24) was the first Reformation hymnal[8] and included four of Luther's hymns together with three from the Bohemian Reformer Paul Speratus (1484–1551). The "Enchiridion" (Erfurt, 1524) included thirty-five songs. In 1524 the "Geistliche Gesangbüchlein," a chorale hymnal with thirty-two polyphonic pieces, was published in Wittenberg by the cantor of Torgau, Johann Walter

6 Opinions on the reason for this differ. Cf. Korth, "Martin Luthers Lied," 40–51.

7 Möller, "16. Jahrhundert," 85.

8 Stalmann, *Kompendium*, 30.

(1496–1570), with whom Luther worked closely. Luther wrote a foreword for his hymnal: "Nor am I of the opinion that the gospel should destroy and blight all the arts, as some of the super-religious claim. But I would like to see all the arts, especially music, used in the service of him who gave and made them."[9]

Luther published the first church hymnal in Wittenberg in 1529; it was printed by Josef Klug (c. 1490–1552) and followed by five reprints until 1545. The printer and cantor at St. Thomas Church, Georg Rhau (1488–1548), published primarily for schools.[10] In 1544 he published 123 pieces. In his foreword to Rhau's *Symphoniae iucundae*, released in 1538, Luther, says with regards to music:

> I would certainly like to praise music with all my heart as the excellent gift of God which it is, and to commend it to everyone... First then, looking at music itself, you will find that from the beginning of the world it has been instilled and implanted in all creatures, individually and collectively. For nothing is without sound or harmony.[11]

"Das Babstsche Gesangbuch" (Leipzig, 1545) was the culmination of this series, and served as a role model for all future publications.[12] It included a foreword by Luther, and was published with elaborate biblical illustrations.

THE HYMNS OF MARTIN LUTHER

Martin Luther (1483–1546) was known to be a good musician, singer, and lutenist. He studied musical theory and sang in the *chorus musicus* at St. George's Church in Eisenach, as well as in its youth choir. However, it was only when he was 40 years old that he first revealed himself as a composer. The occasion was marked by the death of the first martyrs of the Reformation, Hendrik Vos and Johann van Esschen. These Augustinian monks had been arrested due to Reformation sermons on September 29, 1522, and were burnt at the stake on the July 1, 1523, in Brussels. Luther spontaneously composed a song of protest, which spread like wildfire. The first verse addresses the listener, and sets the theme. The third verse designates professors from Leuven as the opponents, and the ninth verse contradicts the

---

9   WA 35:475; Leupold, *Luther's Works* 53:315–16.

10 Stalmann, *Kompendium*, 32.

11 Literary "sounding number," cf. Wisdom 11: 21. See WA 50:369; Leupold, *Luther's Works* 53:321–22.

12 Möller, "16. Jahrhundert," 81.

slander in which they had stated that the martyrs had recanted their faith in the end. In the twelfth verse, which Luther later changed, he expresses his confidence that their death was not in vain:[13]

1. *Ein neues Lied wir heben an,*	*By help of God I fain would tell*
das walt' Gott unser Herre,	*A new and wondrous story,*
zu singen was Gott hat getan	*And sing a marvel that befell*
zu seinem Lob und Ehre.	*To his great praise and glory.*
Zu Brüssel in dem Niederland	*At Brussels in the Netherlands*
wohl durch zween junge Knaben	*He hath his banner lifted,*
hat er sein Wunder g'macht bekannt,	*To show his wonders by the hands*
die er mit seinen Gaben	*Of two youths, highly gifted*
so reichlich hat gezieret.	*With rich and heavenly graces.*
12. *Die Asche will nicht lassen ab,*	*Their ashes will not rest; world-wide*
sie stäubt in allen Landen.	*they fly through every nation.*
Hie hilft kein Bach, Loch, Grub noch Grab;	*No cave nor grave, no turn nor tide,*
sie macht den Feind zuschanden.	*can hide th' abomination.*
Die er im Leben durch den Mord	*The voices which with cruel hands*
zu schweigen hat gezwungen,	*they put to silence living,*
die muss er tot an allem Ort	*are heard, though dead,*
mit aller Stimm und Zungen	*throughout all lands*
gar fröhlich singen lassen.	*their testimony giving,*
	and loud hosannas singing.

Luther had a positive and open attitude towards music, ultimately because he recognized its significance in the ministry of the gospel:

> I am not content with those who scorn music, as all the *Schwärmer* do. For music is a donation and gift from God, and not a gift from man. In this way it expels the devil and makes people happy: for music contributes to forgetting anger, unchastely, haughtiness, and other vices. After theology I give music the next rank and the highest honor.[14]

Luther is known as the "father of the protestant chorales."[15] He wrote catchy spiritual songs which were often upbeat and rhythmic. Of his thirty-seven hymns, only five are original compositions, the rest adaptations.[16] The year 1523 witnessed the beginning of the composition of hymns, which accompanied the reform of the liturgy. The turning of the year 1523/24 saw Luther

---

13 Rüppel, *Ein neues Lied*, 6.

14 Tischreden No. 7034, WA Tischreden 6:348 (English translation Matthias Range).

15 Huchzermeyer, "Luther und die Musik," 18.

16 Albrecht, *Hymnologie*, 14.

ask the composer Georg Spalatin (1484–1545) for a dynamic equivalent version of the Psalms in strophic form:

> Following the example of the prophets and the Church Fathers, I intend to make German Psalms for the people, i.e., spiritual songs so that the Word of God even by means of song may live among the people. Everywhere we are looking for poets. Now since you are so skillful and eloquent in German, I would like to ask you to work with us to turn a Psalm into a hymn as in the enclosed sample of my own work. But I would like you to avoid new-fangled, fancied words and to use expressions simple and common enough for the people to understand yet pure and fitting (*simplicissima vulgatissimaque, tamen munda simul & apta verba canerentur*).[17]

As an example Luther sent his rhymed scoring of Psalm 130, "Aus tiefer Not schrei ich zu dir." However, Spalatin and many other composers did not satisfy Luther's request, so that he ended up having his own long and creative phase over several years thereafter.[18] Within twelve months he composed twenty-four hymns. They were then printed as flyers and thus quickly experienced a wide distribution.[19] In a sixteenth-century document a Jesuit priest states that Luther's hymns alienated more souls from the Catholic faith than all his sermons and writings put together.[20]

On the other hand, many medieval hymns were also used, by taking their melodic motif and modifying it into a new form. Indeed, the oldest hymn in a German hymnal is "Christ ist erstanden" from the twelfth century, with a Gregorian *Vorlage* from the eleventh century.[21] It belongs to the so-called *Leisen*, songs identifiable by their last word "Kyrie-leis."

Vic - ti - mae pas-cha - li lau des im-mo-lent Chris-ti - a - ni.
Christians, to the paschal vic-tim of-fer your thankful praises!

When we compare the melody with Luther's version from 1529, the strong dependence is apparent:

---

17 WA Briefwechsel 3, 220; Leupold, *Luther's Works* 53:221.
18 Albrecht, *Hymnologie*, 15.
19 Huchzermeyer, "Luther und die Musik," 19.
20 Albrecht, *Hymnologie*, 18.
21 Hahn and Henkys, *Liederkunde*, 58–61.

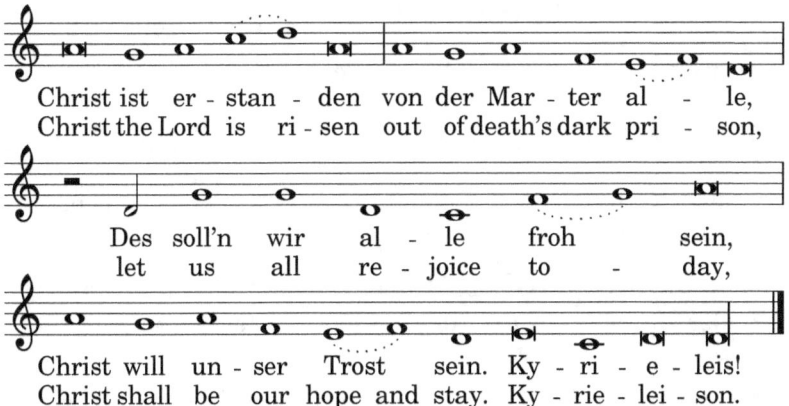

Luther's Easter hymn combines three elements: the Easter greeting "The Lord has risen," the call to Easter exultation, and an interpretation, "*pro nobis*."[22] Every verse flows into the "Hallelujah," which had not been sung throughout the period of Lent. During the Middle Ages a tradition was formed that on Easter morning the preacher would cheer the congregation up with a few jokes. Very popular was the joke that all men who had refused to be henpecked at home should start singing. There was supposedly a man in Waiblingen, so brave that he actually started singing. Afterwards, he was amply fed by his fellow citizens.[23]

The tune of this hymn is not in a minor key, but Dorian, an old church mode which suits serious festivals. For today's ears this melody sounds archaic, as if it was from another world. This is not only caused by the mode, but also by the melody which features almost no half steps, but instead mostly strong whole steps.[24] Luther commented in his "Table Talk" on the hymn, saying that "one ultimately tires of all songs but 'Christ ist erstanden' must be sung every year."[25] Luther recomposed the hymn in 1524 as "Christ lag in Todesbanden" and provided a new melody based on "Christ ist erstanden."

---

22 Weismann, *Handbuch* 1:324.

23 Ibid., 324

24 Ibid., 325.

25 WAT 4:517.

The melody of "Christ ist erstanden" is completely incorporated in the new hymn, but also updated.[26] All seven verses contain six seven-syllable lines and one eight-syllable line.[27] For Luther, this ballad on salvation is clearly all about proclamation in the form of song (*sonora praedicatione*).[28] The song sets the story of Easter to music, but starts with the death of Christ in the first verse.[29] The second verse displays the rule of death and the third verse the coming of the Savior. This verse closes with a "Hallelujah" and leaves no room for doubt that Christ is the victor. In the fourth verse the

26 Weismann, *Handbuch* 1:326.

27 Hahn and Henkys, *Liederkunde*, 60–61.

28 WA 50:372; this expression is already found in a sermon of Ambrosius on Ps 118 (PL 15:1379A).

29 Hahn and Henkys, *Liederkunde*, 60.

conflict is described, drawing on the pre-Reformation traditions of the popular Easter sequence "*Victimae paschali laudes*" (e.g. "*mors et vita duello conflixere mirando*," "how fierce and dreadful was the strife when life with death contended").[30] The fifth, sixth, and the seventh verses are then all about the victory celebration of the redeemed.[31]

Among the medieval songs which were revised, reworked, and extended by one verse are "Nun bitten wir den Heiligen Geist" (thirteenth century) and "Gelobet seist du Jesu Christ" (fourteenth century). In addition, Luther wrote many liturgical songs such as "Wir glauben all' an einen Gott" (a paraphrase of the Nicene Creed), "Vater unser im Himmelreich" (the Lord's Prayer), "Verleih uns Frieden gnädiglich" (benediction), and catechism songs like "Dies sind die heilgen zehn Gebot" (the Ten Commandments) and "Christ unser Herr zum Jordan kam" (on the baptism of the Lord). His free songs include festival songs and children's songs like "Vom Himmel kam der Engel Schar," "Vom Himmel hoch da komm ich her," and "Erhalt uns, Herr, bei deinem Wort."

Last of all, many Psalm paraphrases are found among Luther's works, such as "Ach Gott vom Himmel sieh darein" (Ps. 12), "Es wolle Gott uns gnädig sein" (Ps. 67), and "Wär Gott nicht mit uns diese Zeit" (Ps. 124). The hymn "Aus tiefer Not schrei ich zu dir" is a paraphrase of the penitential Psalm 130 from late 1523. In the beginning of this hymn the falling fifth causes the depth of misery to become audible. The word "Not" (affliction) presents as the highest sound a figurative *exclamatio*.[32] Moreover, it sounds in a half-step (subsidiary second), ultimately embodying the suffering related to the affliction.

Before 1529 Luther composed the famous "A Mighty Fortress," the "Hymn of the Reformation." In 1527 the plague came to Wittenberg, including Luther's own home. In addition to this, one of his followers, Leonhard Kaiser, suffered martyrdom. However, the hymn is intentionally meant to remain universal, and cannot be attributed to a single occasion.[33] Luther furnished the song with a spirited melody. Sadly, today the hymn is usually sung with the monotone rhythm.

In contrast to "Aus tiefer Not" (Ps. 130), only a few lines in "A Mighty Fortress" are taken directly from the biblical original.[34] Luther described his

---

30 Weismann, *Handbuch* 1:327.

31 Rüppel, *Ein neues Lied*, 21.

32 Bernoulli and Furler, *Genfer Psalter*, 42. The falling fifth also appears in the Genevan Psalter.

33 Weismann, *Handbuch* 2:59.

34 Ibid., 60.

original version as a "song of comfort."³⁵ Although the militant language of Psalm 46 is used, Luther nonetheless interprets the Psalm Christologically and applies the depicted fight to the battle between Christ and the Devil. The first and third verses are the so-called "Devil-verses," in contrast to the "Christ-verses." The last lines of the second, third, and fourth verses underline that Christ and the kingdom of God are imperishable and everlasting:³⁶ "He holds the field forever;" "One little word can fell him;" and "The Empire ours remaineth."

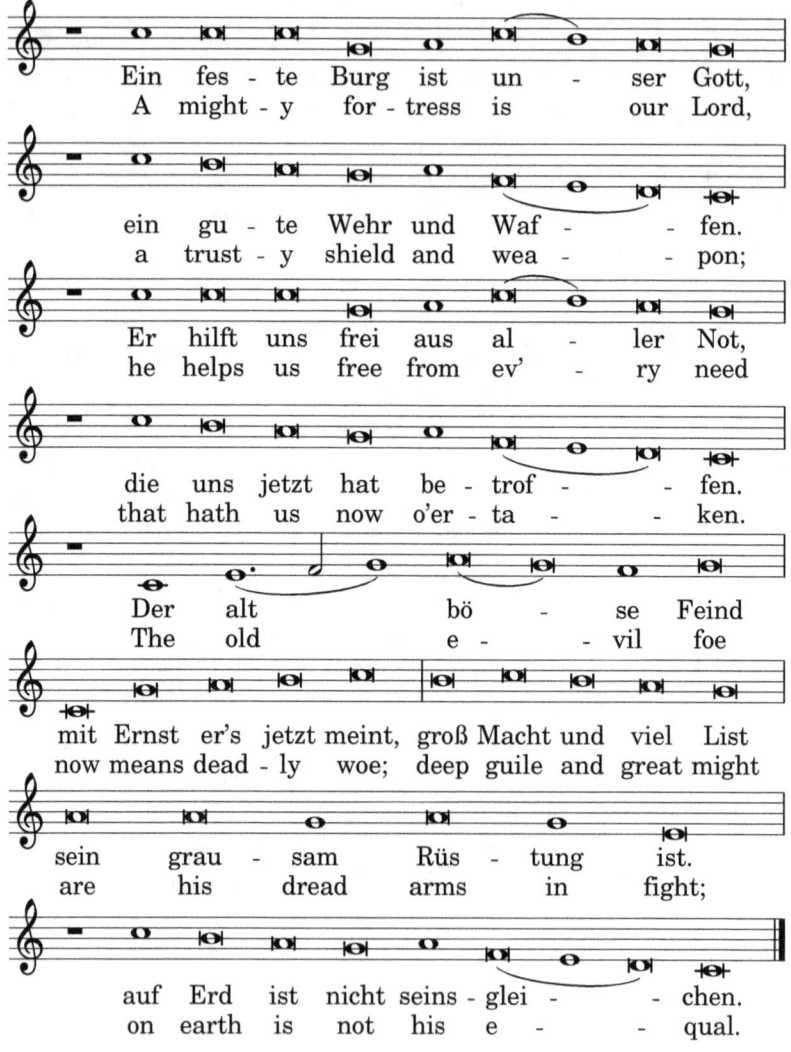

---

35 Rüppel, *Ein neues Lied*, 17.
36 Weismann, *Handbuch* 2:62.

Of Luther's thirty-seven spiritual songs, the majority are included in the German *Evangelisches Gesangbuch*, covering almost every topic. However, Luther did not write a Passion hymn; this theme only appears in a few of his Easter hymns.[37]

CALVIN AND THE GENEVAN PSALTER

Although Huldrych Zwingli himself (1484–1531) was a musician, he banned all music from the church service as "Clamor before the people."[38] The organ of the Grossmünster in Zurich was dismantled at his behest. Various reasons have been given to explain Zwingli's negative attitude regarding music.[39] In contrast, Martin Bucer introduced the German mass in Strasbourg in 1524 and the "Gesangbuch Teutsch Kirchenampt" was released in 1525. In 1537 the pastors of Geneva under the auspices of John Calvin (1509-64) called for the introduction of the use of Psalms in congregational worship:

> Certainly at present the prayers of the faithful are so cold that we should be greatly ashamed and confused. The Psalms can incite us to lift up our hearts to God and move us to an ardor in invoking and exalting with praises the glory of his Name.[40]

Intended was the use of biblical songs set to a rhyme scheme in strophic form.

After his expulsion from Geneva in 1538, Calvin got to know the German-speaking Psalter, which had only recently been finished.[41] The Reformer was apparently so taken with this, that he himself set six Psalms to a rhyme scheme, as well as the Canticle of Simeon, the Ten Commandments, and the Credo. When the first French hymnal was released in 1539 under the title "Aulcuns pseaumes et cantiques mys en chant," it contained thirteen Psalms by the poet Clément Marot (1496–1544) as well as the aforementioned nine songs by Calvin.[42] The melodies originated in part with Wolfgang Dachstein (1487–1553) and Matthias Greitter (c. 1495–1550), while some were taken over from the Strasbourg Hymnal, including Greitter's

---

37. Albrecht, *Hymnologie*, 16.
38. Ibid., 33.
39. Möller, "16. Jahrhundert," 93.
40. "Articles concernant l'organisation de l'Église et du culte à Genève, proposés au conseil par les ministres." Baum et al., *Ioannis Calvini* 10:12. English: Reid, *Calvin*, 54.
41. Friedrich, *Genfer Psalter*, 98.
42. Möller, "16. Jahrhundert," 955.

famous melody "Es sind doch selig alle" from Psalm 68,[43] the "Psaume de bataille" ("battle Psalm"). It was said that Huguenot Francs-tireurs used to sing Psalm 68 when they attacked royal troupes. The soldiers also sang Psalms during the changing of the guard, and before and after meal times. Psalm singing was an essential element of the school programs. Psalms were sung both by craftsmen and by workers in the country. They were even sung by Huguenot rowing slaves on the French galleys and by the women in the prison for Huguenots in Aigues-Mortes.[44]

A year after his return to Geneva in 1541, Calvin published the order of service "La forme des prières et chants ecclésiastiques" with twenty-nine Psalms and six other spiritual songs. Thirty of the texts had been versified by Marot, only five by Calvin himself. In the foreword Calvin writes: "Among all the things adapted to recreate humans and bring them delight, music is the first or at least one of the most important, and we have to regard it as a gift given by God to this end."[45] Music is a gift of God's creation, a gift of the Holy Spirit. However, Calvin consistently warns against abuse of this good gift, if it used outside of its original purpose, viz. the honor of God and the benefit of one's neighbors.[46] For this reason songs such as the Psalms, having been given by the Holy Spirit, were seen as the most suitable for worship and edification. In Calvin's words, such "honest and holy songs will be like spurs to incite us to pray to and praise God, and to meditate upon his works in order to love, fear, honor, and glorify him."[47]

A new hymnal in 1544 contained forty-nine Psalms, the Canticle of Simeon, and the Ten Commandments in song form, all set to a rhyme scheme by Marot.[48] When Marot died, the project was interrupted until Calvin tasked Theodore Beza (1519–1605) to pursue it. Eighty-three Psalms were then published in 1551 with the title "Pseaumes octantetrois de David," including thirty-four compositions by Beza, and melodies by Loys Bourgeois.[49]

The Genevan Psalter was finished in 1562, following the replacement of several melodies. It was published with the title "Les Pseaumes, mise en rime françoise." Forty-nine Psalms originated with Marot, one hundred and one with Calvin's successor Theodore Beza. Grammatically the

---

43. Bernoulli, *Genfer Psalter*, 44.
44. Friedrich, *Genfer Psalter*, 104.
45. Baum et al., *Ioannis Calvini* 6:169–70.
46. Smelik, "Theologie der Musik," 68.
47. Baum et al., *Ioannis Calvini* 6:169–70.
48. Bernoulli and Furler, *Genfer Psalter*, 26–27.
49. Ibid., 27.

compositions rely heavily on the Hebrew originals. Free adaptations, such as Luther's paraphrases of Psalms, did not fit Calvin's ideal. Poets should neither shorten, nor expand the original text; rather the given text should simply be rendered as a rhymed versification.[50] Calvin describes this principle in his foreword to an edition of the Psalms in 1543:

> It is to have honest and holy songs which will be like spurs to incite us to pray to and praise God, and to meditate upon his works in order to love, fear, honor, and glorify him. Moreover, what St. Augustine said is true, that no one is able to sing things worthy of God except that which he has received from him. Therefore, when we have looked thoroughly, and searched here and there, we shall not find better songs and more fitting for the purpose than the Psalms of David, which the Holy Spirit spoke and created through him. Moreover, when we sing them, we are certain that God puts these songs in our mouths, as if he himself were singing in us to exalt his glory.[51]

Psalm 134 is a good illustration of the strong reliance on the biblical text (the melody is by Bourgeois, 1551):

---

50. Joby, *Calvinism and the Arts*, 64.
51. Pidoux, *Les Pseaumes*.

2. Hebt eure Hände auf und geht zum Throne seiner Majestät In eures Gottes Heiligtum, bringt seinem Namen Preis und Ruhm!	2. Lift up your hands, in prayer draw nigh unto his sanctuary high; O bless the Lord, kneel at his feet, and worship him with reverence meet.
3. Gott heil'ge dich in seinem Haus und segne dich von Zion aus, der Himmel schuf und Erd' und Meer. Jauchzt, er ist aller Herren Herr!	3. The Lord now bless you from above, from Zion in his boundless love; Our God, who heaven and earth did frame, blest be his great and holy Name.

Matthias Jorissen (1739–1823), the cousin of Gerhard Tersteegen, completed a "new rhyming of the Psalms" in 1798, in which the night-song character of the Psalm has been extended, but its "day and night" aspect is not inconsistent with the content of the Psalm. The "house of the Lord" becomes the "throne of his glory," suggesting the vision of the heavenly council before God's throne. The blessing in Psalm 134:3 is expanded so as to include sanctification, which also logically fits the content of the Psalm. Incidentally, the images of the original have been kept.[52]

As mentioned before, Calvin did not limit himself to the Psalms, as can be seen in the multiple other biblical passages, and extra-biblical texts such as the Credo, which were set to a rhyme schemes.[53] Often two Bible verses were rendered in one strophe, which ultimately produced a high number of strophes; the 176 verses of Psalm 119 in the Bible produced 88 strophes!

Like Luther, Calvin does not justify music soteriologically, but instead he sees it as grounded in God's creation. As a gift of God it is be utilized for the benefit of one's neighbors and to glorify God. On one hand the "I" in the Psalms becomes the "I" of the individual believer so that the affliction and the praise, the plea, the complaint, and the worship, are in fact his or her own prayers. On the other hand, the community of believers, experiencing the collective "we," is strengthened as it is joined together as one voice in corporate worship. The Old Testament Psalms are especially suitable to express individual experiences, while simultaneously being strongly congregational.[54]

The Genevan cantor Loys Bourgeois (1510–61) composed the majority of the 127 melodies in accordance with Calvin's standards. Other melodies originated with Bourgeois' predecessor Guillaume Franc (c. 1505–70), with "Maître Pierre," probably the cantor and the Hebraist Pierre Davantès (c. 1525–61). All 150 Psalms were set to a new tune, in order to place only

---

52. Weismann, *Handbuch* 2:49.
53. Joby, *Calvinism and the Arts*, 72–73.
54. Watson, *English Hymn*, 44.

the pure Word of God in the mouths of the church members during worship. The melodies have only two note values, long and short. They are quiet, simple, and lack all dotting; they are written without bars and never in triple time. The lines are clearly differentiated, and begin and end with long notes.[55] According to Calvin, music should be characterized by "weight and majesty" ("pois et majesté").[56] Ligatures were only used in a few cases, where one syllable contains two notes. In the case of Psalm 6 there are even three notes on a single syllable. Due to these principles, the Genevan Psalter is stylistically cohesive, although various poets and composers were involved in its production.

In contrast to the Lutheran approach, the Genevan Psalter was not at all like the folk songs of its time. However, like the Lutheran songs, it was written in the vernacular of the Reformers. Direct *Vorlagen* other than the Strasbourg Psalter are not perceivable. The songs were influenced by Gregorian melodies. The interval of a Psalm, and often a single line, consists typically of an octave, with only in a few cases a ninth. The melodies are based on traditional church modes. The different verse forms are based on the different biblical originals, and are therefore not interchangeable.[57]

Unlike Zwingli, Calvin traced the existence of music back to God in the story of Jubal, the biblical father of music (Gen. 4:21). Musical instruments are only an aid, but music is God's endowment to humankind.[58] In his *Institutes of the Christian Religion*, Calvin describes the worship of the church as being grounded in 1 Corinthians 14:15 and Colossians 3:16:

> And certainly if singing is tempered to the gravity befitting the presence of God and angels, it both gives dignity and grace to sacred actions, and has a very powerful tendency to stir up the mind to true zeal and ardor in prayer. We must, however, carefully beware, lest our ears be more intent on the music than our minds on the spiritual meaning of the words.[59]

The widespread use of hymnals in the Reformed Church was necessary in contrast to Lutheranism, simply due to the vast number of verses. Sixty-three different editions of the Genevan Psalter had already been published by 1562–65, so that one must assume that almost every church member possessed their own hymnal. The first version was printed by roughly 45

---

55. Joby, *Calvinism and the Arts*, 68.
56. Baum, *Ioannis Calvini* 6:169.
57. Friedrich, *Genfer Psalter*, 102.
58. Baum et al., *Ioannis Calvini* 23:100; cf. *Institutio* I.11.12 about sculptures.
59. *Institutio* III.20.32.

different printers in Geneva and France. This represents between 30,000 to 50,000 copies.[60]

The Genevan Psalter experienced an extremely fast international distribution. Thomas Sternhold (c. 1500–49) and John Hopkins († 1570) translated the complete Psalter into English in 1562. Peter Datheen published a Dutch version in 1565. The Lutheran, Ambrosius Lobwasser (1515–85), who had been criticized as the "eyeball and siren of Calvinism," started to translate the Huguenot Psalter word for word into rough German in 1565, completng his work in 1573. From this time till the last version came out in 1824, around 1,000 editions of these hymnals were released.[61] Other translations followed shortly thereafter: Italian (1603), Polish (1600/1605), Spanish (1606), Hungarian (1607), and Czech (1587/1618), until the Psalter had been translated into 22 different languages. Among the Catholics, a Psalter was released in 1585 by Kaspar Ulenberg, followed by a new Lutheran Psalter in 1602 produced by Cornelius Becker.[62] Jorissen's "new rhyming of the Psalms" appeared in 1798, after 60 versions of the Lobwasser Psalter had already been released, but it quickly superseded Lobwasser's and has remained popular up to the present day.

In the Reformed and Lutheran churches, worship was sung without an organ, unisonous, and unaccompanied, well into the seventeenth century, and even later in some areas. The sermon, sacrament, and prayer, including church worship, were the basic elements of the Reformed liturgy. Even today choirs are largely unknown in most Reformed churches. The cantor, a leader with a strong voice, or a youth choir, led the worship. On the other hand, a unique music culture based on the Psalms developed in private homes, including in the beginning the practice of concerts. Well-loved were the simple, homophonic tenor pieces by Claude Goudimel, which had been published in 1565, thereafter experiencing a large international distribution.[63] Some churches in German-speaking Switzerland outside of Basel already began singing four-part pieces in the seventeenth century.[64] The compositions by Jan Pieterszoon Sweelinck (1562–1621), the greatest Dutch composer and organist, who worked at the Oude Kerk in Amsterdam, represent the ultimate culmination of this trend. His Psalm motets came out in four parts (1604, 1612, 1613, and posthumously in 1621), all as four- to eight-part pieces. They are characterized by their virtuosity, use of

60. Friedrich, *Genfer Psalter*, 102.
61. Bernoulli and Furler, *Genfer Psalter*, 9.
62. Möller, "16. Jahrhundert," 70.
63. Stalmann, *Kompendium*, 42.
64. Friedrich, *Genfer Psalter*, 104.

counterpoint and an expressive interpretation of the text. Sweelinck's *Collegium musicum*, an exclusive circle of merchants, was the primary audience for his music. They often came together as a private circle of music connoisseurs to enjoy his motets.

CONCLUSION

The role of music in the Reformation can hardly be overestimated. Alongside of the writings and sermons of the Reformers, it was primarily the new songs which popularized and spread the Protestant message among the people. The Reformation was also a musical movement. The songs created identity and ultimately produced a social cohesion in the community of faith. We will do well not to underestimate the importance of music in the church service.

Music is understood by the Reformers as a gift of God. It does not primarily find its raison d'être in Christology or soteriology but in the doctrine of creation.[65] Music is not an end in itself, but ultimately contributes to the proclamation of the Gospel. It is actually prayer and proclamation in song form (*sonora praedicatione*).

From a musical point of view the songs of the Reformation are in continuity and discontinuity with the music of the Middle Ages. The Reformers sometimes drew from the musical traditions they were acquainted with, but modified them for their specific purposes, and above all created new melodies and texts. These songs are characterized by their use of the vernacular, their simplicity, their dependence on the Bible, and their liturgical significance. The melodies of the Reformation were neither populist nor exclusively classical. They were simple and accessible to all, while simultaneously being dignified and appropriate according to their holy content.[66] Because of their intermediate position, they acquired a timelessness which has now persevered for more than half a millennium. At the same time, because of their international distribution, they have also had an ecumenical impact.[67]

Luther's songs and particularly the Genevan Psalms cover the whole spectrum of praise and lament. Through their close reliance on the biblical text, they are able to represent the whole spectrum of religious experience from the deepest separation from God to an overflowing praise of his Name. This breadth avoids the pitfalls of a restricted view of music, often present in many modern collections of songs in which, for example, God is often

---

65. Smelik, "Theologie der Musik," 76–77.
66. Harrell, *Martin Luther*, 34–6.
67. Bernoulli and Furler, *Genfer Psalter*, 32.

primarily worshiped as Father, and Jesus as King. Which of the modern songs take up the topic of repentance? Is there any room for lament in our services and in our songs? The Reformation songs are based on deep life experiences and often reflect difficult circumstances. Their biblical content and authentic faith experiences continue to possess an abiding relevance.

BIBLIOGRAPHY

Albrecht, Christoph. *Einführung in die Hymnologie*. 4th ed. Göttingen: Vandenhoeck & Ruprecht, 1995.

Baum, Wilhelm, et al., eds. *Ioannis Calvini, Opera Quae Supersunt Omnia*. Corpus Reformatorum 29–87. Braunschweig: Schwetschke, 1863–1900.

Bernoulli, Peter Ernst, and Frieder Furler, eds. *Der Genfer Psalter: Eine Entdeckungsreise*. 2nd ed. Zürich: Theologischer, 2005.

Dürr, Alfred, and Walther Killy, eds. *Das Protestantische Kirchenlied im 16. und 17. Jahrhundert: Text-, musik- und theologiegeschichtliche Probleme*. Wiesbaden: Harrassowitz, 1986.

Eckert, Eugen. "Reformatorische Risiken und Nebenwirkungen auf Kirchenlieder der Gegenwart." *Ansätze: esg-Nachrichten* 4–5 (2012) 4–10.

Friedrich, Verena. "Der Genfer Psalter." In *Musik und Gottesdienst* 63 (2009) 98–104.

Hahn, Gerhard, and Jürgen Henkys, eds. *Liederkunde zum Evangelischen Gesangbuch*. Vol. 12. Handbuch zum Evangelischen Gesangbuch 3. Göttingen: Vandenhoeck & Ruprecht, 2005.

Harrell, Robert D. *Martin Luther: His Music, His Message*. Greenville, SC: Musical Ministries, 1980.

Huchzermeyer, Helmut. "Luther und die Musik." *Luther* 1 (1968) 14–25.

Joby, Christopher Richard. *Calvinism and the Arts: A Re-Assessment*. Leiden: Brill, 2007.

Korth, Hans-Otto. "Martin Luthers Lied 'Vom Himmel hoch': Zur Herkunft der beiden jüngeren Melodien." In *Das deutsche Kirchenlied: Bilanz und Perspektiven einer Edition*, edited by Wolfgang Hirschmann and Hans-Otto Korth, 40–51. Kassel: Bärenreiter 2010.

Leupold, Ulrich S. *Luther's Works* 53. Philadelphia: Fortress, 1965.

Luther, Martin. *D. Martin Luthers Werke*. 121 vols. Weimarer Ausgabe. Weimar: Böhlau, 1883–2009.

Möller, Christian. "Das 16. Jahrhundert." In *Kirchenlied und Gesangbuch: Quellen zu ihrer Geschichte*, edited by Christian Möller, 69–127. Tübingen: Francke, 2000.

Pierre Pidoux, ed. *Les Pseaumes mis en rime francoise par Clément Marot et Théodore de Béze* [1565]. Kassel: Bärenreiter, 1935.

Reid, J. K. S., ed. *Calvin: Theological Treaties*. LCC 22. Philadelphia: Westminster, 1977.

Rüppel, Johannes. *Ein neues Lied wir heben an: Betrachtungen zu Liedern Martin Luthers*. Kassel: Evangelischer Presseverband Kurhessen-Waldeck, 1983.

Sixt, Johann Michael. *Reformationsgeschichte der Reichsstadt Schweinfurt*. Schweinfurt: Volkhart, 1794.

Smelik, Jan. "Die Theologie der Musik bei Johannes Calvin als Hintergrund des Genfer Psalters." In *Der Genfer Psalter und seine Rezeption in Deutschland, der Schweiz und den Niederlanden: 16.–18. Jahrhundert*, edited by Eckhard Grunewald et al., 61–78. Tübingen: Niemeyer, 2004.

Stalmann, Joachim. *Kompendium zur Kirchenmusik: Überblick über die Hauptepochen der evangelischen Kirchenmusik und ihrer Vorgeschichte*. Hannover: Lutherisches Verlagshaus, 2001.

Watson, John R. *The English Hymn: A Critical and Historical Study*. Oxford: Clarendon, 1997.

Weismann, Eberhard, et al. *Handbuch zum evangelischen Kirchengesangbuch*. Vol. 3/1–2, *Liederkunde*. Göttingen: Vandenhoeck & Ruprecht, 1970, 1990.

5

The Reformation and Historical-Critical Research in Biblical Interpretation

Gert Kwakkel

INTRODUCTION

The unique authority of Scripture was part and parcel of the theological convictions of Luther, Calvin, and other Reformers of the sixteenth century. As opposed to the Roman-Catholic doctrine of the authority of the church and its tradition, they formulated the principles of *sola scriptura*, "by Scripture alone," and *sacra scriptura sui ipsius interpres*, "Holy Scripture is its own interpreter." Scripture did not need any external authority to decide its status and interpretation.

Luther, for example, wrote in one of his apologies against the bull of Pope Leo X that Scripture should be given the first position among everything ascribed to the Fathers; that is, "that in and of itself it is the most certain, the most accessible, the clearest explainer of itself, as it tests, judges, and illumines everything."[1] Calvin, for his part, stated that "Scripture has its authority among believers on no other grounds than that they declare that

---

1. Luther, *Assertio* 97: "ut sit ipse per sese certissima, facillima, apertissima, sui ipsius interpres, omnia omnium probans, judicans et illuminans."

it has come down from heaven, and as though therein God's own spoken words are heard."[2]

All this seems to differ much from the principles which guide the historical-critical research of the Bible as it has developed since the eighteenth century. Notwithstanding its great diversity, a basic characteristic of historical-critical research is that it does not accept any biblical utterance just because it is found in Scripture. Biblical information on past events, authorship of books, dates of composition, and any other things has to be critically judged. It can only be accepted after having stood the test.

The critical approach is well illustrated by a metaphor used by Abraham Kuenen, one of the fathers of historical-critical research of the Old Testament in The Netherlands. In his view, the historical-critical researcher acts like a judge, who examines all the witnesses and formulates a hypothesis which accounts for the statements of all the witnesses, even if it contradicts some of them. Next, he tests the hypothesis by going through the evidence once again, and finally gives judgment as to what really happened.[3]

Nevertheless, it has often been asserted that in one way or another the Reformers gave the impulse to the later rise of historical-critical research, or that historical-critical research keeps and passes on the heritage of the Reformation.[4] As is well-known, Luther's high view of Scripture did not stop him from denouncing the Epistle of James as "a straw letter" nor from criticizing the Book of Esther. Calvin, though more moderate in this respect, could still speak about an error in Matthew 27:9 (the mistaken reference to Jeremiah instead of Zechariah) or state that Acts 7:16 (about the transport and burial of the bodies of the patriarchs) should be amended.[5] Apparently, if the Reformers were not the fathers of historical-critical research, their approach was not identical with that of present-day inerrantists either.

OUTLINE AND METHOD

This contribution will present two views of the relationship between the Reformers and historical-critical research. The first is that of Hans-Joachim

2. Calvin, *Institutio*, 1559, I.vii.1: "non alio iure plenam apud fideles authoritatem obtinent, quam ubi statuunt e caelo fluxisse, acsi vivae ipsae Dei voces illic exaudirentur."

3. Kuenen, "Critical Method," 485–88.

4. Cf. Kraus, *Geschichte*, 40, 80. One assertion Kraus has in mind is that of Ebeling, "Bedeutung," 42, to the effect that the historical-critical method is the consequence of the Reformed doctrine of justification by faith, *sola fide*.

5. Calvin, *Commentarius in harmoniam evangelicam*, 749: "certe Ieremiae nomen errore positum est pro Zacharia"; *Acta apostolorum* 1, 187: "Quare hic locus corrigendus est."

Kraus in his *Geschichte der historisch-kritischen Erforschung des Alten Testaments*, the first edition of which was published in 1956.[6] Kraus (1918–2000) was a Reformed theologian from Germany. I got acquainted with his book when I was enrolled on the Master program of the Theological Seminary of the Reformed Churches (Liberated) in Kampen, The Netherlands, where it was used as a textbook for many years. The second view is taken from *Pandora's Box Opened* by Roy A. Harrisville, a professor emeritus at Luther Seminary, St. Paul, Minnesota. He published the book in 2014, when he was already in his nineties. Unlike Kraus, Harrisville does not focus on historical research of the Old Testament, but takes most of his examples from the New Testament. Moreover, he writes from a Lutheran perspective.

After the presentation both views will be evaluated, first from a historical and then from a theological perspective. My aim in all this is to define the extent to which historical-critical research can be used by biblical scholars who adhere to the basic convictions of the Reformers.

HANS-JOACHIM KRAUS

According to Kraus, the main task of a historical inquiry into Protestant research of the Bible is to find an answer to the question what has become of the Reformed confession of *sola scriptura* since the rise of historical criticism.[7] As a result, the relationship between the convictions of the Reformers and historical-critical research is a recurring topic in his book.

For Kraus, it is clear that the Reformers initiated the process leading to the rise of historical-critical research. This was the consequence of their decision to concentrate fully on Holy Scripture and its literal or historical sense. The historical circumstances in which the biblical authors were doing their work came to the fore. Precise study of the biblical texts led to many new observations and discoveries. Interpreters became increasingly aware of the human shape of Scripture and critically examined traditional views on, for example, the authorship of biblical books.[8]

However, several other factors and intellectual currents also contributed to the rise of historical-critical research, until it finally took shape as a scholarly method in the Age of Enlightenment. The first to be mentioned is Humanism. Although the Reformers adopted many aspects of humanist research, Reformation and Humanism must clearly be distinguished. The main point of difference was that the Reformers emphasized God's

---

6. Enlarged editions were published in 1969 and 1982.
7. Kraus, *Geschichte*, 3–4.
8. Ibid., 4, 8–18, 92.

authority whereas Humanism focused on humanity and human authority.[9] Humanism greatly influenced Socinianism, which argued for the use of human reason as the highest criterion in biblical interpretation. It also affected Hugo Grotius, whose approach differed from the Reformed tradition in which he was raised in that he excluded all dogmatic premises from his exegesis. According to Kraus, both Socinianism and Grotius were part of the intellectual history that led to the Enlightenment and thus to the rise of historical-critical research.[10] Furthermore, Grotius, for his part, influenced English deism, another intellectual movement that must be taken into account in order to get a full picture.[11]

With respect to critical research of the Old Testament in particular, Kraus gives pride of place to two other scholars from the seventeenth century, namely Baruch Spinoza and Richard Simon. Spinoza was the first to draw attention to literary-historical problems in Old Testament research and he formulated the hermeneutical principles that should guide historical-literary research. In his view, Scripture had to be investigated in the same way as nature, that is, based on reason alone.[12]

In similar vein, Richard Simon advocated the use of a purely critical and rationalistic method and thus coined the principles and rules of the historical-critical method. Kraus hails Simon's work as the real beginning of historical-critical scholarship because of Simon's impact on Johann Salomo Semler in the second half of the eighteenth century. Moreover, historical-critical scholars in the nineteenth century, such as Eduard Reuss and Karl Heinrich Graf, explicitly honored Simon as the intellectual father of their method.[13]

According to Kraus, it was Semler who definitively launched historical-critical research in Germany. His background was in Pietism, but an intellectualistic thirst for knowledge in line with the ideals of the Enlightenment dominated his work. His indebtedness to Simon can be gathered from the fact that he published a German translation of Simon's *Histoire critique du Vieux Testament* and adopted many of his views. In agreement with the Enlightenment principle of free research guided by human reason, Semler propagated a critical investigation of the canon. In all this, he brought

---

9. Ibid., 27–28.
10. Ibid., 41–43, 50–53.
11. Ibid., 56, 93–94.
12. Ibid., 61–64.
13. Ibid., 65–70, 86.

about the revolution in Protestant biblical studies that led to the victory of historical-critical method.[14]

So far, mention has been made of scholars and currents which positively contributed to the development of historical-critical research. In addition, Kraus refers to Reformed and Lutheran orthodoxy as representatives of the opposite approach. Unlike Luther, orthodox theologians completely identified Scripture with the Word of God. They defended their dogma of inspiration in a rationalistic way and did not allow for any error in Scripture. All this provoked the criticism that ushered in historical-critical research of the Old Testament, until Semler finally accomplished the destruction of the orthodox dogma.[15]

Still other factors could be mentioned, for example, text-critical research in the first half of the seventeenth century.[16] Anyway, this overview suffices to point out the two main elements of Kraus' view of the relationship between the Reformation and the rise of historical-critical research. First, although the historical-critical method used in biblical studies in modern times was born at the end of the eighteenth century, it cannot be regarded as a product of the Age of Enlightenment alone, as many other factors contributed to its development.[17] Second, Spinoza and Simon, who were very influential in shaping critical research, were anything but heirs of Reformed theology. Baruch Spinoza was a Jew and Richard Simon was a Roman-Catholic, who tried to combine his critical approach with respect for the doctrine of the church. Consequently, it would be incorrect to state that historical-critical research has merely adopted the heritage of the Reformation.[18]

In keeping with this, Kraus concludes his discussion of Semler's work by drawing attention to the difference between his convictions and those of the Reformers. Luther and Calvin testified to the presence of the Word of God issuing from Scripture.[19] Characteristic for Semler was the perspective of a human critic who is committed to the present time and judges the past. By virtue of his human authority, the critic selects the reasonable and moral divine truths from Scripture, as distinguished from the human and historical elements. In Kraus' view, this implies that the biblical concept of

---

14. Ibid., 104–10.
15. Ibid., 31–38, 92–93, 107.
16. See ibid., 46–50.
17. Cf. ibid., 70, 80.
18. Cf. ibid., 40, 68, 111; cf. also 335–36, 426.
19. Ibid., 109: "Bezeugten die Reformatoren das Ereignis der Gegenwart des Wortes Gottes aus der Heiligen Schrift, . . . "

revelation and a fundamental insight of the Reformers are abandoned, in favor of a modern form of Gnosticism.[20]

For Kraus this state of affairs does not imply that historical-critical research should be rejected, however. He agrees with Karl Barth and Gerhard von Rad that it should be accepted as a useful element of a theological interpretation of the Old Testament, but not as its goal. Interpreters must focus on the *kerygma*, because the ultimate purpose of their research has to correspond to the essential object (*die Sache*) of the biblical texts; that is, God himself, his Word, and an encounter with him. Within this framework, historical-critical research is justified by the human shape of Scripture, by analogy with the incarnation of Christ, in agreement with Luther's view of Scripture. Furthermore, God did not act in a special and isolated history of redemption, but in and by contingent historical events. Accordingly, historical-critical research provides an important service to theological exegesis in that it clarifies the concrete circumstances in which God acted according to the testimony of the biblical authors and in which they wrote their texts.[21]

Kraus happily welcomes the results of this approach in the works of Martin Noth, Walther Zimmerli, Claus Westermann, and, of course, Von Rad.[22] However, he also acknowledges that there are still several questions that have not yet received a definitive response, one of which relates to the theological function of historical-critical exegesis.[23] Apparently, the debate on this question, which occupied Barth and Von Rad so much, still has to be pursued.

ROY A. HARRISVILLE

The main part of Harrisville's book *Pandora's Box Opened: An Examination and Defense of Historical-Critical Method and Its Masters Practitioners* is dedicated to the rise of the historical-critical method from the seventeenth century onward. The author portrays a large number of scholars who have contributed to its development or critically interacted with it. He begins with Baruch Spinoza, who is credited with the invention of the method "as

---

20. Ibid., 107–13.

21. Cf. ibid., 416–20, 432–33, 492–95, 497–500, 506–7, 525–27, 569–73; cf. also 386–89 (on Martin Kähler), 389–91 (on Hans Emil Weber), and 426–29 (on Wilhelm Vischer).

22. Ibid., 447, 449–50, 486–87, 505–9, 540. See also 502–3, on the series of commentaries *Biblischer Kommentar Altes Testament*.

23. Cf. ibid., 578.

currently construed,"²⁴ and ends with Otto A. Piper, who was Harrisville's doctoral supervisor at Princeton Seminary. In the final three chapters he defends the method against attacks from several sides as well as against recent synchronic alternatives, which isolate the texts from their authors and their external objects. This part of the book particularly addresses the relationship between the Reformation and the historical-critical method; accordingly, the emphasis is on theological evaluation rather than on historical explanation.

Harrisville admits that some scholars developed the historical-critical method in order to undermine the authority of Scripture, but in his view the use of the method can be separated from such intentions. He infers the right to criticism from the distinction between gospel and Scripture. Although Scripture is the normative witness to the gospel, it is not identical with it. The gospel of "God's reclamation of the world through the death and resurrection of Jesus Christ" is the core of Scripture "from out of which the whole could be understood." Historical criticism is helpful for an interpretation which focuses on the core, because of the historical nature of Christian faith. It analyzes the historically contingent contexts in which God was made manifest and protects against Docetism. Without this method the church would be unable to claim any scholarly basis for its exegesis. It would forsake its task to make the gospel heard on the public square, and put an untimely end to the age-old quest for an understanding between faith and reason.[25]

However, in order to fulfill its task profitably, the historical-critical method must be adjusted in several respects. It should give up its claim to objectivity.[26] With Karl Barth, Rudolf Bultmann, and others, Harrisville maintains that the nature of the object of research (i.e. the biblical texts) requires that interpreters take a stance on the Bible's subject matter. They should do their work in faith and thus allow the text to become the interpreter's interpreter.[27] Moreover, they should work within the context of the Christian community, with its confessions, which, however, must always be submitted to the Bible, in agreement with the priority of Scripture.[28]

---

24. Harrisville, *Pandora's Box*, 252.

25. See ibid., 302, 317–18, 326–27, 333, 348; quotations taken from 327 and 326 respectively.

26. Ibid., 304–6, 328.

27. Ibid., 306–13, 330–31, 336–41, 350.

28. Ibid., 313–19, 332–36.

In developing this view, Harrisville obviously takes issue with fundamentalism and biblicism.[29] At the same time, he is convinced that he is in line with the basic tenets of the Reformation, which he sharply distinguishes from post-Reformation orthodoxy, just as Kraus did.[30] Taking Scripture as the normative witness to the gospel agrees with the principle of *sola scriptura*, while focusing on its core corresponds to *sola fide* and *solus Christus*.[31] Furthermore, Harrisville connects his opposition to the idea of a neutral interpreter to Calvin's doctrine of the internal testimony of the Holy Spirit as a prerequisite of interpretation.[32]

Apparently, the most essential element in this connection is Luther's view of the authority of Scripture. According to Harrisville, Luther did not attribute a formal or abstract authority to Scripture (as later orthodoxy would do). For him, the authority of the Bible was derived from its scope, Jesus Christ. The biblical writings were authoritative because—and to the extent that—they announced Christ.[33] Evidently, for Harrisville this view leaves much room for the use of critical methods including a critical evaluation of any claims found in the text (*Sachkritik*).[34]

HISTORICAL EVALUATION

What is the historical relationship between the Reformation and the rise of historical-critical research? It goes without saying that the mere examination of two studies on the subject does not suffice to pass final judgment. A thorough study of the work of the Reformers is needed. This should also consider the differences between, for example, Luther and Calvin, as both Kraus and Harrisville appeal to the former more than to the latter in their defense of the legitimacy of historical-critical method. Furthermore, it should be checked whether the Reformers really differ so much from later orthodoxy as has been asserted.[35]

Nevertheless, it seems correct to conclude that if the Reformers contributed to the rise of historical-critical research, their hermeneutics was by no means the only factor responsible in the development of the method. Kraus' historical investigation provides substantial evidence in support of

---

29. Cf. ibid., 348.
30. Cf. ibid., 23, 261.
31. Ibid., 326.
32. Ibid., 307, 339.
33. Ibid., 18–19, 261–62, 324, 337–38.
34. See, e.g., ibid., 310, 341.
35. See also the essay by A. T. B. McGowan in this volume.

this conclusion. In addition, it should be noted that in their defense of the method, both Kraus and Harrisville make a somewhat selective use of the hermeneutics of the Reformers, the former by appealing to Luther's view of the human shape of Scripture and the incarnation analogy, the latter by appealing to Luther's emphasis on Christ as the scope of Scripture. Other elements, such as the role of Scripture as the supreme judge of all controversies, are not explicitly addressed in their final evaluations.

Like Reformed and Lutheran adherents of historical-critical research, advocates of biblical inerrancy also may feel inclined to seek allies among the Reformers. This likewise seems to be a hazardous undertaking, for two interrelated reasons. First, as has been pointed out above, Calvin, for example, could speak of an error or a need for correction in biblical texts. How does this relate to Article IX of the Chicago Statement on Biblical Inerrancy, which affirms that the inspiration of the Bible "guaranteed true and trustworthy utterance on all matters of which the Biblical authors were moved to speak and write"? It would be interesting to know how the Reformers might have evaluated this Statement, but evidently we will never know.

Second, in formulating their doctrine of Scripture and principles of biblical interpretation, the Reformers were interacting with the issues of their day, namely the Roman-Catholic view of the authority of the church and its tradition and spiritualist ideas on the so-called left wing of the Reformation.[36] They were obviously not in a position to pronounce on what would be at stake centuries later between advocates of historical-critical research and inerrantists. Of course, it is relevant to compare their statements with those of people living in later eras, but it is historically incorrect to force them to take sides with either historical-critical research or inerrancy as developed and defended in the nineteenth and twentieth centuries.

THEOLOGICAL EVALUATION

It will be clear that evangelical theologians who want to define their position with regard to historical-critical research should seriously consider the views of the Reformers, but still have to formulate their own position, in accordance with their biblical principles and in response to the issues of their time. When they do so, the aspect called "historical" will not be problematic as there seems to be a consensus on the historical nature of God's revelation; it is rather the element expressed by "critical" that requires further reflection. In this connection, four observations can be made.

---

36. See, e.g., Harrisville, *Pandora's Box*, 18.

1. "Critical" is always a relative term, never an absolute. One is always critical with respect to something. Moreover, a critical judgment requires a criterion or a norm, which is not criticized for the time being. As Kraus has pointed out, many practitioners of historical-critical research use human reason as a criterion to determine what is historically plausible and what is not. Conversely, the Protestant principles of *Sola Scriptura* and of Scripture as the supreme judge of everything suggest that whatever Scripture teaches is the norm and must be accepted without criticism. In this connection, it is of interest to note that most—not all—examples of critical comments of Luther and Calvin reviewed by Kraus relate to tradition, not to Scripture itself, as he himself acknowledges.[37]

2. For Harrisville it is legitimate to evaluate critically much of what is taught in Scripture, because he locates Scripture's authority in its scope, the gospel of Jesus Christ, and he confines it to that. In other words, a critical stance towards Scripture as in historical-critical research is allowed and the scope is the norm. This may seem to be an attractive solution, but it does not work.

    First, it is impossible to do justice to the gospel of Jesus Christ within the limits of the current historical-critical approach. The mere incarnation of God's Son, not to mention other things, shows that God must actively intervene in the course of history in order to save the world. It does not suffice that he acts in and by the contingent events of history (as Kraus puts it); that is, such events as can be investigated by historical-critical research. Something is needed beyond what is historically plausible according to human experience and reason.

    Second, if Jesus Christ is accepted as the only Savior, it seems strange to renounce his view of Scripture (i.e. the Old Testament, in his days). For him, Scripture was the highest authority in all discussions. This can be inferred from his appeal to biblical texts introduced with "It is written," over against the devil's suggestions and misuse of the Bible (Matt 4:1–11). With his Jewish opponents Jesus shared the principle that Scripture cannot be broken (John 10:35). It is true, he did not consider all elements of the Old Testament to be applicable law anymore (see, e.g., Matt 5:38–42; 19:3–9; Mark 7:18–19), but he never put a biblical prescription into perspective because of its human origin or nature. It seems more probable that he did so because its validity had expired, since the time of fulfillment had arrived (cf. Matt 5:17).

---

37. Kraus, *Geschichte*, 16–18.

No doubt, he heard in Scripture the living voice of his heavenly Father, through the Spirit (cf., e.g., Matt 22:43; John 5:37,39).[38]

3. The incarnation analogy, to which Kraus refers, is often used in discussions about the nature of Scripture, for example in the solid and highly appreciated *Reformed Dogmatics* of Herman Bavinck.[39] Yet, in spite of being obvious, the analogy is not really helpful.

   First of all, it fails to do justice to the unique mystery of the incarnation of the Son of God. Jesus Christ is God and man in one person; he has both a divine and a human nature. Conversely, Scripture has neither a divine nor a human nature. To be sure, it was given by God through inspiration and its authors did their work using their human capacities; but it has only one nature, namely that of a book.

   Furthermore, it is anything but evident which aspects of the divine and human nature of the Son of God must be related to which aspects of Scripture. According to Kraus and many other theologians, the weaknesses of Christ's human nature have their parallel in the fallible human elements in Scripture, which are open to historical criticism. It is equally justified to draw a line from the immaculate conception of Jesus Christ to Scripture's infallibility or inerrancy. It follows that the incarnation analogy cannot predict anything with respect to Scripture. It can merely be used retrospectively, to illustrate aspects of Scripture that have already been established on other grounds.[40]

4. In one of his *Tischreden* (*Table Talk*), Luther said that Holy Scripture requires humble readers who constantly say: "Teach me, teach me, teach me!"[41] In line with this conviction, believers (theologians and others) should allow Scripture to teach them about its own nature. Some elements of this "self-witness" of Scripture have already been reviewed above (i.e. in the comments on Jesus' view of Scripture). Space does not permit to add others. Anyhow, it is clear that for Jesus and the apostles the divine authority of Scripture was beyond dispute. Discussions did not relate to the question as to whether what was taught in Scripture should be accepted, but only to the right interpretation of the

---

38. See also Wells, *James Barr*, 371, 373.

39. Bavinck, *Gereformeerde dogmatiek*, 1:352, 405 (= *Reformed Dogmatics* 1:380–81, 434–35).

40. For a penetrating critique of the incarnation analogy, see Wells, *James Barr*, 340–49. As for his own preference, Wells says: "If we wish to speak of analogies in connection with Scripture, perhaps we can find no better one than the sovereignty of divine grace expressed in inspiration and conversion"; ibid., 363.

41. Luther, *Tischreden*, vol. 4, No. 5017. Cf. also Kraus, *Geschichte*, 20.

biblical texts.[42] Accordingly, a critical attitude informed by Scripture and by Jesus' teaching in particular limits itself to the question: "*What does Scripture teach? Have I or have we correctly understood what it says?*" It does not dwell upon the possibility to critically reject any element of what Scripture actually teaches.

A nice example of this approach can be found in Calvin's discussion of the authorship of 2 Peter. Calvin agrees with those who argue that the style of the letter differs so much from that of the historic Peter that the apostle can hardly be the writer. In addition, there are some "other probable conjectures" (*aliae probabiles coniecturae*)—which Calvin does not specify[43]—from which it can be inferred that another person wrote the letter. Yet nothing unworthy of Peter can be found in it, as it gives evidence of the power and grace of an apostolic spirit. If the letter is accepted as canonical (as Calvin evidently does), Peter's authorship must be recognized, because his name is mentioned in 2 Peter 1:1 and the writer affirms that he has lived with Christ. Pseudepigraphy is not an option for Calvin, as it is unworthy of a minister of Christ. In the end, Calvin maintains that the letter stems from Peter, but at the same time he tries to account for its peculiarities by assuming that one of Peter's disciples wrote the letter instead of the apostle himself.[44]

It turns out that for Calvin the claims made by the canonical text are decisive and have to be accepted. However, within those limits he ponders the possibility of reading or interpreting the text in another way than the most obvious one, if the data urge him to do so. The details of his argument as to Peter's authorship need not be discussed here. The question whether he always applied these principles consistently can also be left open. Even so, it is clear that Calvin points toward a viable course which can still be taken by evangelical scholars. Critical research should submit itself to what Scripture says; its critical aspect relates to *what exactly* Scripture intends to say, not to the trustworthiness of what it says.

---

42. Cf. Bavinck's extensive overview of Scripture's teaching about itself in *Gereformeerde dogmatiek*, 1:358–72 (= *Reformed Dogmatics*, 1:389–402); cf. also ibid., 1:393 (= *Reformed Dogmatics*, 1:423–24).

43. On 2 Pet 3:15, where Paul is referred to as "our dear brother," Calvin comments that Peter would never has spoken in this way; see Calvin, *Commentarii in epistolas canonicas*, 370.

44. Calvin, *Commentarii*, 321–22.

CONCLUSION

Obviously, historical-critical research has provided biblical scholars with many useful insights. More than in the past, they are aware of the complex processes that may have led to the actual shape of the biblical books. The diversity and specificity of the genres found in the texts have come to light. The historical background of the biblical stories has been elucidated by archaeology. All this has contributed to a better understanding of how the original audiences or readers may have interpreted the texts.

Nevertheless, current historical-critical research is unable to do justice to the deepest divine intention behind Scripture. By limiting itself to what can be demonstrated within a human and reasonable perspective, it risks losing sight of the core message of the Bible, that is, God's miraculous intervention for the redemption of the world. This does not imply that evangelical theologians cannot make any use of it. They can profitably use several of its elements, such as genre analysis and the reconstruction of the editorial process behind the books, as long as the teaching of Scripture is accepted and the true nature of historical-critical research is taken into account. As a scholarly method it shares the possibilities and limits of all modern academic research; it can only clarify matters within the set boundaries of what is accessible to human perception.

BIBLIOGRAPHY

Bavinck, Herman. *Gereformeerde dogmatiek*. Vol. 1. 4th ed. Kampen, Netherlands: Kok, 1928.

———. *Reformed Dogmatics*. Vol. 1, *Prolegomena*. Translated by John Vriend. Grand Rapids: Baker Academic, 2003.

Calvinus, Johannes. *Commentarii in epistolas canonicas*. Edited by Kenneth Hagen. Ioannis Calvini opera exegetica 20. Geneva: Droz, 2009.

———. *Commentarius in harmoniam evangelicam*. Corpus Reformatorum 73. Brunswick: Schwetschke, 1891.

———. *Commentariorum in acta apostolorum liber primus*. Ioannis Calvini opera exegetica 12/1, edited by Helmut Feld. Geneva: Droz, 2001.

———. *Institutio christianae religionis* I and II. Joannis Calvini opera selecta 3: Institutiones Christianae religionis 1559 libros I et II, edited by Petrus Barth and Guilelmus Niesel. Munich: Kaiser, 1928.

"The Chicago Statement on Biblical Inerrancy." *Journal of the Evangelical Theological Society* 21 (1978) 289–96.

Ebeling, Gerhard. "Die Bedeutung der historisch-kritischen Methode für die protestantische Theologie und Kirche." *Zeitschrift für Theologie und Kirche* 47 (1950) 1–46.

Harrisville, Roy A. *Pandora's Box Opened: An Examination and Defense of Historical-Critical Method and Its Master Practitioners*. Grand Rapids: Eerdmans, 2014.

Kraus, Hans-Joachim. *Geschichte der historisch-kritischen Erforschung des Alten Testaments*. 3rd ed. Neukirchen-Vluyn: Neukirchener, 1982.

Kuenen, A. "Critical Method." *Modern Review* 1 (1880) 461–88, 685–713.

Luther, Martin. *Assertio omnium articulorum M. Lutheri per bullam Leonis X. novissimam damnatorum* [1520]. D. Martin Luthers Werke: Kritische Gesamtausgabe 7:94–151. Weimar: Böhlau, 1897.

———. *Tischreden*. Vol. 4. D. Martin Luthers Werke: Kritische Gesamtausgabe. Weimar: Böhlau, 1916.

Wells, Paul Ronald. *James Barr and the Bible: Critique of a New Liberalism*. Phillipsburg, NJ: Presbyterian and Reformed, 1980. 2nd ed., Eugene, OR: Wipf and Stock, 2016.

6

Justification by Faith
Are Protestants and Catholics Irreconcilably Divided?

A. N. S. (Tony) Lane

The doctrine of justification by faith is like a shopping mall with many entrances. One can enter the arcade via different shops and, having done so, then proceed to look at all the other shops. With justification by faith likewise there are many different entry points. One can focus on the definition of the word justification, on the formal cause of justification, on imputed versus imparted righteousness, on justification, *sola fide*, on the merit of good works, on assurance of salvation, etc. Our entry point will be different. We will examine the question of the (im)perfection of our righteousness, implying the need for mercy at the Last Judgement. In tackling this issue we will find ourselves touching on many of the other issues.

But first we will prepare the ground by giving some definitions and by considering three general points about the doctrine.

DEFINITIONS AND GENERAL CONSIDERATIONS

Definitions

There are three types of righteousness that will be discussed below and it is important to be clear about the distinction between them:

- *Inherent righteousness* (sometimes called infused or imparted righteousness) refers to the inward change brought about by regeneration and renewal. This is seen as Christ's righteousness, which is imparted to us by the Holy Spirit.

- The *righteousness of works* refers to our outward works. Roman Catholics generally take the position that our inherent righteousness is perfect, but the righteousness of our works is not.

- *Imputed righteousness* refers to the imputation to us of Christ's righteousness, by which we are reckoned to be righteous, despite the fact that we remain sinful, despite the imperfection of our inherent righteousness and the righteousness of our works. Protestants have generally held to this but most Catholics have not. Inherent and imputed righteousness together are sometimes referred to as "twofold righteousness" (*duplex iustitia*).

Tension

In the New Testament we see a tension. In the parable of the Pharisee and the Tax Collector (Luke 18:9–14) the Pharisee thanks God for all his good works and that he is better than others. The tax collector by contrast beats his breast and says, "God have mercy on me, a sinner." It is the tax collector, not the Pharisee, who is accepted by God. The grace of God is shown to the worst of sinners and this is the only ground on which we can approach God. But that is only half of the story. A few chapters earlier in the same Gospel (Luke 14:25–33) Jesus speaks uncompromisingly of the demands of discipleship and warns that, "those of you who do not give up everything you have cannot be my disciples" (14:33). The promise of acceptance to the worst sinner does not rule out the demand for total commitment from all believers.

The same tension is found in Paul. He teaches justification by faith alone, that we are accepted by God not on the ground of our good works or merits but solely on the basis of Christ's death for us on the cross. But alongside this comforting message of grace, the same Paul also warns the

Corinthian Christians that those indulging in a variety of activities, such as adultery, theft, or drunkenness, will not inherit the kingdom of God. "And that," he says, "is what some of you *were*"—before they came to Christ (1 Cor 6:9–11). The good news of free acceptance does not rule out the need for obedience. "If anyone is in Christ, the new creation has come." (2 Cor 5:17)

A key test for any doctrine of justification is whether it succeeds in holding this tension.

Differing Concerns

In looking at the issue of justification we need to compare the Catholic and Protestant doctrines. But before doing so it is helpful to examine the underlying *concerns* of each side. Some of the recent ecumenical dialogues have focused on this issue.[1] Protestants are concerned to emphasize the seriousness of sin, the gratuity of salvation, and our dependence upon God's grace and mercy. They focus attention on "the misery of their sins, their resistance against God, and their lack of love for God and their neighbor" and therefore "in faith put their whole trust in the saving God, are sure of his mercy, and try in their lives to match up to this faith." The corresponding danger is that they "think too little of God's regenerative power." Roman Catholics, by contrast, are concerned to stress the reality of God's transformation of our lives by his grace/the Holy Spirit, together with the need for and value of good works. Catholics

> deeply penetrated by the limitless power of God, stress above all, in the event of justification also, God's glory and the victory of his gracious acts on behalf of men and women, holding human failure and half-heartedness toward these gracious acts to be, in the strict sense, of secondary importance.

The corresponding danger is that they do not take the misery of sin sufficiently seriously.

It is not hard to see that both sets of concerns are valid, but one-sided. Each side can acknowledge the validity of the other's concerns. In the early 2000s I wrote a book on *Justification by Faith in Catholic-Protestant Dialogue*.[2] Writing that book made me much more sensitive to areas that are of concern to Roman Catholics. For example, I was made aware that some

---

1. E.g., Lehmann and Pannenberg, eds., *Condemnations*, 40, from where the following quotations are taken.

2. Some of the material in this paper is taken from this book.

Protestant formulations that emphasize human sin and our dependence upon mercy may go so far that they can be accused of belittling the regenerating work of the Holy Spirit.

Status of Theological Language

We must beware the danger of treating theological doctrines as if they were mathematical formulae. If they were, there would be no scope for diversity. If a column of figures add up to 115, all other answers are simply wrong. To approach theology this way would imply an extreme and naive form of realism foreign to the way in which the discipline actually works. We sometimes meet people who think that quoting one biblical passage settles an issue, ignoring all the rest of what Scripture says. If this naive approach were correct there would be no hope of reconciling a document that proclaimed justification by faith alone with another that denies it. I am referring, of course, not to the Reformers and Trent but to Paul and James.

IMPERFECTION OF HUMAN RIGHTEOUSNESS

We turn now to our chosen topic of the imperfection of human righteousness. We will examine how this was understood by the Reformers Luther and Calvin, by Catholic Humanists, in the Reformation dialogues between the two sides (especially at Regensburg in 1541), and at the Council of Trent. We will also ask whether recent dialogues, culminating in the *Joint Declaration on the Doctrine of Justification* (1999), have resolved the issue and consider the Second Vatican Council and the *Catechism of the Catholic Church* (1994).

Luther: simul iustus et peccator

At the Reformation both sides agreed that all baptized believers are still plagued by concupiscence, by sinful inclinations, and lustful desires. The difference comes over the status of these desires. It is because he saw them as sin that Luther viewed the Christian as *simul iustus et peccator*—at the same time righteous and a sinner. This slogan can be given two different meanings. First, Luther held that the Christian is both completely righteous *in Christ* because covered by his righteousness and completely a sinner *outside of Christ* and so in constant need of mercy. But, secondly, Luther also held that *in themselves* Christians are both righteous and sinners, because of the imperfection of their inner renewal—a tension described in Romans 7:14–24.[3] Without the second of these meanings the slogan becomes problematic not just for Catholics but also for the Reformed, who are concerned to maintain a clear doctrine of sanctification.

Calvin: Twofold Grace (duplex gratia)

Calvin's approach to justification was rather different from Luther's. Having set out what Christ has done for the salvation of the human race in Book 2 of the *Institutes*, Calvin devotes Book 3 to the means by which we lay hold of this grace. This begins with our union with Christ by the Holy Spirit through faith. In Christ we then receive a double or twofold grace: being reconciled to God and regeneration (3:11:1). In other words we receive the grace of justification and of sanctification. For Calvin these two are inseparable as they both flow from our union with Christ. There is no possibility of being justified without being sanctified. Calvin compares this with the heat and the light of the sun. It is by the light that we see, not by the heat; it is by the heat that we are warmed, not by the light. These two are not to be confused. But nor are they to be separated since it is impossible to have the one without the other. If the sun shines there is both heat and light.

What then of the righteousness of the Christian? Calvin approaches this differently in different contexts. His chapters on regeneration and sanctification (3:3–10) are all about an inward renewal by the Holy Spirit and he is happy to refer to this as righteousness. Thus, righteousness is one of the fruits that follow renewal (3:3:8–9). As we grow in the Christian life we become increasingly like God, righteous (3:3:9).

When turning to the chapters on justification (3:11–18) the emphasis changes. Calvin recognizes that believers are those who pursue and obey righteousness and that relative to the wicked they are righteous (3:17:14). Yet experience teaches that "the traces of sin always remain in the righteous" (3:11:11).[4] In short, while they are called righteous because of their holiness of life, this consists more in the pursuit of righteousness than actually fulfilling it (3:17:10). In these chapters there is a strict contrast between human righteousness, which is soiled, and the imputed righteousness of Christ.

---

3. For Luther's understanding of the formula, see Althaus, *Theology of Luther*, 242–45.

4. Quotations from Calvin's *Institutes* are taken from the edition by McNeill and Battles.

When the issue is growth in the Christian life, Calvin is happy to refer to human righteousness, but when the issue is acceptance by God he emphasizes the worthlessness of human righteousness. In the former context the reality of human righteousness is the issue, in the latter its imperfection. Calvin never mentioned Luther's *simul iustus et peccator* slogan, but the two emphases noted above correspond to the two meanings of that slogan.

Catholic Humanism

The doctrine of justification had not been defined by the Catholic Church prior to the Reformation, so in the early years Catholic theologians took many different approaches to the Reformation doctrine, ranging from uncompromising (and often uncomprehending) hostility to almost complete agreement with it. Genuine dialogue was possible between the two sides as the Roman response to the Protestant doctrine was not predetermined.

Among those in the Roman Catholic Church most sympathetic to Luther's doctrine was an Erasmian reforming group in Italy, which included leading cardinals. One of these, Gasparo Contarini, underwent a conversion experience which he described in a private letter of 1511 and which has affinities with Luther's (later) Tower-experience (*Turmerlebnis*).[5] In Germany also there was a significant group of Catholic humanists seeking reform within the Roman Catholic system. Noteworthy among these was Johann Gropper, who in 1538 published his highly influential *Enchiridion*, a handbook for reform of the diocese of Cologne. Gropper shared Luther's theological concerns and embraced ideas such as the awareness of ongoing sin in the justified. Justification involves an inner renewal, but in this life our righteousness is always imperfect. Our good works (even as believers) remain imperfect and do not satisfy God's law.[6]

The Reformers' conviction about the imperfection of our inherent righteousness was shared widely by Catholic humanists such as Gropper and Contarini. Yarnold notes that "the sense that the converted Christian still needs to throw himself on the mercy of God seems to have been in the air independently of Luther."[7] This concern was in line with much patristic

---

5. Contarini to Giustiniani (24 April [1511]) in Gleason, *Reform Thought*, 24–28.

6. *Enchiridion Christianae Institutionis*, 167b–68a, 174b. On Gropper's doctrine of justification, see Braunisch, *Theologie der Rechtfertigung*.

7. The different doctrines are set out by Yarnold, "*Duplex iustitia*," quotation at 213. The theme of the perpetual need for God's mercy runs throughout Yarnold's chapter.

and medieval piety.⁸ Among such Catholic humanists there was widespread sympathy for the Protestant idea that Christ's righteousness is imputed or reckoned to us. Because our inherent righteousness is imperfect, Christ's righteousness needs to be imputed to us in order for us to be acceptable to God.

Regensburg Colloquy (1541) and Aftermath

From 1530 there was a series of colloquies aimed at reconciling the two sides in Germany—to avert civil war and to enable a common front against the Turkish threat. The greatest chance of success came at Regensburg in 1541. At this colloquy six debaters were selected: Martin Bucer, Philipp Melanchthon, and Johann Pistorius on the Protestant side; Johann Gropper, Johann Eck, and Julius Pflug on the Catholic side. Their most significant achievement was to draw up an agreed statement (Article 5) on justification in five days. This success led to a burst of optimistic enthusiasm. Contarini, who was present as papal legate, was jubilant and expressed his joy to Cardinal Alessandro Farnese, the pope's grandson, in Rome: "God be praised, these Catholic and Protestant theologians resolved to agree on the article of justification, faith, and works."⁹ The joy and the hope engendered were to be short-lived, however. The colloquy soon began to founder, but that was because of differences on *other* doctrines, such as the infallibility of councils and transubstantiation,¹⁰ not because of shortcomings in the statement on justification.

Article 5 teaches that faith gives birth to a twofold righteousness (without using those words), namely inherent righteousness (inner renewal) and imputed righteousness (Christ's righteousness reckoned to our account). As regards our present theme, imputed righteousness is needed because of the imperfection of inherent righteousness:

> It is by this faith [faith which is effectual through love] that we are justified (i.e. accepted and reconciled to God) inasmuch as it appropriates the mercy and righteousness which is imputed to us on account of Christ and his merit, not on account of the worthiness or perfection of the righteousness imparted to us in Christ. (4:6)¹¹

8. Zumkeller, "Ungenügen," documents this in detail.
9. Contarini to Farnese (3 May) in Pastor, "Correspondenz," 372.
10. For details, cf. Matheson, *Cardinal Contarini*, chaps. 9 and 10, respectively.
11. Here and below the translations are my own.

> In our standing before God we are not to rely upon our inherent righteousness: Although the one who is justified receives righteousness and through Christ also has inherent [righteousness], . . . nevertheless, the faithful soul depends not on this, but only on the righteousness of Christ given to us as a gift, without which there is and can be no righteousness at all. (5:1).

Sanctification and growth in the Christian life are important, but because they remain imperfect they are not sufficient to make us pleasing to God:

> Although fear of God, patience, humility and other virtues ought always to grow in the regenerate, because this renewal is imperfect and enormous weakness remains in them, it should nevertheless be taught that those who truly repent may always hold with most certain faith that they are pleasing to God on account of Christ the mediator. (6)

After Regensburg, Gropper found himself in extended controversy with Bucer and Melanchthon over the attempted Reformation of the Cologne diocese. His stance towards Bucer became increasingly polemical, but he continued for a time at least to affirm twofold righteousness and, in particular, the need for imputed righteousness. In his *Christliche und Catholische Gegenberichtung* he teaches that we are to rely and trust principally on the imputed righteousness of Christ. Because inherent righteousness is imperfect we are not to rely on it primarily, but the inward experience of it is proof that we are forgiven, that Christ's righteousness is imputed to us, and that he dwells in us by faith. Our inner renewal through love is a pledge or at least a taste of forgiveness and imputed righteousness.[12] He was rebuked for this by the Louvain Theology Faculty, but stuck to his guns. Contarini also maintained this stance after the colloquy until his death the following year. This shows that their acceptance of the Regensburg article was an act of conviction, not of ecumenical inconsistency.

Council of Trent

The Tridentine *Decree on Original Sin* (1546) viewed concupiscence as a result of sin and as an inclination towards sin, but not itself as sin or as meriting eternal death. This means that Christians are acceptable to God despite suffering from lustful desires and even light and daily (venial) sins do not impair their righteousness.

---

12. *Christliche und Catholische Gegenberichtung*, 20a–b.

The Tridentine *Decree on Justification* (1547) was the response of the Roman Catholic Church to Regensburg. There was ongoing debate concerning the idea of twofold righteousness. The various drafts of the decree were drawn up by Girolamo Seripando, who held strongly to the belief in the Christian's ongoing need for mercy. He held that the imperfect righteousness which the justified are able to attain deserves to be rewarded with eternal life only when it is complemented by Christ's righteousness.[13] Therefore the Christian at the last judgement should "appeal to God's mercy and put his trust in the merits of Christ."[14] Seripando introduced these ideas into successive drafts of the decree and the bishops each time voted to remove them.[15] The idea that we need mercy at the last judgement was excluded from the decree. Some of the bishops spoke of demanding eternal life as of right at the Last Judgement.[16] Diego Lainez branded twofold righteousness a Lutheran novelty and warned against turning the throne of justice into a throne of mercy.[17]

Following Seripando's failure the decree contains two significant statements relating to our theme, both contingent upon the view of concupiscence as not itself as sin or as meriting eternal death just outlined. The decree understands justification to be "not merely remission of sins but also the sanctification and renewal of the inner person." Because of this it follows that "we are not merely considered to be righteous but are truly called righteous and are righteous."[18] Christian initiation involves both being *made* righteous and being *counted as* righteous, but this distinction does not imply a doctrine of *duplex iustitia*. For Trent we are counted as righteous because we actually *are* righteous. The *Decree* rejects the idea that we need imputed righteousness to be acceptable to God since our inherent righteousness suffices to make us acceptable before the throne of God's justice.

Given the previous two points it is not surprising that the *Decree* teaches that we can merit eternal life.

> We must believe that nothing further is wanting to the justified,
> to prevent their being accounted to have, by those works which

---

13. Jedin, *Papal Legate*, 335. Cf. Yarnold, "*Duplex iustitia*," 214, 223.
14. Jedin, *Council of Trent*, 2:284.
15. On these debates, see Lane, *Justification by Faith*, 61–65.
16. Pas, "Doctrine de la double justice," 23, 35, gives examples of those holding that eternal life may be demanded as a debt.
17. Jedin, *Council of Trent*, 2:253–58. For these and Lainez's ten other arguments against twofold righteousness, cf. Maxcey, "Double Justice," 269–78.
18. *Decree on Justification*, chap. 7. For the Tridentine decree I use my own translation, based on the existing ones.

have been done in God, fully satisfied the divine law according to the state of this life, and to have truly merited eternal life, to be obtained also in its due time, so long as they depart in a state of grace (Rev 14:13).

The language is unequivocal. "Nothing further is wanted . . . fully satisfied the divine law . . . truly merited eternal life." A number of Catholic theologians argue that imputed righteousness is unnecessary not because our works are perfect but because our inherent righteousness is perfect.[19] That is not what Trent teaches. We have "fully satisfied the divine law" and "truly merited eternal life" by "those *works* which have been done in God."

Catholic piety is sometimes different from theology. In his late sixteenth-century *Controversy on Justification*, Cardinal Bellarmine argues, in opposition to Protestantism, that the confidence of believers is born not of faith alone but of good merits. But he then concludes that "on account of the uncertainty of our own righteousness and the danger of vain glory it is safest to repose one's entire confidence in the mercy and kindness of God alone."[20]

Contemporary Dialogues

Since Hans Küng's epoch making *Justification: The Doctrine of Karl Barth and a Catholic Reflection*[21] there has been a series of ecumenical dialogues between Roman Catholics and Protestants on the doctrine of justification, culminating in the *Joint Declaration on the Doctrine of Justification* (1999).[22] Some of these deal specifically with our theme. *Justification by Faith*, seventh in an American series of *Lutherans and Catholics in Dialogue*, considers the

19. Bellarmine brings out this difference when he describes justification as being "made and constituted righteous by obtaining an inherent righteousness and a righteousness that is not imperfect but absolute and perfect" (*De Iustificatione* 2.3 in *Disputationum Roberti Bellarmini*, 4:897).

20. A translation of Bellarmine, *De Iustificatione* 5.7 in *Disputationum Roberti Bellarmini*, 4:1092–96, a passage that has been much quoted over the centuries. Bellarmine followed his own advice since in his will he beseeches God "not as the valuer of merit, but as a giver of pardon, to admit me among His Saints and Elect" (Broderick, *Robert Bellarmine*, 2:441).

21. For the second edition Küng wrote an "Introductory Chapter" entitled "Justification Today" (ix–xxvii). The German original was published in 1957.

22. I have expounded these in my *Justification by Faith*. A shorter version with an update will be found in my "Justification," forthcoming in the *Oxford Handbook of Ecumenical Studies*.

There have been further dialogues since 1999, the most significant being Almen and Sklba, *Hope of Eternal Life*.

theme of the "Sinfulness of the Justified."[23] The differences between the two sides are stated and then seen as "symptoms of continuing differences in their concerns." In particular Lutherans fear that the Catholic view will lead Christians to anxiety or complacency and to insufficient reliance on God's mercy; Catholics fear that the Lutheran position will lead to a neglect of good works and insufficient motivation to thank God for our inner renewal. *The Condemnations of the Reformation Era: Do They Still Divide?*, published in German in 1986, considers the issue of concupiscence, concluding that "modern Catholic theology has come much closer to the Protestant view."[24]

Finally, in the *Joint Declaration on the Doctrine of Justification* one of the seven issues discussed is "The Justified as Sinner."[25] Here Catholics affirm their traditional position that concupiscence or inclination to sin is not strictly sin and "does not merit the punishment of eternal death" (§30). Lutherans affirm the view of the Christian as *simul iustus et peccator*. Looking at ourselves through the law we see that we remain "totally sinners," but the sin that remains in the Christian is "ruled" by Christ rather than ruling the Christian, so in this life "Christians can in part lead a just life" (§29). The *Joint Declaration* was first published in 1997 and the Roman Catholic Church responded officially the following year. They considered the Lutheran explanation of *simul iustus et peccator* to be unacceptable and this and other issues needed to be resolved in an "Annex" which was added to the Joint Declaration. On Reformation Day 1999 there was an official signing of the Joint Declaration, together with the Annex, at Augsburg. It is important to note that the Joint Declaration has only been approved *together with* the Annex.

The Annex affirms the reality of our inward renewal (2 Cor 5:17) and that "in this sense" the justified do not remain sinners. On the other hand, as Christians we still need to pray "God, be merciful to me, a sinner" (Luke 18:13). "To this extent, Lutherans and Catholics can together understand the Christian as *simul justus et peccator*, despite their different approaches to this subject as expressed in JD 29–30" (Annex §2A). Although the two sides differ in their understanding of concupiscence, both can agree on holding together "the reality of salvation in baptism and the peril from the power of sin" (Annex §2B). This statement is to be applauded for two reasons: for recognizing the different concerns of each side and also for acknowledging the New Testament tension between the universality of sin and the call to lead righteous lives.

---

23. Anderson, Murphy, and Burgess, *Justification by Faith*, 51–52.
24. Lehmann and Pannenberg, *Condemnations*, 44–46.
25. Also published as an Appendix in my *Justification by Faith*.

Second Vatican Council

The Council produced very little that relates directly to justification, but it did make one very significant statement relevant to our theme. The *Dogmatic Constitution on the Church* describes the church as "at the same time holy and always needing reform," echoing Luther's slogan.[26] This is because "on earth the church is adorned with true though imperfect holiness."[27] One of the ecumenical dialogues, *Church and Justification*, notes that "it is not in dispute between us that the church is "holy" and "sinful" at the same time" (§156).[28]

Catechism of the Catholic Church

The *Catechism of the Catholic Church*, in its sections on Justification (§§1987–95) and on Merit (§§2006–11) restates traditional teaching, drawing on Trent in particular, but the section on merit concludes with a significant quotation from Teresa of Lisieux:

> After earth's exile, I hope to go and enjoy you in the fatherland, but I do not want to lay up merits for heaven. I want to work for your *love alone* . . . In the evening of this life, I shall appear before you with empty hands, for I do not ask you, Lord, to count my works. All our justice is blemished in your eyes. I wish, then, to be clothed in your own *justice* and to receive from your *love* the eternal possession of *yourself*.[29]

This affirmation of the inadequacy of our works and of "all our justice [righteousness]" can be seen as an acknowledgement of the validity of Seripando's concerns that were brushed aside at Trent.

CONCLUSION

What are our expectations for dialogue? Total agreement is totally unrealistic. Even in my local congregation we do not agree totally about everything. We agree sufficiently that we recognize each other as acceptably orthodox

---

26. *Lumen Gentium* 1:8 (Tanner, *Decrees*, 2:855).

27. *Lumen Gentium* 7:48 (Tanner, *Decrees*, 2:888).

28. Cf. *Church and Justification* §§129, 148–65, for discussion of the tension between the church as holy and sinful. Neuhaus, "Catholic Difference," 189–92, discusses the holiness of the church in the context of Luther's *simul iustus et peccator*.

29. §2011. The italics and ellipsis points are from the original.

and can work together. It is unrealistic to expect Protestants and Catholics to agree totally on this doctrine. There are significant points of difference within Evangelicalism, let alone within the wide spectrum of Protestantism.

So what can we realistically expect? We can hope that each side can express the doctrine in such a way that the other side can see that its concerns are met. I would also suggest that maintaining the New Testament tension set out above is an important criterion for acceptability. When it comes to the imperfection of our righteousness I would suggest that the evidence is that this criterion has been met.

We started this paper with the New Testament tension and at the end we saw that tension in the Annex to the Joint Declaration. We started by looking at differing concerns and at the end we saw the *Catechism of the Catholic Church* addressing a major Protestant concern. There are still serious issues to be resolved, there is still need for further progress, but the signs so far are very encouraging.

BIBLIOGRAPHY

Almen, Lowell G., and Richard J. Sklba. *The Hope of Eternal Life: Lutherans and Catholics in Dialogue XI*. Minneapolis: Lutheran University Press, 2011.
Althaus, Paul. *The Theology of Martin Luther*. Philadelphia: Fortress, 1966.
Anderson, H. George, T. Austin Murphy, and Joseph A. Burgess, eds. *Justification by Faith. Lutherans and Catholics in Dialogue VII*. Minneapolis: Augsburg, 1985.
Bellarmine, Robert. *Disputationum Roberti Bellarmini Tomus Quartus*. Cologne: Gualtherus, 1619.
Braunisch, Reinhard. *Die Theologie der Rechtfertigung im "Enchiridion" (1538) des Johannes Gropper*. Münster: Aschendorff, 1974.
Broderick, James. *Robert Bellarmine*. Vol. 2. London: Longmans, Green and co., 1950.
Calvin, John. *Institutes of the Christian Religion*. Edited by John T. McNeill. Translated by Ford L. Battles. LCC 20–21. London: SCM, 1960.
Church and Justification: Understanding the Church in the Light of the Doctrine of Justification. Geneva: Lutheran World Federation, 1994.
Gleason, Elisabeth G., ed. *Reform Thought in Sixteenth-Century Italy*. Chico, CA: Scholars, 1981.
Gropper, Johann. *Christliche und Catholische Gegenberichtung eyns erwirdigen Dhomcapittels zu Cöllen*. Cologne: Gennepaeus, 1544.
———. *Enchiridion Christianae Institutionis*. Cologne: Quentel, 1538.
Jedin, Hubert. *A History of the Council of Trent*. 2 vols. London: Nelson, 1957, 1961.
———. *Papal Legate at the Council of Trent: Cardinal Seripando*. London: Herder, 1947.
Joint Declaration on the Doctrine of Justification. Grand Rapids : Eerdmans, 2000.
Küng, Hans. *Justification: The Doctrine of Karl Barth and a Catholic Reflection*. London: Burns & Oates, 1964.
———. *Justification: The Doctrine of Karl Barth and a Catholic Reflection*. 2nd ed. London: Burns & Oates, 1981.

Lane, A. N. S. *Justification by Faith in Catholic-Protestant Dialogue: An Evangelical Assessment*. London: T. & T. Clark, 2002.

Lehmann, Karl, and Wolfhart Pannenberg, eds. *The Condemnations of the Reformation Era: Do They Still Divide?* Minneapolis: Fortress, 1990.

Matheson, Peter. *Cardinal Contarini at Regensburg*. Oxford: Oxford University Press, 1972.

Maxcey, Carl. E. "Double Justice, Diego Laynez, and the Council of Trent." *Church History* 48 (1979) 269–78.

Neuhaus, Richard J. "The Catholic Difference." In *Evangelicals and Catholics Together: Toward a Common Mission*, edited by C. Colson and R. J. Neuhaus, 175–227. London: Hodder & Stoughton, 1996.

Pas, Paul. "La doctrine de la double justice au Concile de Trente." *Ephemerides Theologicae Lovanienses* 30 (1954) 5–53.

Pastor, Ludwig von. "Die Correspondenz des Cardinals Contarini während seiner deutschen Legation (1541)." *Historisches Jahrbuch* 1 (1880) 321–92, 473–501.

Tanner, Norman P., ed. *Decrees of the Ecumenical Councils*. Vol. 2. London: Sheed & Ward, 1990.

Yarnold, Edward. "*Duplex iustitia*: The Sixteenth Century and the Twentieth." In *Christian Authority*, edited by G. R. Evans, 204–23. Oxford: Oxford University Press, 1988.

Zumkeller, A. "Das Ungenügen der menschlichen Werke bei den Deutschen Predigern des Spätmittelaters." *Zeitschrift für Katholische Theologie* 81 (1959) 265–305.

7

The Reformation and the Questions of Authority and Truth

Andrew T. B. McGowan

INTRODUCTION

The subject I was given for this paper is, "The Reformation and the questions of authority and truth." Since this conference is intended to mark the fast-approaching 500th anniversary of the Reformation, marking the moment when Martin Luther issued his Ninety-five Theses in October 1517, I want to focus in this paper on Luther. The Reformation, of course, did not spring ready-made in October 1517. It was a complex movement and, for Martin Luther himself, many factors came together in its origins, including personal, ecclesial, political, biblical, and theological factors. It was also a slow, developing process, although punctuated by moments of crisis.

The thesis of this paper is that Luther's understanding of truth was determined by the question of authority. In 1517, he still maintained the authority of the church as represented by the ope. By the end of his life, he affirmed the full authority of Scripture, in opposition to the pope.[1] As he

---

1. Several writers have sought to trace Luther's relationship to the pope and his changing attitudes to the authority of the church as exercised by the pope. The most

made that transition from the authority of the church to the authority of Scripture, his concept of truth developed and with it, his understanding of Christian doctrine, not least his doctrine of justification by faith.[2]

Along the way we shall suggest that the overall impact of Luther's move in terms of authority was weakened by two factors: first, by Luther's doctrine of Scripture itself; and second, by the failure to articulate an alternative strong doctrine of the authority of the church. In conclusion, we shall argue that the trajectory in many churches today is in the opposite direction from that of Luther. There is clear evidence that the movement back from the authority of Scripture to the authority of the church is prevalent, not least in Europe and that this move is most obvious in controversial moral and ethical issues.

In order to pursue this thesis, we are going to divide the material into three parts. First, Luther and the Church; second, Luther and Scripture; and third, some analysis and conclusions.

LUTHER AND THE CHURCH

Prior to the publication of his Ninety-five Theses, Luther had already challenged elements of the prevailing theology of the church in his *Disputation against Scholastic Theology* (1517).[3] In particular, he challenged the place given to Aristotelian philosophy in relation to Christian theology. For example, in *Thesis 41* of that work, he went so far as to say that "Virtually the entire *Ethics* of Aristotle is the worst enemy of grace."[4] In this document, Luther also gives hints of what would later become his developed doctrine of justification by faith. He wrote, "We do not become righteous by doing righteous deeds but, having been made righteous, we do righteous deeds."[5] Although the expression "made righteous" later becomes "declared righteous" in Reformed theology (following Paul's language in Romans 3 and Romans 5), this does show Luther's movement in that direction. By the time the Lutheran position on justification was clarified in Article 4 of the Augsburg Confession (1530),[6] we have justification by faith alone and the doctrine of the imputation of the righteousness of Christ.

---

recent of these is Hendrix, *Luther and the Papacy*.

2. For a Catholic perspective on Luther's trial and subsequent excommunication, see Olivier, *Trial of Luther*.

3. Pelikan and Lehmann, eds., *Luther's Works*, 31:3–16.

4. Ibid., 31:12.

5. Ibid., 31:112.

6. http://bookofconcord.org/augsburgconfession.php, accessed 18 August 2016.

It is clear that, from 1517 onwards, Martin Luther was seeking the reformation of the church rather than the creation of a new church. Indeed, the very idea of a new church was something entirely foreign to the mindset of medieval Christians. Whereas the publication of his Ninety-five Theses in October 1517[7] is regarded by many as the spark which created the Protestant churches, nothing was further from Luther's mind. As a priest and university professor, he had identified a pastoral problem relating to the sale of indulgences. When he issued his Ninety-five Theses, he intended to begin a debate so as to reform the practice. These Ninety-five Theses did not, in themselves, offer any significant challenge to the authority and teaching of the church. The only real point of challenge concerned the right of the pope to commute time in purgatory. Luther argued that the pope could only commute penances or penalties which he himself had imposed. Notice, at this point Luther is not challenging the authority of the Church or the hierarchy, nor the practice of selling indulgences, nor the reality of purgatory but only the authority of the pope himself to offer remission from purgatory.[8] Even when Luther asserts that the pope does not have "the power of the keys" (*Thesis 26*) this is not a challenge to his authority. As H.J. Grimm notes, "This is not a denial of the power of the keys, that is, the power to forgive and to retain sin, but merely an assertion that the power of the keys does not extend to purgatory."[9] Indeed, Luther was clear that, if only the pope had realized what was being said and done in respect of the sale of indulgences, he himself would be the first to object and to deal with the matter. He wrote, "Christians are to be taught that if the pope knew the exactions of the indulgence preachers, he would rather that the basilica of St Peter were burned to ashes than built up with the skin, flesh, and bones of his sheep" (*Thesis 50*).[10] This is further demonstrated when he says, after raising a series of questions regarding indulgences, that if "indulgences were preached according to the spirit and intention of the pope, all these doubts would be readily resolved. Indeed, they would not exist" (*Thesis 91*).[11]

Having said that Luther did not in these Ninety-five Theses seek to undermine the authority and teaching of the church but merely challenge abuses of the system of indulgences, there were elements in the Ninety-five

---

7. Pelikan and Lehmann, *Luther's Works*, 31:17–33.

8. Oberman tells us that when Luther was in Rome in 1510, he climbed the steps of the Santa Scala on his knees because he wanted to free his grandfather from purgatory. Clearly at that stage he still believed in purgatory and sought to work within the teaching of the church. Oberman, *Luther*, 147.

9. Pelikan and Lehmann, *Luther's Works*, 31:27n7.

10. Ibid., 31:30.

11. Ibid., 31:33.

Theses which contained the seeds of Luther's later theology. For example, what he says about repentance being different from the sacrament of penance (*Theses 1–3*)[12] and his assertion that "Any truly repentant Christian has a right to full remission of penalty and guilt, even without indulgence letters" (*Thesis 36*).[13]

In these earliest expressions of Luther's theology, then, he did not directly challenge the authority of the church, nor did he set another authority alongside that of the church. This changed over time, on the basis of deeper theological work, not least due to his serious academic engagement with the text of Scripture in his work as a professor of biblical studies. The evidence of this changing perspective is seen in the various debates and publications, and it can be traced with reasonable accuracy.

The beginning of Luther's challenge to the authority of the church and the truth of its theology came in response to the critique of his Ninety-five Theses. Albert of Brandenburg, the Archbishop of Mainz, was the man responsible for promoting the St Peter's indulgence and who had commissioned John Tetzel as his agent in this matter. After Luther published his Ninety-five Theses, sales of the indulgence fell away and Albert was furious. In December 1517, he sent a copy of Luther's work to the pope, together with a request that Luther be charged with heresy. In August 1518, after several delays, Luther published his *Explanation of the Ninety-five Theses*.[14] Luther arranged for a copy to be sent to the pope with a respectful covering letter but the pope had already, by this time, initiated proceedings against him.

In his *Explanation* Luther moves a few steps further. H.T. Lehmann sums up the progress in Luther's thinking:

> He writes respectfully of the pope but questions his primacy as bishop of Rome; he quotes the church fathers and canon law but treats the Bible as the primary—but not yet sole—authority in religious matters; he recognizes the ultimate authority of general church councils in matters of faith but opposes the burning of heretics, as was done at the Council of Constance; he still accepts purgatory and "the treasure of the church" but interprets them in an evangelical fashion; he dislikes tumult and disobedience but asks in unmistakable terms for a reformation of the church.[15]

12. Ibid., 31:25.
13. Ibid., 31:28.
14. Ibid., 31:81–252.
15. Ibid., 31:79.

It is neither necessary nor possible in a paper of this length to consider in detail all that followed, including ecclesiastical process, a vast array of publications, and various controversies. A serious examination of the literature alone would merit a book rather than a paper. For our purposes, in establishing Luther's developing views on authority and truth, it is sufficient to note briefly and chronologically some developments in Luther's attitude to the authority of the church and to its theology.

In the Spring of 1518, Luther defended his theology before a meeting of his fellow Augustinians in Heidelberg. Luther prepared the theses to be discussed in Heidelberg and later published his commentary and explanation of the theses.[16] One change we see here, which is of interest for Luther's later theology, is that he describes the true theologian as a theologian of the Cross.[17] The real defense of his position, however, would come later in the year. Following the request from Albert that Luther's theology be examined, Pope Leo X ordered that Luther be summoned to Rome and instructed his court theologian, Sylvester Mazzolini (Latin name Prierias), to respond to Luther's Ninety-five Theses. Prierias duly wrote his *Dialogue Concerning the Power of the Pope* (*Dialogus de potestate papae*) in 1518 and Luther replied with his *Responsio*.[18] In this response, Luther spoke of three authorities: Scripture, the Fathers, and Canon Law and, as Lohse points out, "Now, for the first time, he stated bluntly that pope and Councils could err."[19] When the summons to Rome came, Frederick III, the Elector of Saxony, intervened, insisting that Luther be tried in Germany. It was then arranged that this should take place in Augsburg.

In October 1518, the pope's representative, Cardinal Tomas de Vio (known as Cajetan) met with Luther at Augsburg. Cajetan was a Dominican and a distinguished theologian. The two main areas where Cajetan pressed Luther were on papal authority and on the sacraments. Luther denied having said or written anything contrary to Scripture, the Fathers or the papal decrees. Despite repeatedly being urged by Cajetan to recant, Luther maintained his position.

Luther later wrote his own account of the proceedings at Augsburg.[20] He said that Cajetan had failed to engage with Scripture and had been unable to respond to Luther's exegesis of Scripture in relation to the themes of indulgences, faith, and grace. Instead, Cajetan had simply urged him to re-

16. Ibid., 31:35–70.
17. Ibid., 31:53.
18. Ibid., 1:647–86.
19. Lohse, *Luther's Theology*, 111.
20. Pelikan and Lehmann, eds., *Luther's Works*, 31:253–92.

cant.[21] During the debate Luther appealed to a future council of the church to settle the matter. This was somewhat topical since the University of Paris had just done precisely that on another matter. We see then that even at this stage Luther was denying that he was out of step with official church teaching, insisting that he had said or written nothing of which he should recant.

The following year, in July 1519, there was another debate, this time at Leipzig. This was intended to be a debate between August Bodenstein (known as Karlstadt), one of Luther's colleagues at Wittenberg and John Eck, the papal representative, who was Vice Chancellor of the University of Ingolstadt. After a few days of debate between Eck and Karlstadt, Luther stepped up, and he and Eck debated from the 4th to the 14th July. These two had clashed in writing but not in person: Eck had published his *Obelisks* against Luther's Ninety-five Theses and Luther had replied with his *Asterisks*. One important development in Luther's thinking surfaced at the Leipzig debate. For the first time, Luther openly and clearly denied papal authority as taught by Eck. Among other arguments, Luther argued that for 1100 years there had not been papal authority in the church.

The next stage of development followed some pro-papal publications by Augustine Alveld of Leipzig. In 1520, Luther published his *On the Papacy in Rome Against the Most Celebrated Romanist in Leipzig*.[22] Here Luther advanced his argument still further, concluding, "I shall accept whatever the pope establishes and does, on condition that I judge it first on the basis of Holy Scripture."[23] This is a significant stage in the move towards the final authority of Scripture. Luther also denied that conciliar decisions were infallible and said that he did not feel bound in his conscience by such decisions. In the Leipzig debate, Eck had pressed Luther regarding the authority of the decisions made at the Council of Constance, which had condemned Huss, and accused Luther of being a Hussite. This Luther denied, yet by 1520 he was openly declaring himself to be a Hussite.[24] Luther's report on the Leipzig debate makes a good deal of Eck's charge regarding Hus.[25] Once again we see a slow but clear development. It is perhaps not insignificant that Philip Melanchthon, now a professor at Wittenberg, was with Luther at Leipzig.

After years of thinking, writing, consulting, preaching, and debating, Luther had, by the end of 1520, reached fairly settled convictions on most

21. Ibid., 31:275–76.
22. Ibid., 39:49–104.
23. Ibid., 39:101.
24. Hendrix, *Luther and the Papacy*, 97–98.
25. Pelikan and Lehmann, eds., *Luther's Works*, 31:313–25.

of the key areas of dispute. Whereas in 1519 he had advocated three sacraments, including the sacrament of Penance,[26] by the time he wrote *The Babylonian Captivity of the Church* in 1520,[27] Luther felt sufficiently sure of his interpretation of Scripture to reduce the number of sacraments to two, Baptism and the Lord's Supper. This was, of course, a major challenge to the authority of the church and the hierarchy, since Luther was claiming the right to define the sacramental theology of the church.

Luther's developing attitude to the papacy is demonstrated by the difference between two publications, one in 1520 and one in 1545. In 1520, having been encouraged by Karl von Miltitz, supported by Johann von Staupitz and Wenceslas Link, Luther wrote an open letter to Pope Leo X entitled, *The Freedom of a Christian*.[28] In this letter, Luther could still insist that he had nothing against Leo personally and, in some ways felt quite sorry for him, regarding him as "a lamb in the midst of wolves."[29] In 1545, towards the end of his life, Luther wrote *Against the Roman Papacy, An Institution of the Devil*.[30] This was published on the day the Council of Trent was due to convene and when Pope Paul III was in office. Here the tone is very different. The editor describes it as "the most bitter of Luther's polemical writings"[31] and certainly the language is extreme. For example, "what are prayer and God's word to the pope? He must serve his own God the devil!"[32]

By the time of his speech at Worms in 1521, Scripture has become Luther's only authority.[33] Indeed, Luther is famously reputed to have said at Worms, "My conscience is captive to the Word of God."[34] Luther's changing views in respect of authority led to striking changes in doctrinal formulation. This is very evident both in his catechism of 1529 and in the Augsburg Confession of 1530. Luther's final doctrinal position stands in complete contrast to the theology of the Catholic Church.

What we see, then, in this brief account is that, when Luther published his Ninety-five Theses, he was simply protesting against the abuse of the system of indulgences. At this stage, he still submitted to papal authority and argued that the pope himself would be horrified if he knew what was

26. In his *Sacrament of Penance*, ibid., 35:9–22.
27. Ibid., 36:3–126.
28. Ibid., 31:327–77.
29. Ibid., 31:336.
30. Ibid., 41:257–376.
31. Ibid., 41:259.
32. Ibid., 41:295.
33. See "Luther at the Diet of Worms," ibid., 32:101–31.
34. Ibid., 32:112.

going on. As the debate on his Ninety-five Theses continued, Luther moved to the position that the pope's authority was limited and that the supreme authority in the church was a general council. Later still, he denied the final authority of general councils and indicated that he did not feel bound by their decisions. Finally, he came to regard the papacy as an institution of the devil! In his earliest days, he believed in purgatory, seven sacraments and most other Catholic doctrines, by the end of his life he had articulated what would be called Protestant theology, as expressed in the catechisms and confessions of the Reformation churches.

LUTHER AND SCRIPTURE

Having argued that Luther's theological development was driven by a change in his understanding of authority, namely, moving from a place where the church had final authority to the place where Scripture had final authority, we must now look more closely at Luther's understanding of Scripture.[35]

It is important to remember that the inspiration and authority of Scripture was not in itself a contested issue at the Reformation. As Richard A. Muller has demonstrated, there was continuity of conviction about the inspiration and authority of Scripture from the late medieval period through to the post-Reformation scholastics.[36] The problem, rather, was one of interpretation. Muller writes,

> The problem of the doctrine of Scripture in the age of the Reformation and the era of orthodoxy was, in other words, not so much a problem of a new view of inspiration and authority as it was a problem of a very traditional view of inspiration and authority in the context of an altered approach to exegesis and hermeneutics.[37]

Hence the key question was whether Scripture was to be interpreted through the lens of tradition or by means of the new exegetical and hermeneutical tools furnished by Humanism. Luther's controversy at Leipzig with John Eck demonstrated that they were using two different ways of interpreting Scripture. Luther insisted on exegeting what the text said, irrespective of what others had said about the text in the past, whereas Eck insisted that

---

35. See the excellent summary of Luther's teaching on Scripture, particularly in relation to the authority of the church, in Lohse, *Martin Luther's Theology*, 187–95.
36. Muller, *Post-Reformation Reformed Dogmatics*.
37. Ibid., 9.

the proper interpretation of any text was what the tradition and the church said.[38]

Luther held to the tripartite doctrine of the word of God being Christ, Scripture, and the preached word[39] but, whereas Calvin tended to place more emphasis on the Scriptures as being the completed, inscripturated form of revelation, Luther was far more concerned with the preached word. He underlined the historical primacy of the oral proclamation, looking upon Scripture as a later development.[40] Jaroslav Pelikan wrote a "Companion Volume" to the American edition of Luther's Works entitled, *Luther the Expositor: Introduction to the Reformer's Exegetical Writings* in which he explains that when Luther uses the expression the "Word of God" he is most often referring to the "oral Word of proclamation."[41] Similarly, Althaus writes, "Written Scripture is necessary because of the danger that preaching could be heretically distorted if the normative apostolic message were forgotten."[42] The reason for this is that Luther cannot separate the preaching of the gospel from justification by faith, that is, he cannot separate the gospel from its fruit. It is in the proclamation that human beings are convicted and transformed (Romans 10:14). The necessary relationship thus envisaged between the preaching and the awakening of faith has as its corollary a dialectical tension between the objective and subjective authority of Scripture. As J.K.S. Reid has noted,

> The authority of Scripture was indeed objective, but it could not be understood as merely objective. Rather it carried with it a relation to the subject to whom it commended itself and upon whom it impinged by the agency of the Holy Spirit. Instead of an authority of a purely objective kind or of a purely subjective kind, Luther maintains that the authority of the Bible lies in an objective-subjective relationship.[43]

It is not possible, then, to separate Scripture from the one to whom it testifies, or from the one to whom it is attested, or even from the one (the Holy Spirit) whose work it is to be the vehicle of this attestation. Truly it can be said that the

---

38. Pelikan and Lehmann, eds., *Luther's Works, Companion Volume*, 110–11.
39. Ibid., 22:528.
40. Ibid., 45:360.
41. Ibid., *Companion Volume*, 64.
42. Althaus, *The Theology of Martin Luther*, 73.
43. Reid, *The Authority of Scripture*, 64.

authority which Scripture possesses is objectively grounded, spiritually commended and subjectively acknowledged. This threefold aspect of the authority of Holy Scripture constitutes Luther's distinctive contribution to the matter.[44]

Luther had a very high doctrine of Scripture. He was in no doubt that "The Holy Spirit Himself and God, the Creator of all things, is the author of this book."[45] The identification of the words of the Bible with the word of God is so complete that if we wish to discover the latter we look to the former, hence, "Let the man who would hear God speak read Holy Scripture."[46] Luther is very much opposed to the idea that the Scriptures are human testimony to God; rather he insists that, "Scripture is God's testimony concerning himself."[47] This is a general principle throughout his writings and is related to the question of origin, that is, if these writings are merely of men then what authority can we possibly ascribe to them? Or, how can we know what is true and what is false? Thus, "Scriptures, although they too are written by men, are neither of men nor from men, but from God."[48]

This general principle of authorship is particularized when Luther speaks of the individual writers, and their very words are said to be those of the Holy Spirit. For example, "This is the speech of St. John or rather of the Holy Spirit"[49] and "St. Peter's words are God's words. . ."[50] At first it might appear as if Luther is speaking in a poetic or non-literal sense, but it soon becomes clear that he is speaking precisely. He writes, "Not only the words which the Holy Spirit and Scripture use are divine, but also the phrasing."[51] He carries this to its logical conclusion when he writes, "Not one letter in Scripture is purposeless . . . for Scripture is God's writing and God's word."[52] We could multiply such quotations[53] but let us conclude with one which summarizes the position, "This book, the Holy Scripture, is the Holy Spirit's book."[54]

---

44. Ibid., 65.
45. *Luthers Werke*, 43:6.
46. Ibid., 54:263.
47. Ibid., 50:282.
48. Pelikan and Lehmann, eds., *Luther's Works*, 35:153.
49. *Luthers Werke*, 54:55.
50. Pelikan and Lehmann, eds., *Luther's Works*, 39:237.
51. *Luthers Werke*, 40/2:254.
52. Ibid., 50:282.
53. For example ibid., 43:671; 42:23; 15:43.
54. Ibid., 48:43.

An important corollary of Luther's view of Scripture is his conviction that it is entirely trustworthy. Luther insists that, "The Scriptures cannot err"[55] and even that, "The Scriptures have never erred."[56] Some argue that this is untenable in the light of apparent contradictions within Scripture but Luther did not accept this: "It is impossible that Scripture should contradict itself, only that it so appears to the senseless and obstinate hypocrite."[57] This is continually reasserted in both a positive way, "Scripture agrees with itself everywhere,"[58] and a negative way, "it is certain that Scripture cannot disagree with itself."[59] He saw his task as an exegete, to some extent, as being the work of reconciling such apparent disagreements. "Passages of Scripture that are opposed to one another must, of course, be reconciled, and to one must be given a meaning which agrees with the sense of the other."[60] He is even prepared to argue that, properly understood, both of two contradictory statements can be true.[61] The method of exegesis then, is to compare Scripture with Scripture[62] allowing the clearer passages to interpret the less clear. Althaus writes, "Luther uses self-interpretation of Scripture and interpretation through the Holy Spirit as a pair of synonymous expressions."[63] There seems to be little question, then, that Luther held to a high view of the authority of Scripture.

One of the most significant keys to understanding Luther's doctrine of Scripture is his understanding of the relationship of the Scriptures to Christ. Under this general topic we have two important issues. First, Luther's belief that the entire canon, both Old and New Testament, points to Christ and has him as its center, around which everything else revolves. Second, the question of the extent of the canon, since it is Luther's contention that whatever does not testify to Christ is not Scripture and therefore does not deserve to be in the canon. These are significant points and we shall consider them in turn.

---

55. Walch, *Luthers Saemmtliche Schriften*, 19:1073.
56. Ibid., 15:1481.
57. Ibid., 9:356.
58. Ibid., 3:18.
59. *Luthers Werke*, 23:123.
60. Ibid.
61. Ibid., 54:66.
62. Ibid., 8:237, 239; 7:639; 14:556.
63. Althaus, *Theology of Martin Luther*, 78; cf. Pelikan and Lehmann, eds., *Luther's Works*, 26:57–58.

Firstly, the Christocentricity of the Scriptures. Luther writes, "For this much is beyond question, that all the Scriptures point to Christ alone."[64] This is not only a descriptive definition of the Scriptures, but a prescriptive one, since a basic premise is that, "Christ is the incarnate Word of God. Therefore the Bible can be the word of God only if its sole and entire content is Christ."[65] Some might assume that Luther is here referring only to the New Testament but that is not the case. Luther believed that Christ is the center of both Testaments.[66] Indeed, he prefers to limit the term "Scripture" to the Old Testament,[67] in the light of what we noted earlier about the New Testament being basically a verbal proclamation. He is in no doubt that the Old Testament has Christ as its center and is so consistent in this interpretation that, as Bornkamm writes, he can speak of Christians in the Old Testament:

> For whoever believes in Christ, be it only in the promised Christ, was a Christian. That was why Luther unhesitatingly called Moses and the patriarchs Christians whenever he spoke of their faith in the promise of the future Redeemer.[68]

Luther was even so bold as to compare the relative significance of the Father and the Son in Scripture saying,

> Holy Scripture has more to say about the Son than about the Father because the entire Scripture exists for the sake of the Son. In the Old Testament too, there are more testimonies to the Son than to the Father.[69]

At this point, Luther is undoubtedly overstating his case. We can agree that Christ is the focal point of God's work of redemption and that everything prior to the incarnation was leading up to it, as prolegomena. At the same time, we must suggest that Luther's Christocentricity appears to be asserting more than is justified by the evidence. There are many passages, even books, in the Old Testament which speak constantly of God the sovereign Creator but speak only occasionally (and then, usually typologically) of the Son.

Second, the extent of the canon. Luther writes, "Whatever does not teach Christ is certainly not apostolic even though St. Peter or St. Paul teaches it. Again whatever preaches Christ would be apostolic even though

---

64. Pelikan and Lehmann, eds., *Luther's Works*, 35:132.
65. Althaus, *Theology of Martin Luther*, 74.
66. *Luthers Werke*, 5:633; 39:47.
67. Kooiman, *Luther and the Bible*, 204–5.
68. Bornkamm, *Luther and the Old Testament*, 257.
69. WA TR, No. 5585.

Judas, Ananias, Pilate or Herod were doing it."[70] This does not mean that he rejected the canon as received; rather he appears to form a canon within the canon. As Althaus says, "He allows the canon to stand as it was established by the ancient church. But he makes distinctions within the canon. He evaluates the books according to the norm of their apostolic content."[71] This emphasis on the centrality of Christ as a criterion for decision-making with respect to the canon is not concerned so much with the human Jesus and his coming but rather with the Christ of soteriological formulation.[72] It can be said in this connection that Luther looked at the whole Bible through the eyes of Paul's Epistle to the Romans and indeed he admits as much in his preface to that book where we read, "it is a bright light, almost sufficient to illuminate the entire Holy Scriptures."[73] Hence Luther believed that the Christ as testified to in Romans was the real Christ, and if the other writers did not speak of this Christ, then their writings were not apostolic Scripture.

The best known example of this is the book of James. Luther begins by saying that the ancients had rejected this book but he considered it to be a good book because, "it sets up no new doctrines of men but vigorously promulgates the law of God."[74] Having said this, however, he goes on to state that "it is flatly against St. Paul and all the rest of Scripture in ascribing justification to works."[75] Luther concludes, "St. James' epistle is really an epistle of straw, compared to these others, for it has nothing of the gospel about it."[76] He passed similar judgements on Jude and Revelation.[77]

One issue was how the authority of Scripture was to work in practice. Who determined what Scripture was saying? In his *To the Christian Nobility of the German Nation Concerning the Reform of the Christian Estate* in 1520, Luther argued that the right to interpret Scripture belonged to all believers and not just to the Roman hierarchy although, at the same time, he denied the right of "private interpretation."[78] In *The Papacy in Rome* Luther developed this argument and defined "the priesthood of all believers."[79] It was due to these convictions that Luther's translation of the Bible into German

---

70. Pelikan and Lehmann, eds., *Luther's Works*, 35:396.
71. Althaus, *The Theology of Martin Luther*, 81.
72. Kooiman, *Luther and the Bible*, 208.
73. Pelikan and Lehmann, *Luther's Works*, 35:365.
74. Ibid., 35:395.
75. Ibid., 35:396.
76. Ibid., 35:362.
77. Landeen, *Luther's Religious Thought*, 95.
78. Pelikan and Lehmann, *Luther's Works*, 44:115–217.
79. Ibid., 39:15–159.

had as one objective the enabling of all believers to read, understand, and interpret Scripture for themselves.

Before dealing with varying interpretations of Luther's views, let us deal briefly with his response to the Roman Catholic view that Scripture gains its authority from the testimony of the church because the church selected the canon and so determined what is Scripture and what is not. The consequent argument is that, this being the case, only the church can decide upon the proper interpretation Scripture. Luther's response to this charge was to emphasize that the authority of Scripture is determined by God and not by the church. In his controversy with Eck, Luther wrote, "The Church cannot give any more authority or power than it has of itself. A council cannot make that to be of Scripture which is not by nature of Scripture."[80] The Scriptures are thus self-authenticating[81] and are dependent upon no-one, thus they can rightly be asserted as an objective authority, apart from any external testimony to them. Luther also said that, if the church argued that it was superior to the Scriptures because it determined the canon, the logical outcome of their position was to consider John the Baptist to be superior to Jesus because he pointed to him![82]

Having given this summary of Luther's doctrine of Scripture, emphasizing his high view of the authority of Scripture, his Christocentric approach, and his views on the extent of the canon, let us now consider some responses to Luther.

A number of theologians have taken Luther's comments on the extent of the canon, especially his critical remarks concerning those books of whose apostolicity he was not convinced, to imply that he did not hold a high view of the authority of Scripture. One example is Adolf Harnack who wrote,

> But—when so bravely carrying on his battle against the authority of the Councils—Luther took up at the same time an adverse attitude towards the infallibility of Scripture; and how could he do otherwise? . . . The content of a person who gives himself to be our own never can be coincident with a written word however clear and certain it may be. Thus Luther necessarily had to distinguish even between Word of God and Holy Scripture . . . Luther refused to be dictated to and to have his mouth stopped even by the apostolical testimony . . . There can be no doubt that the position Luther took up towards the New Testament in

---

80. Cited by Briggs, *Biblical Study*, 107.
81. *Luthers Werke*, 7:175ff.
82. Ibid., 26:57.

his prefaces, and even in special discussions elsewhere, was the correct one . . .[83]

Unfortunately, Harnack provides no references or other evidence to support his argument, especially his contention that Luther distinguished between Scripture and the Word of God.

C.A. Briggs also denied that Luther taught a high view of Scripture. He wrote, "Luther does not hesitate to dispute the validity of Paul's argument in Gal. 4:22."[84] He also asserted that, "The Reformers laid down no theory of inspiration such as would cover accent and letter, word, logic, and grammar."[85] Briggs fails to take into account those passages in Luther, which we mentioned earlier, where the very letters of Scripture are said to be inspired and even the phrasing is attributed to the work of the Holy Spirit. More significantly, neither Harnack nor Briggs takes Luther's Christocentricity seriously enough.

Paul Lehmann, speaking of both Luther and Calvin, wrote,

> Textual literalism in the sense of the infallibility of the Biblical words was never held in the Church before the seventeenth century. It achieved extreme and solitary formulation in the Formula Consensus Helvetica (1675) . . . which declared even the vowel points of the Hebrew alphabet to have been inspired by the Holy Spirit. This . . . was as remote as could be from the mind of the Reformers.[86]

We can agree that the Reformers did not hold to the inspiration of the Masoretic traditional pointing. For example, Luther wrote of Genesis 47:31,

> Here the interpreters are at variance because of the differences in the points, which in the Hebrew language lead to many instances of ambiguity because the method of pointing is uncertain in a high degree.[87]

This, however, does not stop Luther from making claims on behalf of the inspiration of individual words and letters, as we have tried to show, and should not be used as an argument to suggest otherwise. Lehmann himself is prepared to say,

---

83. Harnack, *History of Dogma*, 7:224.
84. Briggs, *Biblical Study*, 140.
85. Ibid., 141.
86. Lehmann, "Reformers' Use of the Bible," 342–43.
87. Pelikan and Lehmann, eds., *Luther's Works*, 8:141.

the Reformers not infrequently speak about the Bible in ways that suggest its literal inerrancy. But the verbal inspiration is a consequence of their view that God is the author of Scripture, not the basis of it.[88]

This somewhat liberal view of Luther's doctrine of Scripture is countered by some on the more conservative side. J.T. Mueller, for example, in his article "Luther and the Bible" asserts that, "Luther held the Bible to be the infallible divine Word"[89] and in a later section speaks of Luther as one "to whom the whole Bible was God's inspired, inerrant Word."[90] With regard to the "canon within the canon" which we have mentioned, Mueller writes, "This emphasis is indeed found in Luther's writings, but it is not to deny the verbal and plenary inspiration of the Bible, but to stress the gospel of God's grace in Christ as the essential message of the Scriptures. . ."[91] To use the terms "plenary" and "Bible" suggest that Mueller is attributing Luther's doctrine of inspiration to the sixty-six books which make up the canon as we know it, since that is what these words have come to mean in contemporary theological debate. We may agree with Mueller's doctrine of Scripture but we cannot agree with his interpretation of Luther. Mueller might speak of the "Bible" but we remain convinced that his Bible does not put James, Hebrews, Jude, and Revelation in a secondary category at the end, as Luther seems to do.

The problem with Mueller is that he subordinates Luther's Christological approach and implies that inspiration was the only significant key to understanding his doctrine of Scripture.

Mueller makes great use of F. Pieper and M. Reu in his work and their views are worth considering. Pieper, like Mueller, criticizes those who suggest that Luther took a more liberal attitude to the Scriptures than the later Lutheran dogmaticians,[92] and states that such "alleged difference" is "pure fabrication."[93] He then goes on to document all the references to inerrancy and chronological precision. He uses phrases such as "all parts of Scripture"[94] and hence makes the same mistake as Mueller. In response to Luther's view of canonicity, Pieper argues that the "hay, straw, and stubble" quotation, as he calls it, refers to, "those periods in the lives of the prophets

---

88. Lehmann, "Reformers' Use of the Bible," 339.
89. Mueller, "Luther and the Bible," 88.
90. Ibid., 95.
91. Ibid., 101.
92. Pieper, *Christian Dogmatics*, 1:276.
93. Ibid., 277.
94. Ibid., 285.

when they were not moved as the infallible organs of the Holy Spirit to write the Holy Scriptures."[95] When he argues that Luther's openness on the extent of the canon is a separate question from the "inspiration" question, we must disagree.

Reu broadly supports Mueller and Pieper but at two points he goes further. First, he attempts to prove that Luther ascribed inerrancy to the autographs,[96] yet he fails to provide evidence from Luther's own writings that he held to this view. Second, Reu spends a great deal of time on the "dictation theory"[97] arguing that while Luther himself was in no way guilty of this, his successors were heading in that direction. This argument compromises Pieper's claim that there were no differences between Luther and the later dogmaticians.

Harnack, Briggs, and Lehmann argue that Luther's high view of Scripture was undermined by his views on the extent of the canon. Mueller, Pieper, and Reu argue that Luther's views on canonicity do not fundamentally affect his high view of Scripture. Our argument would be that Luther did indeed hold to a high view of Scripture, believing in the verbal inspiration of the Scriptures. At the same time, however, he applied a Christological lens to the doctrine of Scripture, which led to his various comments on canonicity. In other words, the key issue is not whether Luther held to a "low" view of Scripture (Harnack *et al*) or to a "high" view of Scripture (Mueller *et al*) but rather the impact of his Christological method. In this respect we might wonder if Luther's doctrine of Scripture has more in common with the theology of Karl Barth than with some of his fellow Reformers.

ANALYSIS AND CONCLUSIONS

Let me now try to draw together the threads of this chapter by offering three points of analysis and conclusion.

First, Martin Luther's great contribution was the affirmation that Scripture, interpreted on its own terms by grammatical-historical exegesis and compared with other Scriptures, is the final authority for God's people. His progression to this conclusion concerning the authority of the Scriptures, from his earlier view of the authority of the church, led to a new understanding of biblical doctrine, not least in relation to justification by faith. It was as he moved towards the sole authority of Scripture that he was enabled to liberate the doctrines of Scripture from the strictures and false

---

95. Ibid., 288.
96. Reu, *Luther and the Scriptures*, 103–8.
97. Ibid., 109–32.

expressions of medieval scholasticism. At the same time, Luther's achievements were somewhat restricted by his Christological method, hence the clarity of doctrinal formulation that we see in Calvin was not present in Luther. To some extent, of course, this was because Calvin came later and was able to build on the achievements of Luther and the other early Reformers, but it was also due to Calvin's clear understanding that *all* of Scripture, having been breathed out by God, carried full authority, rather than simply those books which were more obviously Christ-focused.

Second, it is to be regretted that Luther ultimately failed in his attempt to reform the church. Instead, a new church was formed. Shortly afterwards, another division took place, with Zwingli and others, leading to the formation of yet another church. Since then, Protestantism has demonstrated an infinite capacity for disruption, schism, secession, and division. It might well be argued that the great gains of the Reformation were the rediscovery of the doctrine of justification by faith and an affirmation of Scripture as supreme authority. At the same time, we must recognize that a coherent doctrine of the church was lost. It seems to me that one of the great unresolved theological tasks of Protestantism is to articulate a doctrine of the authority of the church, in relation to the doctrine of the authority of Scripture.

Third, one of the main lessons to be learned from Luther is that, when he moved progressively from a conviction that the church had supreme authority to the place where he understood that Scripture had supreme authority, he was then able to articulate clearly the doctrines of the Christian faith. Unfortunately, in our day church theologians are moving in precisely the opposite direction. Church courts, councils, and synods are taking to themselves the right to articulate doctrine, irrespective of the clear teaching of Scripture. Protestant theology, in other words, is moving away from the conviction that Scripture has final authority in doctrinal deliberations to the place where the courts of the church have full authority. In some churches this had led to further divisions as evangelicals have left their churches to form yet more denominations. In other churches, evangelicals have been disciplined by the courts of the church for refusing to accept decisions which are contrary to the plain teaching of Scripture. This has been particularly apparent in the recent debates on same-sex relations.

As European evangelical theologians, it is incumbent upon us to address these issues and to work and pray for a new Reformation.

BIBLIOGRAPHY

Althaus, Paul. *The Theology of Martin Luther*. Translated by Robert C. Schultz. Philadelphia: Fortress, 1975.

Bornkamm, H. *Luther and the Old Testament*. Philadelphia: Fortress, 1969.

Briggs, C.A. *Biblical Study*. New York: Scribner's, 1890.

Harnack, Adolf. *History of Dogma*. Translated by Neil Buchanan. Boston: Little, Brown, 1894-99.

Hendrix, Scott H. *Luther and the Papacy: Stages in a Reformation Context*. Philadelphia: Fortress, 1981.

Hodge, A. A. and Warfield, B. B. "Inspiration." *Presbyterian Review* 2 (1881) 225-60.

Kooiman, W. J. *Luther and the Bible*. Philadelphia: Muhlenberg, 1961.

Landeen, W. M. *Martin Luther's Religious Thought*. Nampa, ID: Pacific, 1971.

Lehmann, Paul L. "The Reformers' Use of the Bible." *Theology Today* 3, no. 3 (1946) 328-44.

Lohse, Bernhard. *Martin Luther's Theology: Its Historical and Systematic Development*. Edinburgh: T. & T. Clark, 1999.

Luther, Martin. *D. Martin Luthers Werke: kritische Gesammtausgabe* (Weimarer Ausgabe) various eds. 121 vols. Weimar, 1883-2009.

Muller, Richard A. *Post-Reformation Reformed Dogmatics*. Vol. 2, *Holy Scripture: The Cognitive Foundation of Theology*. Grand Rapids: Baker, 1993.

Mueller, J. T. "Luther and the Bible." In *Inspiration and Interpretation*, edited by John F. Walvoord, 84-114. Grand Rapids: Eerdmans, 1957.

Oberman, Heiko A. *Luther: Man between God and the Devil*. New Haven: Yale University Press, 2006.

Olivier, Daniel. *The Trial of Luther*. London: Mowbrays, 1971.

Pelikan, Jaroslav, and Lehmann, Helmut T., eds. *Luther's Works*. 55 vols. American ed. Philadelphia: Muhlenberg & Fortress; St Louis: Concordia, 1955-86.

Pieper, F. *Christian Dogmatics*. St. Louis: Concordia, 1950.

Reid, J. K. S. *The Authority of Scripture*. London: Methuen, 1957.

Reu, M. *Luther and the Scriptures*. Columbus, OH: Wartburg, 1944.

Walch, J. G, ed. *Dr. Martin Luthers Saemmtliche Schriften*. 22 vols. St Louis: Concordia, 1885-1910.

8

Guilt, Shame, and Forgiveness
Crucial Questions of Life in the Perspective of Reformation Theology

Christoph Raedel

GUILT AND SHAME—QUESTIONS OF LIFE TODAY?[1]

In March 2015 the whole of Germany and the world beyond was shocked when a 27 year old pilot of Germanwings (an air-carrier of the Lufthansa-group) committed suicide by veering an aircraft with 149 people on board into the French Alps. The flight from Barcelona to Düsseldorf had among its passengers a school class returning from a school exchange. Pilot Andreas Lubitz used the moment when the other pilot went to the toilet to lock the cockpit door, making it impossible for his colleague to reenter. Then he slowly and steadily lowered the aircraft, calmly breathing (as the voice recorder revealed later), until the plane finally crashed into the mountains killing all passengers and himself.

---

1. I would like to thank Bernd Wannenwetsch (Kandern) and J. Samuel Hammond for comments on an earlier draft of this paper and Marie Hammond (both Durham, North Carolina) for editing its English version.

Quickly the question arose who was to blame for this act of killing. Obviously it was the pilot who steered the aircraft into the mountains, seemingly clearly aware of his doing and in a healthy condition. But was he really? Investigation revealed that Lufthansa had twice refused to renew Lubitz's medical certificate because of a serious episode of depression. From 2009 onwards the license continued to be renewed on an annual basis. Who takes responsibility for renewing the license of someone who had been in therapy for suicidal tendencies? Many questions remain even after the case has been closed, but this much is certain: to be a pilot had been Lubitz' childhood dream, and while this dream had come true, it had been put in jeopardy by the diagnosed depression. Depression, we know, is a deeply painful condition, usually marked by withdrawal, ruminative sadness, self-blame, and excessive feelings of guilt. Was it a sense of shame over the prospect of losing a position that guided his premeditations as he conducted an internet research on "cockpit doors" and "suicide" only days before crashing the plane into the French Alps? The question remains: How could he so calmly steer the aircraft into the rocks when he must have been aware of ringing alarms and the second pilot banging at the door and screaming at him?

Germanwings flight 4U9525 has created a narrative of guilt and shame. Citizens of the town of Montabaur, where Lubitz lived, felt shame fearing their town might henceforth be known as the home of a mass murderer. Parents felt guilty of having sent their children on the school exchange. The media searched for a scapegoat and memorial services were held trying to find ways expressing the pain, guilt, and shame that seem unbearable.

Feelings of guilt and shame, it seems, are known to us, but what is the concept behind these feelings? Are they more than just that—subjective expressions of an emotional state? The German philosopher and journalist Ulrich Greiner, for example, argues that our Western societies have constantly moved away from the inherited "culture of guilt" and the even older "culture of shame" towards what he calls a "culture of embarrassment." In his book *Schamverlust* (*Loss of Shame*)[2] he follows—mainly through the lens of European literature—the path we have travelled towards a shameless culture. His key point is this: The notion of shame refers to the moral awareness of the human being, that is, the capacity to see oneself as a moral subject and to be conscious of one's responsibility to obey the dictates of a recognized authority. Failure to act according to the moral standards on which civilization rests causes a "bad conscience." Hence, a "culture of shame" presupposes an objective moral law and the personal conscience that signals divergence

---

2. See Greiner, *Schamverlust*.

from this law, finding expression in shame. For Greiner, the shift is exactly here: transcendent moral law is no longer generally accepted in late modern societies, and its place is being filled by the many rules of "political correctness" that every person has to yield to. Therefore, embarrassment, replacing shame, is the result of having neglected one or several of those many, changeable and, in fact, changing rules. Life is awkward when all that matters is to behave in a politically correct way, but this, Greiner maintains, is the core condition of survival in the West.

Greiner's book contains many valuable insights. Though it cannot count as a full-scale analysis of the phenomenon of shame in Western societies, two points in his analysis are especially worth pondering:

- The *first* is indeed a significant shift in the way our societies relate to authority. Kant's moral law still implied the awareness of a transcendent reality. One's life had to stand the test of time, even after one's time on earth was over. Goodness, for Kant, was found in enacting the good will, that is, in following the categorical demand for a maxim that is universally applicable. It is the dignity of the human being as "Spirit" to follow a validated ethical command rather than changeable impressions. The rules of "political correctness" work entirely differently, because in substance, Greiner argues, they aim at saving one's personal competitiveness based on good health.[3] Greiner mentions chastity as an example: Though ridiculed as a virtue today, chastity has not disappeared but has been thoroughly co-opted into the fitness-cult and the art of body-performance. "You shall style your body and keep it in good condition" proves for many today a more demanding commandment than obedience to a religious rule was for previous generations.

- A *second* valid point of Greiner's book is his demonstration that the promise of unbounded individualism to live one's life as one prefers is, in fact, a liberty that comes at the price of constantly bowing to the changing commands of professional career, social environment, and fashion trends. The world in which everybody is wired to conforming to imperatives that keep changing is marked by extreme insecurity.[4] This insecurity, I would add, makes us good consumers because peo-

---

3. Ibid., 76. An example from daily life would be the constant admonition that every person—children and the elderly in particular—needs to drink about two liters of liquid a day. To send children to school without a water-bottle is widely regarded as irresponsible in Germany nowadays. My childhood memory tells me that under the same climate conditions nothing of that sort was discussed when I was a schoolboy in the 1980s.

4. Ibid., 74.

ple tend to compensate the sense of insecurity preferably by acquiring goods that promise to make life safe.

So what about *guilt* in our societies? In 1946, still amidst smoking ruins resulting from a disastrous war, the existentialist philosopher Karl Jaspers reflected on the concept of guilt. Among its layers he counts "metaphysical" guilt as something Germans in particular needed to face.[5] This guilt is based on the "solidarity" of all human creatures who are held responsible for injustices around the world because they have not done everything possible to prevent evil. For Jaspers, this guilt cannot be justified by humans but calls for "jurisdiction" that belongs to God only. However, within just a few decades from the time of Jaspers's writing God was increasingly moved to the rear as an actor to be reckoned with in history. As a result, people are less bothered by having to face God's wrath than by the impression of God's absence from the world. As Tillich pointed out, the existential problem of modern humans is not sin but life's apparent "meaninglessness."[6] So the focus was shifting from the justification of sinners to the justification of God for allowing terrible things to happen. As C.S. Lewis observed: People today "want to know, not whether they can be acquitted for sin, but whether He [God] can be acquitted for creating such a world" as the one we find ourselves in.[7]

Today our societies have by and large probably moved even "beyond" this concern. For many people, the eclipse of God is so complete that God is not even considered for the role of the scapegoat that can be blamed for natural disasters. The tribunal for metaphysical guilt, it seems, has been firmly closed. But to get rid of *God* does not necessarily mean to be rid of *guilt*. The focus, though, is now radically anthropocentric. With God out of the picture, the human desire and need to have one's existence justified leads to desperate attempts of self-justification, a merciless enterprise marked by competition for recognition and "praise." So guilt and shame are still with us. The "blame-game" is in full swing, for example when we say: "It is not my fault" and begin to blame someone else. People still seem to know that shame is an appropriate response to certain types of behavior when they exclaim: "Shame on you." In short: we are far from having outgrown guilt and shame as questions of life that call for an answer.

---

5. See Jaspers, *Question*, 32.
6. See Tillich, *Courage to Be*, 46–51.
7. Lewis, "Christian Apologetics," 95.

GUILT, SHAME, AND THE CONCEPT OF MUTUAL RECOGNITION. A PHILOSOPHICAL PERSPECTIVE

We began with the disastrous killing of 149 people in a crashed airplane carried out by the pilot to whom they had been entrusted. But is this kind of reference not something of a theologian's trick? To introduce the notion of guilt and shame by bringing up an atrocity where nobody can really identify with the actor? Do we really need to go to such extremes to establish the validity of concepts like guilt and shame—in order that we can then offer forgiveness as the way out? It was Dietrich Bonhoeffer who rejected the strategy of exploiting human weakness for the sake of introducing "God." Bonhoeffer intended to speak of God "not at the boundaries but at the center, not in weakness but in strength," i.e. in the strongest hours of human life.[8] Bonhoeffer's point can, in some way, be complemented by C.S. Lewis who, in his reflections on the task of apologetics, argued for a descent to the level of everyday life when probing the depth of contemporary notions of guilt and shame. He writes:

> our continual effort must be to get their [the audience's] mind away from public affairs and "crime" and bring them down to brass tacks—to the whole network of spite, greed, envy, unfairness and conceit in the lives of "ordinary decent people" like themselves (and ourselves).[9]

Following the general direction hinted at by Bonhoeffer and Lewis, I would like to employ here the philosophical concept of "recognition" (*Anerkennung* in German) in order to identify the matrix underlying contemporary understandings of guilt and shame. To receive and to grant recognition is something that stands at the very center of our lives. It is also a concept that will prove helpful in elaborating forgiveness as the theologically sound response to the questions of life dealt with here.[10]

Let us take as our starting point a question of Jesus preserved in the Gospel of John. In the context of discussing why the Jews would not accept his messianic authority, Jesus asked: "How can you believe since you accept glory from one another but do not seek the glory that comes from the only God?" (John 5:44) Of particular interest here is the analysis of the general human condition implied by this question.[11] A person is a social being, em-

---

8. Bonhoeffer, *Letters and Papers*, 366–67 (letter dated April 30, 1944).

9. Lewis, *God in the Dock*, 96.

10. Widely regarded as the point of reference for the concept of "Anerkennung" in philosophy is Honneth, *Recognition*.

11. For a helpful interpretation of the text, see Ridderbos, *John*, 205–6.

bedded in social structures and strictures by being related to other people. A fundamental form of relating to each other and, in that process, of discovering one's own identity is recognition, expressed in biblical terms as "receiving glory," that is: by being praised, recognized by others as an agent who matters. Our self-perception is to a significant degree rooted in relations of recognition to parents and the family we have not ourselves chosen. As humans we long for recognition, for signs of goodwill and praise, or even of correction and critique if they are themselves acts of goodwill. We dwell on recognition by others, and without it die the death of social isolation. Our soul hungers for recognition like our body longs for food and water. The "hook" in the biblical quote given above, as I see it, is the question: From whom do we actually care to receive recognition? Our self-perception may vary significantly depending on whose recognition we think really matters. And here is the fork in the road: the (post)modern project is built on the assumption that there is no such "thing" as God to be taken into account when it comes to recognition. All that matters is what other *people* think of us, though actually not just *any* people but certain people whose praise really counts for us because we acknowledge them as subjects whose judgment is important.

The voices that matter in this realm of constructing identity relentlessly call out: "Be yourself, be authentic!—and we will praise you." To achieve the good life in this highly individualist sense, however, is actually rather hard work. To be "authentic" carries a requirement of originality that is incompatible with trust in traditions, role-models, and cultural frameworks. The actualizing of the original self knows of no referential authority but is staged in front of expectations of what it means to lead the good life. To live up to the expectations of others earns you praise, while failure to do so earns you disregard or disrespect.[12] So the need to be wholly authentic and the pressure to conform to wider expectations of what it means to "Be yourself" turn out to be an inescapable paradox.

Due to the socially structured reality of human life, self-esteem cannot be developed in isolation from others.[13] To be sure, to care for yourself you do not need the other ("You take care of your own stuff. And I don't care what you think about me"), but self-*care* is not the same as self-*esteem* that

---

12. E.g., with the current moral vision, having sex outside the marriage of a man and a woman is widely accepted, though some rules apply that everyone must know: don't touch children under the age of fourteen; above that age, make sure of mutual consent. So there is no longer a shared narrative of the good of marriage in terms of regulating sexual desire, but merely a shifting pattern of rules one needs to be aware of.

13. An insightful study that lies behind some of the thoughts developed in this section is Majer, *Scham, Schuld und Anerkennung*.

presupposes relations of mutual recognition.[14] To have self-esteem means to hold convictions concerning what kind of behavior would be appropriate towards myself,[15] even when I am being shamed by contrary attitudes or actions.

Guilt and shame may (philosophically) be understood as conflicts in relations of recognition. They may be distinguished in various ways. For Herbert Morris guilt (and innocence) deal with *morals* (rights and wrongs), while shame deals with *models*, i.e., our sense of what is heroic, measured in terms of honor and glory on the one side and shame on the other.[16] One might say that guilt deals with *rules* while shame deals with *roles* in society. A sense of guilt is caused by the violation of a set of rules: I have not lived up to the expectations others have of me. The feeling of shame is rooted in the painful (though not necessarily public) loss of trust in oneself as to being acceptable to others: I cannot play my self-scripted role anymore; I have failed in aspiring to the (heroic) model that I regard as authoritative for a good life. To put it another way: To feel guilty is to sense the consequences of the *power* of my thoughts, words, and deeds. To be ashamed is to feel their *powerlessness*. In Sartre's terms, shame arises when one feels oneself as a mere object stared at by others.[17] This "objectification" is humiliating because it hurts the self-esteem: My self-perception is crumbling because I have no say anymore, my look at others meets no response, and consequently I cannot fill the role I had crafted for myself.

To summarize this point: Both guilt and shame deal with conflicts of recognition, but in different ways. Shame is more self-referential, focusing on one's own failure and the loss of authority to count as a valued agent in the network of mutual recognition, while guilt refers to other people's expectations expressed in rules society upholds.[18] Embedded in a framework of (ideally) mutual recognition life becomes a constant struggle for acceptance by others and to uphold the authority to be some person whose judgment of others really matters. This struggle is intensified by the widely-shared assumption that the life we have is limited to our earthly existence, and that there is no source or subject of recognition beyond the human sphere. Without God in view, the struggle for mutual recognition among

14. In the terminology of Majer, mutuality is a core characteristic of recognition while respect is different in this regard: to respect the other in his or her dignity as a human creature does not necessarily imply mutuality. I owe respect to every human being no matter how he or she responds or behaves generally.

15. Majer, *Scham, Schuld und Anerkennung*, 53.

16. Morris, *Guilt and Shame*.

17. Sartre, *Being and Nothingness*.

18. Majer, *Scham, Schuld und Anerkennung*, 96.

humans easily turns into a vicious cycle. The question is: Can the vicious cycle in which people strive to "accept glory from one another but do not seek the glory that comes from the only God" (John 5:44) be overcome by God's action on their behalf? And would the gift of forgiveness be a theologically appropriate description of the way in which God breaks the vicious cycle?

"FREE AT LAST": THE PROMISE OF FORGIVENESS IN CHRISTIAN PERSPECTIVE

Keeping in mind the valuable contributions philosophy has made to the concepts of guilt and shame, we turn to biblical and theological thinking to answer crucial questions of life. God needs to break the vicious cycle—and that for two reasons:

- *First,* contrary to modern intuition it is not of primary importance what *we* think about God but what *God* thinks about us. Reflecting on who may be the "others" whose recognition matters, we need to become aware of recognition by God as the one who has made us. There is no way to answer questions of life without taking into account the Giver of life, God.

- *Secondly,* apart from God, revealed as the God "for us," as Karl Barth liked to put it, humans lack the ability to consider seriously the *depth* and the *nature* of guilt and shame. Sin will not enter the picture as long as guilt and shame are seen as subjective feelings that may be overcome by technical (therapeutic) means or handled by moral strategies of rehabilitation. To recognize oneself as a sinner falling short of God's command is simply unbearable as long as no redeemer is in sight. Hence, without God entering the circle of the struggle for mutual recognition humans will not find the courage to be serious about the human condition as it really is. Consequently, to justify the "good life" one lives takes the form of *self*-justification, expressed in acts of mutual (non)recognition between individuals competing for praise by others and, at the same time, ignoring the only subject who does not enter the competition, God.

In considering the Christian response to human guilt and shame, I shall primarily draw on Romans 8 and the theologies of Martin Luther and John Calvin. We take as our starting point Romans 8, "the inner sanctuary within the cathedral of Christian faith; the tree of life in the midst of the Garden of Eden; the highest peak in a range of mountains," as this chapter has been called by interpreters.[19] A short expression of what is happening here would be: The *questions* of life meet the *Spirit* of Life who opens up human existence to the *fullness* of life.

It is not my intention here to expound the marvelous texture of this Pauline chapter but simply to identify some of the keys woven into the text that may open the door to a solid Christian response to human feelings of guilt and shame. My point, in brief, is this: The Gospel promise of forgiveness offers what humans need: on the one hand *acquittal* from the accusation of (metaphysical) guilt and on the other a new identity by *adoption* into the family of God.

Acquittal: "No Condemnation Now I Dread"[20]

With the eclipse of God in Western societies it does not suffice to simply state that "God" is the solution to our deeply felt problems. Rather we must clearly identify who we actually mean when speaking about God. Paul indicates in a subtle but effective way that God is the Father of our Lord Jesus Christ, present in the Spirit. This is what Douglas Moo writes: "Note how Paul involves Father, Son, and Spirit in the work of redemption."[21] The only appropriate way to narrate the story of God's redemptive work in history is to unfold this drama by high-lighting Father, Son, and Holy Spirit as the triune actors for the sake of salvation. In other words, the gift of forgiveness is inseparable from the identity of the giver, who is the triune God. Regarding the concept of recognition, we note that God as the triune One eludes human definitions. In the circle of mutual recognition God is the subject that cannot be objectified under human scrutiny because God transcends our notions of "person" or "being." God is, as a subject, the "radical other" (Kierkegaard) on whose recognition human self-perception depends but who does not depend on the praise of creatures.

For Paul, the presence of the Holy Spirit makes a world of difference to the human life, for "natural" human life is subdued to the "law of sin and death" (v. 2). According to Moo, this expression could refer to the Mosaic Law but is more plausibly understood in a figurative sense (as becomes obvious from the opposite of the "law of the Spirit").[22] Paul speaks of the "principle" or "authority" of sin and death that hold humans captive to despair

---

19. Moo, *Romans* (NICNT), 467.
20. Charles Wesley, "And Can It Be that I Should Gain." In *United Methodist Hymnal*, no. 363, verse 5.
21. Moo, *Romans* (NIVAC), 256.
22. Moo, *Romans* (NICNT), 474–7.

and decay. But by the gracious activity of God in Jesus Christ this "scheme" has been met with the "authority" of the life-giving Spirit who breaks the bonds of sin and death.

What is the significance of Paul's metaphorical speaking of the "law of sin and death" for the question at hand? Paul would not be surprised to learn that throughout history this "law" takes on different forms and manifests itself in changing ways. Our condition recognizes no all-persuasive moral law with binding force but an "inner" law that could well be described as the craving for recognition and acceptance by the human "other." But this focus on human recognition alone, bereft of the divine "other," fails to achieve the fullness of life offered in Christ. The good news of the Gospel according to Romans 8 is that for all those who are "in Christ" (v. 1) the higher law of the Spirit breaks the power of the principle that condemns humans to struggle for the ultimate acceptance by God, unattainable by human effort.

The defeat of the law of sin and death is pronounced by Paul with the words, "no condemnation" (v. 1), a judicial term used here to point out what is accomplished by Christ's redemptive work. To be "in Christ," i.e. to be united to him by faith through the Spirit of Christ (v. 9), is to receive acquittal from sin and guilt by the hands of the supreme judge. The sentence "not guilty" proclaimed by Christ breaks the chains of mutual accusations that hold people captive, making them crave for the recognition without which no one can live. For Paul, this is not simply the change of a psychological condition that may follow from the advice: "Simply do not care what others think about you." It is a real "realm-transfer" (Rom 8:8–9). The fear and fate of condemnation is no longer a threat to believers because they have been transferred to a kingdom ruled by the law of the Spirit. Moo declares:

> "No condemnation" is the banner triumphantly flying over all those who are 'in Christ' (v. 1) only because 'in Christ' we have been set free by the Spirit from that realm, ruled by sin, in which condemnation (= death) is one's ineluctable fate.[23]

The penalty of ultimate exclusion that "natural" humans deserve was laid on Jesus Christ, who "suffered outside the city gate" (Heb 13:12).

According to the apostle, the new life free from accusation and guilt is not bought at the price of diminishing the weight of sin as rebellion against God. The vicious cycle of counterfeit recognition and lack of acceptance is not broken by claiming that there would not actually be any reason to disregard the other; we are, in fact, signed by sin. Rather, the gift of forgiveness means that God allots to himself, in his Son, what humans deserve, while

---

23. Moo, *Romans* (NICNT), 477.

they receive, free of charge, what belongs solely to God by putting their trust in Jesus Christ. Paul expresses this as follows: "And so he [God] condemned sin in the flesh, in order that the righteous requirement of the law might be fully met in us, who do not live according to the flesh but according to the Spirit." (Rom 8:4)

The concept of union with Christ has been aptly taken up in Luther's theology of the cross.[24] In his well-known treatise, *The Freedom of the Christian*, he uses the image of the marriage, in which Christ is the bridegroom and the soul of the faithful the bride, to express the miracle of a mysterious exchange realized in faith: "Christ is full of grace, life, and salvation; the soul is full of sin, death, and condemnation. Let faith step in, and then sin, death, and hell will belong to Christ, and grace, life, and salvation to the soul."[25] Marriage is, and not only for Luther, the supreme image to portray the complete surrender to the other. In this sense there is mutuality in recognition. At the same time, one should not overlook the ultimate asymmetry within this reciprocity, for what Christ gives is a gift worthy to be received: salvation, grace, and life, while the gift of the human soul is, as it were, a non-gift: it is the acknowledgment of having nothing to offer, the act of giving up all claims to having deserved the grace bestowed. So the mystery of this marriage is God's accepting a non-gift for what it is not: a gift. Hence, the exchange of asymmetric gifts establishes a real union grounded in the full surrender of both partners.[26]

The Finnish school of Luther interpretation especially emphasizes that God's gift is actually Christ himself.[27] Understanding the *personal* character of the gift received in faith helps to avoid the misconception that is implicitly present in the discussion of the forensic versus the effective understanding of justification. I prefer to follow those interpreters who read Luther as keeping these aspects close together. To receive Christ as the giver of forgiveness is to allow Christ to be henceforth the ruling principle of the believers' life. In Luther's own words (from 1539): "Christ did not only earn *gratia*, 'grace,' for us, but also *donum*, 'the gift of the Holy Spirit,' so that we might have not only forgiveness of sin," but may also cease sinning.[28] Christ did not lay down his life so that forgiven sinners might refuse to live the new life.

---

24. Elert, *Lutheranism*, 166–76.
25. Grimm, ed., *Luther's Works*, 31:13.
26. Holm, "Justification and Reciprocity."
27. Mannermaa, *Christ Present in Faith*.
28. Gritsch, ed., *Luther's Works*, 41:114 ("On Councils and the Church"). In the edition quoted the final sentence is: "also cessation of sin."

Faith in Christ introduces a new mode of recognition: divine recognition. Faith opens the eyes to the awareness that God recognizes in the believer not only the outward person (the body "subject to death"; Rom 8:10) but something more than that, the righteousness of Christ bestowed on all who are "in Christ" by faith. This *personal* recognition is framed by Christ presenting the Church *collectively* to himself "without stain or wrinkle or any other blemish, but holy and blameless" (Eph 5:27). While humans as sinners have every reason to see in themselves and in the church *less* than there actually is (despairing at their shortcomings), God recognizes *more* in them than there is to be seen by human eyes.[29] The reality of sin is taken seriously and not simply glossed over, but at the same time God grounds the believers' identity in a gracious act of forgiveness. Being forgiven, believers are enabled to recognize in others, by faith, what no one else can see in them, namely, God's creatures, for whose sin Christ died the sinners' death.

Adoption: "Dear Lord and Father of Mankind"[30]

We saw that Paul could express in judicial language that believers are released from the threat of condemnation under the law of sin and death. He complements this by using the participatory language of adoption. Whoever is united to Christ through the life-giving Spirit becomes a child of God, calling God "Abba, Father" (v. 15). The language of adoption goes to the very heart of relationships grounded in recognition, because adopting someone is, in a fundamental way, an act of recognition. Turning our attention to Calvin, we find him to be distinctively a theologian of "adoption," because the adoption of believers "is at the heart of John Calvin's understanding of salvation."[31] According to Sinclair Ferguson, Calvin "does not treat sonship as a separate locus of theology precisely because it undergirds everything he writes."[32]

While Calvin is prepared to speak, though only in a qualified sense, of a sonship of all humankind since they are created by God into God's image, sonship, properly speaking, is the peculiar privilege of those who belong to the church of Christ. Adoption as children of God is made possible by

---

29. For an excellent study of justification within the framework of recognition (from a Roman Catholic perspective), see Hoffmann, *Theologie der Gabe*.

30. John Greenleaf Whittier, "Dear Lord and Father of Mankind." In *United Methodist Hymnal*, no. 358.

31. Griffith, "First Title of the Spirit," 135. The following section of this paper owes several insights to Griffith as well as to Westhead, "Adoption."

32. Sinclair B. Ferguson, cited in Griffith, "First Title of the Spirit," 135–36.

the incarnation of Jesus Christ. Calvin points out that there is no sonship of the believers without the incarnation of the Son of God: "He being the true Son, has been given to us as a brother, so that that which he possesses as his own by nature becomes ours by adoption, if we embrace this great mercy with firm faith."[33] The fruit of redemption, wrought by Christ's atoning death, is received by faith and cannot be earned by human deeds. To be sure, adoption in this theological, metaphorical sense is different from the human practice of adopting a child. Usually, adoptive parents had no relationship to the child before the adoption process began, while God, as Calvin acknowledges when using "adoption" in a broader sense, is from the very beginning related to the creature as the Creator.

Calvin is well known for the pneumatological overtones in his teaching on salvation that resonate well with Paul's interest in Romans 8 to give the Spirit of Christ a prominent place. For both Paul and Calvin, it is the communication of the Holy Spirit that makes sinners sons by adoption. Calvin identifies "Spirit of adoption" as the "first title" of the Spirit, because the Spirit "is witness to us of the free favor with which God the Father embraced us" in his Son, so as to become our Father "and give us boldness of access to him" by crying in us "Abba, Father."[34] Adoption is sealed by the inner testimony the Spirit gives and by which the believers are assured of their salvation (Rom 8:15), which is, in effect, "union with Christ," the well-known focus of Calvin's soteriology.[35]

Whether this inner witness gives assurance of a salvation that cannot be lost has remained a matter of dispute between Calvinists and Arminians, but Calvin and Wesley are very close in arguing that adoption does not simply inaugurate a new status but initiates a process of conformity to Christ. Adoption is not only a matter of having a good conscience but of obedience to the law of Christ and the indwelling reality of the Spirit. To quote Calvin: "Whomsoever, therefore, God receives into his favor, he presents with the Spirit of adoption, whose agency forms them anew into his [Christ's] image."[36] Weaving the words of Romans 8 together, Calvin arrives at the conclusion that the grace of adoption has its end in good works that glorify God. Like Luther, Calvin emphasizes the sufferings of Christ that are the model for the pilgrimage of the believer (Rom 8:17), while Wesley and the evangelical movements tend to emphasize the power of the resurrection life imparted to believers by the Spirit of Christ (Rom 8:13–14). In any case,

33. Calvin, *Institutes* III.20.36.
34. Calvin, *Institutes* III.1.3.
35. Canlis, "Fatherhood of God," 412.
36. Calvin, *Institutes* III.11.8.

they would have agreed when Calvin claims that "the Lord adopts us for his sons on the condition that our life be a representation of Christ."[37]

How does this promise of adoption relate to the contemporary sense of shame understood as the fear or the state of losing my role, my authority, in relations based on recognition? The answer is twofold:

- *First*, adoption into God's family creates a new conception of the self. The Christian is brought into a personal relationship based on unconditional recognition by God, the "other," whose recognition ultimately matters because God *created* this person. While the person as visible to human eyes—a frail body and failing to perform the Master's plan time and again—does not as such fit into the family formed by faith, God in Christ is not ashamed of the adopted child. "Both the one who makes people holy [Christ] and those who are made holy are of the same family. So Jesus is not ashamed to call them brothers and sisters" (Heb 2:11 NIV). There is no reason to be ashamed of oneself when God—who would have every reason to be ashamed of his creatures—is not ashamed to call them "my children," giving them an ultimate sense of belonging which no human relationship can ever provide.

- *Secondly*, the Son through whom they are adopted provides a trustworthy role-model for the pilgrimage of the many sons and daughters who are being adopted into God's family. While the denial of mutual recognition is expressed in blaming others for what they have done (to me), Jesus Christ presents a life based on the concept: "Love your enemies, do good to those who hate you, bless those who curse you, pray for those who mistreat you" (Luke 6:27–28 NIV). The vicious cycle of craving for recognition at almost any price is powerfully broken by Jesus Christ who interrupts the spiral of mutual accusation and blame by taking upon himself the shameful penalty of human guilt. At the same time one needs to be clear about the implications for the daily Christian discipleship. Jesus' advice to his disciples just quoted does not follow the logic of success-orientated self-promotion. It is about faithfulness to God that may (and often will) result in suffering of many sorts. Believers, following the Servant King who was cast out by the "powers" and "authorities" of his time, may well experience acts of shameful social exclusion themselves. It is the Spirit of Christ who frees them from fearing such rejection and disregard and who upholds them as members of the community of Christ's brothers and sisters.

---

37. Calvin, *Institutes* III.6.3.

In summary, the biblical Christian response to crucial questions of life like feelings of guilt and shame is not just another concept proposed for consideration, but a person, Jesus Christ, present in the power of his Spirit as the one who forgives and renews. If personal relationships of recognition are as fundamental to human life as I indicated above then it seems fully plausible that frail human relations can find an anchor in, and broken ones can be healed by, a personal relationship, by being rightly related to the triune God through Christ.

The Weight of Glory: "Thou my Everlasting Portion"[38]

In presenting the Gospel as response to human needs, there is always a danger of accepting uncritically the questions of life raised in contemporary society. Due to the human condition there may be something wrong with the questions themselves. Failing to see this leads to what we may call the "existentialist fallacy," which is the attempt to model the Gospel according to contemporary questions even at the price of a substantial reduction of the message. The truth is, however, that in answering the existential human *questions* of life the Gospel changes the questioner by broadening the *world and life view* from which the questions emerge.

Both for the New Testament writers and the Reformers the Gospel of forgiveness is more (and certainly not less) than a consolation for troubled souls. It is the proclamation of *salvation* inaugurated by the resurrection of Jesus Christ from the dead by the power of God's Spirit. Both Luther and Calvin were keeping together the tension they found in Paul's Letters between the *cosmic expanse* and the *anthropological concentration* of Christ's redemptive work.[39] The Gospel is impoverished once the promise of forgiveness is disconnected from God's acting in history to destroy the powers of evil and to bring about a new creation. "It is well, it is well with my soul"[40] is certainly a confession that has its place in worship, but the expanse of God's renewing work comprises *soteria* for the "cosmos"—humans being God's representatives (Gen 1:28)—with far-reaching consequences, as Paul points out in Romans 8:19–22. Among others Wolfhart Pannenberg argued strongly for a "critical revision" of the way Reformation theology has been widely received. He criticizes the identification of "salvation" with "forgiveness" which resulted from an understanding of the Gospel that was shaped

---

38. Fanny J. Crosby, "Close to Thee." In *United Methodist Hymnal*, no. 407, verse 1.

39. This is the point strongly made by Peters, *Rechtfertigung*, 313.

40. Horatio G. Spafford, "It Is Well with My Soul." In *United Methodist Hymnal*, no. 377.

by the juxtaposition of law and Gospel as prevalent in *some*, but not all of Paul's writings.[41] With Paul's letters *and* the Gospels in view, Pannenberg insists that the Gospel message is the proclamation of eschatological *soteria*, of the in-breaking of the Kingdom of God inaugurated by the resurrection of the Son of God. "The forgiveness of sins abolishes the separation between God and us. [But] Basic [for it] is the presence of the rule of God in the work of Jesus."[42] Peter Brunner was another noted German theologian concerned about an existentialist reduction of the Gospel. Brunner argued that salvation is a thoroughly eschatological concept that is often bereft of the future notion of everlasting life.[43] According to him, the ministry of the church is not to help the world to solve its problems but to resolutely transcend the vision of human life. The church should understand itself as the chosen means of grace for the eschatological salvation of those who believe in Christ, offering a broader vision of life to people enticed by the illusion "that they are alone in this world with themselves, without an [divine] other, without God who created, sustains, and finally judges them."[44] I agree with Brunner that it is this illusion that needs to be unmasked, refuted, and rejected.

Returning to Romans 8 we find that the vision of earthly human life is definitely broadened when Paul uses the concept of *inheritance* "to introduce his qualification of our adoption in terms of its future aspects"[45] by saying: "Now if we are children, then we are heirs—heirs of God and co-heirs with Christ, if indeed we share in his sufferings in order that we may also share in his glory" (v. 17). In his interpretation Douglas Moo emphasizes the proximity of this metaphor to family-life: "a child who has been adopted into a family, while truly part of that family, does not (usually) receive all the benefits of that adoption until a later time."[46] The privileges believers enjoy in this life are incomplete until the Kingdom of God becomes fully manifest in the second coming of Jesus Christ and the final transformation of the believers which Paul mentions in several places. For the apostle this eschatological transformation of the believers will be accomplished by the same Spirit who raised Jesus from the dead (v. 11). Consequently, the experience of having one's sins forgiven and one's mind renewed is not at once identical

---

41. Pannenberg, *Systematic Theology*, 460-61.

42. Ibid., 461. (The English translation obscures the climax in the second sentence the original conveys.)

43. See Brunner, "Rechtfertigung heute," 128-29.

44. Ibid., 129; translation mine.

45. Moo, *Romans* (NICNT), 504.

46. Ibid.

with the eschatological consummation of all things, which remains a revelatory event eagerly expected by the followers of Christ.

Paul's distinction between salvation received and consummation expected rests in his conviction that God in Christ has won a victory over the "powers and authorities" (Col 2:15; Eph 6:12), but has not yet destroyed them. Though they cannot separate believers from Christ anymore (Rom 8:38), they can still assault them by spreading their venomous influence. Only when Christ returns, assures Paul, "the creation itself will be liberated from its bondage to decay and brought into the freedom and glory of the children of God" (v. 21).

Why is the distinction between the personal acceptance of the Gospel and the cosmic consummation important for answering the crucial questions of life? Because, if salvation was solely the acceptance of being accepted by God (to allude at Tillich's famous phrase), then salvation could well be interchanged with other (religious) messages or psychological therapies that aim at overcoming feelings of guilt and shame. We could deal with subjective experiences that help people to get along better, though we would have to counter the accusation that Christianity offers a solution to a plight (sin as separation from God) which humanity would not have known without Christianity. Paul, however, is convinced that the Gospel of Christ testifies to an objective battle against the principalities and powers of darkness that hold humans captive in their natural condition. The Gospel of grace, therefore, reaches further than humans in their fallen state could possibly anticipate in their questions. The conflict in which they find themselves is of cosmic expanse and has eternal consequences. The resurrection of Jesus and the gift of the Spirit have *begun* to make "all things new" but the *fullness* of life will be celebrated in the heavenly banquet depicted by Jesus. Until that consummation, watching and waiting remain needful elements of Christian discipleship.

A final point: initially I introduced the notion of recognition as a rather *negative* concept; I highlighted the problems that follow once we crave solely for human recognition, leaving God out of the picture, with the consequence of putting unbearable demands on the human "other" as well as on ourselves. This diagnoses stands, but if we rightly confess the triune God to be the same as the Creator and the Redeemer, we should expect that the human longing for recognition and acceptance is not fully explained as a sinful desire. Rather, we may expect it to be a pointer to the Creator, expressing a sense of belonging instilled into man and woman at creation. So another reason why longing for recognition is so persistent with human nature lies in the fact that we were created for recognition—for a recognition, however, that links the earthly with the heavenly life.

We may, therefore, fully share C.S. Lewis's surprise to find that "such different Christians as Milton, Johnson and Thomas Aquinas [take] heavenly glory quite frankly in the sense of fame or good report. But not fame conferred by our fellow creatures—fame with God, approval or (I might say) 'appreciation' by God."[47] For Lewis, this notion made full sense considering the biblical teaching that we are to come to God like children, and "nothing is so obvious in a child . . . as its great and undisguised pleasure in being praised."[48] Christian believers who find their new identity in Jesus Christ seek to please the One who made them by doing the "good works, which God prepared in advance for us to do" (Eph 1:10). Lewis saw even more of the glorious recognition that is to come:

> The sense that in this universe we are treated as strangers, the longing to be acknowledged, to meet with some response, to bridge some chasm that yawns between us and reality, is part of our inconsolable secret. And surely, from this point of view, the promise of glory, in the sense described, becomes highly relevant to our deep desire. For glory means good report with God, acceptance by God, response, acknowledgement, and welcome into the heart of things. The door on which we have been knocking all our lives will open at last.[49]

BIBLIOGRAPHY

Bonhoeffer, Dietrich. *Letters and Papers from Prison*. Edited by John W. De Gruchy. Translated by Isabel Best et al. Dietrich Bonhoeffer Works 8. Minneapolis: Fortress, 2010.

Brunner, Peter. "Rechtfertigung heute: Versuch einer dogmatischen Paraklese." In *Pro Ecclesia: Gesammelte Aufsätze zur dogmatischen Theologie*, 2:122–40. Berlin: Lutherisches, 1966.

Calvin, John. *Institutes of the Christian Religion*. Grand Rapids: Eerdmans, 1989.

Canlis, Julie. "The Fatherhood of God and Union with Christ in Calvin." In *"In Christ" in Paul. Explorations in Paul's Theology of Union and Participation*, edited by J. Thate Michael et. al., 399–425. Tübingen: Mohr/Siebeck, 2014.

Elert, Werner. *The Structure of Lutheranism*. Saint Louis: Concordia, 1962.

Greiner, Ulrich. *Schamverlust: Vom Wandel der Gefühlskultur*. Hamburg: Rowohlt, 2014.

Griffith, Howard. "'The First Title of the Spirit': Adoption in Calvin's Theology." *Evangelical Quarterly* 73 (2001) 135–53.

Grimm, Harold J., ed. *Luther's Works*. Vol. 31. Philadelphia: Fortress, 1955.

---

47. Lewis, "Weight of Glory," 101.
48. Ibid.
49. Ibid., 103.

Gritsch, Eric W., ed. *Luther's Works*. Vol. 41. Philadelphia: Fortress, 1966.
Hoffmann, Veronika. *Skizzen zu einer Theologie der Gabe. Rechtfertigung—Opfer—Eucharistie—Gottes- und Nächstenliebe*. Freiburg: Herder, 2013.
Holm, Bo Kristian. "Justification and Reciprocity: 'Purified gift-exchange' in Luther and Milbank." In *Word—Gift—Being. Justification—Economy—Ontology*, edited by Bo Kristian Holm et al., 87–116. Tübingen: Mohr/Siebeck, 2009.
Honneth, Axel. *Recognition or Disagreement: A Critical Encounter on the Politics of Freedom, Equality, and Identity*. New York: Columbia University Press, 2016.
Jaspers, Karl. *The Question of German Guilt*. Translated by E. B. Ashton. New York: Capricorn, 1961.
Lewis, C. S. "Christian Apologetics." In *God in the Dock: Essays on Theology and Ethics*, 89–103. Grand Rapids: Eerdmans, 1970.
———. "The Weight of Glory." In *Essay Collection and Other Short Pieces*, edited by Lesley Walmsley, 96–106. London: HarperCollins 2000.
Majer, René. *Scham, Schuld und Anerkennung: Zur Fragwürdigkeit moralischer Gefühle*. Berlin: de Gruyter, 2013.
Mannermaa, Tuomo. *Christ Present in Faith: Luther's View of Justification*. Minneapolis: Fortress, 2005.
Moo, Douglas J. *The Epistle to the Romans*. NICNT. 1996. Grand Rapids: Eerdmans, 2000.
———. *Romans*. NIVAC. Grand Rapids: Zondervan, 2000.
Morris, Herbert. *Guilt and Shame*. Belmont, CA: Wadsworth, 1971.
Pannenberg, Wolfhart. *Systematic Theology*. Vol. 2. Translated by Geoffrey W. Bromiley. Grand Rapids: Eerdmans, 1994.
Peters, Albrecht. *Rechtfertigung*. Handbuch Systematischer Theologie 12. 2nd ed. Gütersloh: Gütersloher, 1990.
Ridderbos, Herman. *The Gospel according to John: A Theological Commentary*. Grand Rapids: Eerdmans, 1997.
Sartre, Jean Paul. *Being and Nothingness: A Study in Phenomenological Ontology*. London: Routledge, 2003.
Tillich, Paul. *The Courage to Be*. New Haven: Yale University Press, 1952.
The United Methodist Hymnal. Nashville: The United Methodist Publishing House, 1999.
Westhead, Nigel. "Adoption in the Thought of John Calvin." *Scottish Bulletin of Evangelical Theology* 13 (1995) 102–15.

9

The Reformation and the Jews

Jean-Paul Rempp

INTRODUCTION

The subject "The Reformation and the Jews" covers not merely the historical inception of the Reformation but also the entire period from that decisive event up to today.[1] The present contribution could not possibly do justice to this vast subject, so I have chosen to focus on the theology of the Calvinist Reformation which enabled a fresh approach to the Jewish issue. Luther's scandalous and incendiary remarks about the Jews are well-known, contrary to the contribution of Calvin's theology to the Jewish issue. I will therefore only briefly put Luther's writings into the theological and sociopolitical context of the day, thus enabling us to appreciate the originality of the theology of Calvin and his followers with regard to the Jewish issue.

JEWS IN EUROPE

In order to understand Luther's attitude, both Marc Lienhard and his student Lucie Kaennel begin by examining the situation of the Jews in the sixteenth

---

1. I am grateful to Michael Ponsford for translating my French text and French book titles into English.

century.² At the end of the Middle Ages the conditions for the Jews in Europe had become extremely difficult. Since the days of the Church Fathers they had faced the ominous accusation of deicide. While the situation had been relatively favorable up to the beginning of the eleventh century, the subsequent centuries saw a worsening of their lot, as a few facts will make clear: the route of the First Crusade (1096–99) to Jerusalem was lined with massacres of Jewish populations;³ Jews were expelled from England in 1290, from France in 1394, and from Spain in 1492 and 1496.⁴

In the German Holy Roman Empire things had also grown worse, reflecting the territorial fragmentation and the weakening of imperial power. The emperors had always attempted to regulate the lot of the Jews, who as the emperors' serfs, enjoyed special status and protection, but in territories where the Habsburgers no longer ruled the situation changed. Jews were expelled from Würzburg, Mecklenburg, Magdeburg, Nürnberg, Esslingen, and Ulm in 1499, from Regensburg in 1519, and Hessen in 1524. In Luther's day Worms, Frankfurt, and Prague were the only major European cities which tolerated Jews.

But this time of trial for the Jews was also a time of renewal, of a quest for origins and fervent expectation of eschatological events. On the quest for origins within Judaism, Kaennel remarks:

> If the history of events within the Empire shows little sign of any notable improvement of the plight of the Jews, the history of ideas confers on them an intellectual dignity and recognition. This rehabilitation is due to the humanist quest for a return to the Graeco-Latin and Hebrew origins of civilization; to Christian Hebraists who in the first half of the sixteenth century renewed the exegesis of the Old Testament; and to Christian kabbalah seeking a synthesis between Jewish kabbalist themes and Christian theology. By teaching the first humanists Hebrew, Jews played an outstanding intellectual role, sadly often forgotten. The development of humanism, the growing interest in Hebrew sources, progress in the art of printing, and the publication of the first Hebrew Bible editions brought Jewish scholars and

---

2. The key French texts are the chapter "Luther and the Jews" in Lienhard, *Martin Luther*; and Kaennel, *Luther était-il antisémite?*, to which I shall be referring.

3. Bernard of Clairvaux intervened against such violence, taking his stand in front of those persecuting the French Jews during the Second Crusade crying, "Do not lay hands on the sons of Israel nor speak to them unkindly, for they are the flesh and blood of the Messiah. By abusing them you touch the apple of the Lord's eye." Cf. Lecat, "L'idée de croisade," 69.

4. This dramatic event has often been considered the Jews' greatest calamity since the destruction of the Second Temple and before the horror of the *Shoah* or *Holocaust*.

grammarians to the fore. During most of the sixteenth century the Christian printer Daniel Bomberg made Venice the "capital of Hebrew literature."[5]

JEWS ON LUTHER

Alongside this quest for origins, this persecuted people had a fervent expectation of the end. The sixteenth-century Messianic movements were strongly influenced by the speculations of Isaac Abravanel (1437–1508), who predicted the Messiah's advent for the year 1503. Other examples could be given, all more or less seen as signs of the end.[6]

In this context it is little known that many Jews saw Luther himself as the precursor of the Messiah. Lucie Kaennel describes the logic behind this thinking:

> As the Reformation emerged, the Jews no longer constituted the sole pocket of dissidence. Up to that point they had been alone in combatting the modern "Edom" (Rome) to safeguard their identity. Luther's defiance of temporal and spiritual authorities at the Diet of Worms in 1521 made him not simply a partner in misfortune, but seemingly the carrier of a message of encouragement for the "remnant of Israel." The hopes of a number of Jews crystallized around Luther as the one who had come to prepare the way for the Messiah by turning Christians from their idolatrous beliefs and practices.[7]

The kabbalist Abraham Ben Eliezer Ha-Levi (*ca* 1460—after 1528) was one of the many who saw in Luther a reformer who wanted to re-establish truth and justice and whose innovations would affect Judaism. In his eyes, as in those of Abraham Farissol (*ca* 1451– *ca* 1525), Luther was a Crypto-Jew. It is thus hardly surprising that the Roman Catholic side suspected Luther of Judaizing and held the Jews responsible for the Protestant heresy on account of the Reformers' biblicism, their struggle with Rome, and their iconoclasm.

---

5. Kaennel, *Luther*, 28–29.
6. Cf. the detailed list in ibid., 75–77.
7. Ibid., 71.

LUTHER ON THE JEWS

There is no doubt that for Luther the "Jewish issue" was an integral part of his theology. At the same time, he remains a man of his time who lived at the turning point between the Middle Ages and modern times and was profoundly influenced by medieval tradition and its anti-Jewish sentiments. Kaennel is right to distinguish between "anti-Jewish" and "anti-Semitic," judiciously recalling that the latter term was not coined until 1873, and goes on to clarify:

> ... these two terms denote the same reality in two differing registers. Anti-Jewish belongs in the religious realm and refers to the opposition of the church to Judaism and the conflict between two antagonistic faiths. Its resource is theological argument, even if its discourse is not always fully free from objections borrowed from anti-Semitism. The latter denotes an aversion against Jews involving concrete measures taken against them, has an undeniably racist connotation, and bases its accusations on myths. History furnishes ample evidence that the two often combine forces in a common struggle for an evil cause.[8]

In fact, Luther wrote a number of benevolent texts about Jews. We limit ourselves to three examples. The first says that all Christians are called to be witnesses to the gospel, so they need to understand that God's love and salvation are also for the Jews. That is why Luther recommends a more fraternal attitude toward them:

> We ought not be unfriendly towards Jews because there are potential Christians among them and every day some are becoming Christians.... The right way to behave is surely to live in a Christian fashion and with goodwill to lead them to Christ. Who would want to become a Christian if they saw Christians behaving in an unchristian manner towards other people? No, dear Christians, that is not the way! Let us tell them the truth with goodwill; if they refuse, let them go their way. How many Christians disregard Christ, do not listen to his words, and are worse than pagans or Jews, yet we let them go their way in peace.[9]

The second Luther text states that it was the Christians' behavior which prevented Jews from believing in Christ:

---

8. Ibid., 11. See also Blocher's remarkable study "Theological Reflections on Anti-Semitism."

9. Luther, *Commentary on the Magnificat* (1521). Cf. Kaennel, *Luther*, 42.

> Our clowns, popes, bishops, sophists, and monks, those baggage mules, have up to now so acted towards the Jews that a good Christian might have rather wished to become a Jew. Had I been a Jew and seen oafs and louts like them running and teaching the Christian faith, I would sooner become a sow than a Christian.
>
> I have good hope that if we treat the Jews as friends and instruct them appropriately by means of Holy Scripture, many of them will become real Christians and return to the faith of their fathers, the prophets, and the patriarchs, whereas now we only turn them off by rejecting their religion, refusing to take it seriously, and treating them with arrogance and contempt. If the apostles, who were themselves Jews, had behaved toward us heathen in the same way we heathen behave toward the Jews, no pagan would have ever become a Christian. So if the apostles behaved towards us heathen in a brotherly fashion, it is up to us in turn to treat the Jews as our brothers if we wish to convert some of them. For we ourselves are all still pilgrims on the way to our goal.[10]

The third text also shows that Luther hoped for the conversion of the Jews if Christians behaved appropriately:

> I request and advise that one deal with them prudently and instruct them by Scripture. In this way some of them might be converted. But if we treat them violently and spread inept lies about them, if we treat them like dogs, how can we do them any good? Equally, if we prohibit them from working among us, from exercising a profession, or entertaining social relationships with others, we drive them into money-lending; how can that improve them?
>
> If we want to help them, we must practice towards them not the Pope's law but the rule of Christian love, welcome them as friends, let them solicit employment, and work alongside us so that they can live among us, listen to our Christian instruction, and observe our Christian way of life. If some remain obstinate, so what? We are not all good Christians either. May God give us His grace. Amen.[11]

We can better grasp how humane and moderate this attitude was by contrasting it with the Constitutions and Decrees of the Lateran Council IX

---

10. Luther, *Dass Jesus Christus ein geborener Jude sei*, 314.28—315.24. Cf. Lienhard, *Martin Luther*, 204–65.

11. Luther, *Dass Jesus Christus ein geborener Jude sei*, 336.22-36. Cf. Leplay, *Les églises protestantes*, 76.

of 1215, which stipulated that Jews "must be distinguishable from Christians by their dress," decided that they were "unfit for public employment," and ruled finally that "to avoid excessive mixing with them they be compelled to inhabit certain quarters of towns and villages, separate from cohabitation with Christians, and as far as possible from the churches."[12]

In these circumstances it is hardly surprising that Jews and Marranos[13] warmly greeted Luther's treatise *Dass Jesus Christus ein geborener Jude sei* (*Jesus Christ was a born Jew*, 1523) in which he proved the Savior's virgin birth (and hence his deity) from Old Testament passages. From Antwerp Marranos distributed it eagerly in Spain and Palestine and were bold enough to have it published in Spanish; the text was most likely also translated into Hebrew.

THE CHANGE IN LUTHER

Up to 1530 Luther spoke of the Jews in a conciliatory tone and during that year he composed a final edict of tolerance for their benefit. But from the second half of 1530 onwards his language becomes harsher, culminating in the odious and scandalous statements in his 1543 pamphlet *Von den Juden und ihren Lügen* (*On the Jews and their lies*) in which he pleaded for the Jews to be expelled and recommended a series of violent measures against Judaism.[14] His increasingly notorious anti-Judaism originally found expression in theological terms but went on to comprise political prohibitions.

What is the explanation for this change of course? It is true that Jewish conversions were few and far between and Luther made no secret of his profound disappointment at the fact.[15] He could not understand why the Jews

---

12. Cf. Leplay, *Les églises protestantes*, 77.

13. Spanish Jews who had—under pressure—formally converted to Catholicism but continued to see themselves as Jews and to practice their religion in secret.

14. This pamphlet appeared in reply to a written Jewish summons to Christians to convert to Judaism, which Luther saw as a serious threat to the work of reform. He felt duty-bound to oppose his detractors and resist their attacks against the universal truth of the gospel and the teaching of the church. He no longer wished to have dialogue with the Jews but to expose them and their acts. See also the later *Vermahnungen wider die Juden* (1546, WA 51).

15. In his negative reply of June 11, 1537, to Jorel of Rosheim's request to intervene on behalf of the Jews, Luther gives vent to his profound disappointment at the Jews' refusal to turn to Christ after the Reformation proclamation of the genuine gospel. The Jews possessed numerous proofs that Jesus Christ was the Messiah, but they abused them shamefully, turning them against the Christians and deforming them by their false rabbinic interpretations. Luther's treatise *Dass Jesus Christus ein geborener Jude sei* had not achieved its purpose and he had to face Jewish rejection.

rejected the purified gospel he presented to them. But it would be incorrect to interpret his reaction as the rebuff of a jilted lover. In fact, Luther felt the danger that Christianity could become Judaized and felt he had to react firmly and even violently. In the words of Kaennel:

> Luther thought that the influence of rabbinic exegesis was disastrous, because it led a number of his contemporaries to overrate the Old Testament. Several went so far as to preach that the Jews would have a special role to play in the establishment of the Kingdom of God. The re-evaluation of Judaism induced by the Reformation and humanism led some Christians to Judaize or even to convert to the Jewish faith, which met with Luther's outright condemnation.
>
> Several movements of religious enthusiasts emerged at this time, appealing to the Old Testament and to special visions. At Münster in Westphalia, taking their lead from ancient Israel's royal and prophetic offices, they tried to institute a theocracy—which ended in a blood-bath in 1535—and re-introduced Old Testament practices such as polygamy. In Silesia some Anabaptists, following Jewish practice, began to observe the Sabbath instead of the Sunday. In Bohemia and Moravia some groups tended to practice circumcision as a result of the proselytism of Jews who were said to have circumcised Christians and compelled them to observe the law of Moses. Elsewhere opponents of the Trinity or Unitarians made their appearance, claiming to affirm the unity of the Godhead by rejecting the Trinitarian dogma. [Among them was] Michael Servetus (1509/11–53), the author of a treatise in which he argued for Jewish monotheism, *De Trinitaris erroribus* (*On the Errors of the Trinity*, Haguenau, 1531).[16]

Luther's reaction to this threat was, as a man of his time, severe and inordinately virulent, so that even some of his friends, like Melanchthon and Osiander, criticized this pamphlet as attacking persons and no longer just Judaism as a religion. The Swiss rejected it and its publication was prohibited by the Strasbourg magistrature in 1543.

On the Jewish side the rupture was now complete, since Luther refused to assist Jorel of Rosheim, the Jews' representative at the court of Charles V, in his approaches to the elector of Saxony, Johann-Friedrich. On a more general level, the institutionalization of the Reformed Churches and the consolidation of Protestant orthodoxy in response to the Counter-Reformation deepened the Jews' disenchantment with the magisterial

---

16. Kaennel, *Luther*, 48–49.

Reformation and underlined the affinity between some Jewish thinkers and the antitrinitarian or Sabbatarian radicals. While they felt solidarity with dissident Protestants in defending their non-conformity, the Jews nonetheless maintained their doctrinal polemic.

Marc Lienhard concludes his chapter on Luther and the Jews thus:

> For a time Luther had hoped to win a number of Jews for Christianity. The Jews, in the person of some of their representatives, had expressed the hope that Luther and his followers would join them. This would have inaugurated the Messianic era and thus put an end to Israel's suffering. Both hopes proved illusory. These disappointed expectations turned to hatred.[17] Only partially, with certain people,[18] did the Lutheran Reformation lead to a new attitude towards Judaism.[19]

CALVIN

Calvin's theology and attitude differ markedly from Luther's and must be seen as a genuine turning point in the relations between Christians and Jews. Calvin was indeed the first to break with the ancient pedigree of anti-Semitism dating back to the Church Fathers to which Luther belonged. He did so by changing the way the Jews were seen theologically.

Can it be shown that Calvin was anti-Semitic on the basis of his polemical work *Ad questiones et objecta Judaei. Réponses aux questions et objections d'un certain Juif?*[20] Here Calvin lists twenty-three critical questions with which Jews confronted Christians in a thirteenth-century treatise (*Eben Boschan*) followed by a Hebrew translation of the Gospel of Matthew, which Calvin uses to set out twenty-three very sharp replies.

In *Huguenots et Juifs* (*Huguenots and Jews*) Myriam Yardeni, professor of history at Haifa University, argues that this document cannot be cited as evidence for the prosecution against Calvin. On the one hand it is hardly an original text and thus disappointing and also marginal in the sense that it exerted no profound influence on Calvin's contemporaries; on the other hand there is an explanation for the particularly harsh language. Francis

---

17. Luther encountered three Jews, one of whom rejoiced that Christians were studying Hebrew, hoping for a general conversion to Judaism. Luther replied he hoped just the opposite!

18. It is worth underlining the important contribution of the Pietist movement within Lutheranism; see Dowdey, *Jewish-Christian Relations*.

19. Lienhard, *Luther*, 273.

20. English: *Replies to Questions and Objections of a Certain Jew*.

Higman has shown that towards the end of his life the Genevan reformer, who too often had recourse to the same hurtful expressions, was compelled each time to sharpen his tone in order not to lose ground. It may legitimately be assumed this was also the case with *Ad questiones et objecta Judaei*.[21]

Calvin is doubtless a product of his times and not unaffected by the animated debates within Christianity. These polemics sometimes needed to establish a point of view or ironic parodies of opposing views, as witness Calvin's often biting criticism of rabbinic commentators. As François Clavairoly writes,

> Calvin is not always free from the negative stereotypes stigmatizing the Jews of his day; far from it, for he knows them and had heard them. One could quote many statements which could lead one to believe he had adopted them himself, but his theology always, against the prevailing opinion, against himself perhaps, prevents him from falling into the trap of hating and despising the Jews.[22]

Careful, critical study of Calvin's works reveals two things: not only is Calvin no anti-Semite, but he adopts a completely new approach towards the Jews. He may not be a philo-Semite, but he does not hate the Jews as anti-Semites do and thus opens the way for those who come after him and who as genuine philo-Semites love them. The extent of Calvin's writings, which were largely preserved by his successor Theodore Beza, is apparent in Clavairoly's inventory:

> There is first of all the *Institution de la religion chrétienne* (*Institutes of the Christian Religion*), then hundreds of sermons, commentaries on books of the Bible, notably Genesis, Deuteronomy, the Prophets, the Psalms . . . .. Finally, there are his essays and a vast correspondence in both French and Latin.[23]

This enormous *œuvre* allows us a good picture of Calvin's relationship to the Jews and to Judaism.

THE LAW

The Reformation's search for origins, in particular the Hebrew sources of the Old Testament, has already been noted. In this connection Calvin's positive

---

21. Yardeni, *Huguenots et Juifs*, 30.
22. Clavairoly, "Calvin et les Juifs," 539.
23. Ibid., 537.

attitude to the Torah, i.e. to the law, is remarkable. He goes beyond Luther, in whose dualist theology the law was essentially the instrument for convicting sinful humans of guilt and condemnation. Calvin does confirm the role of the law in condemnation, but on the ground of the law's permanence he maintains its importance and usefulness for believers and their life of sanctification. The law is the revelation of God's thought for humankind and a means to holiness, since it shows believers what God regards as righteous and the goal toward which he aims. While believers do not have to observe the law in order to be made righteous, they must strive to please God because they have been justified through Christ and their end is to conform as closely as possible to what the law teaches. Calvin also says of the law that "this word is teaching and instruction."[24]

Noteworthy are also the following words: "Whence did our Lord Jesus Christ and his apostles derive their teaching if not from Moses? When all has been examined, one will discover that the Gospel is simply an exposition of what Moses announced previously."[25]

Calvin regards the Pauline epistles, the starting point of his commentary and exegesis, as a vast meditation on the law: "Not only was it not the evangelists' intention to abolish the law and the prophets, but one should seek in Jesus Christ all that is attributed to him by the law and the prophets."[26]

As for the role of the law in the believers' sanctification he wrote:

> The teaching of the law aims to attach man to God in holiness and, as Moses says in another place, to stick to him. It would therefore be folly to imagine that the law only taught a few minor rudiments of righteousness to introduce men in a perfect way, since we could not desire a greater perfection than what is included in Moses' and Paul's pronouncements.[27]

All this leads to the conclusion that the point of dispute between Jews and Christians is not the law itself but its interpretation. Calvin felt that the rabbis stopped at a purely formal reading while he claimed to read the inner promise of the law in the Messiah. The fulfilment of the promise does not, however, annul the validity of the law. The following few words on the covenant, written five centuries ago, still sound amazingly apposite: "The covenant made with the ancient Fathers [= Israel] in its substance and truth

---

24. Calvin, "Second Sermon on Deuteronomy of March 25, 1555." Cf. Clavairoly, "Calvin et les Juifs," 540.

25. Calvin, "Third Sermon on First Timothy," 301.

26. Ibid.

27. Calvin, *Institution de la religion chrétienne* II.8.51.

is so similar to ours that one can regard it as one and the same; it differs only in the order of dispensation."[28]

THE JEWS NOT GUILTY OF DEICIDE

Calvin's theology opens vistas on the Jewish issue which contrast to the tradition of the Fathers up to Thomas Aquinas and to Luther. In his commentary on John 4:22, "salvation is from the Jews," he wrote: "They were set apart from other peoples for a time in order that ultimately the pure knowledge of God should flow from them to the whole world,"[29] thus explaining that the Jewish people are above all positively qualified as messianic people who bring the knowledge of God to the whole world, not as a people guilty of deicide, an expression Calvin in fact never employs. The Fathers had used the term "deicide" to suggest that the Jews had "killed God" in the person of Jesus, the Son of God, but this expression appears in no single Reformed catechism—and this in a period which the nineteenth-century historian of doctrine, Francis Bonifas, described as "the age of confessions of faith."[30]

Calvin even scoffs the very notion of deicide: God is immortal, therefore he cannot be killed, so the charge does not stick anyway. Above all he insists that all humans are sinners and so of equal status in sin. The Jews are wicked, it is true, but not because they are Jews but because they are humans and like all humans wicked sinners. Jews are no better than Christians but no worse either since all humans are sinners.[31] This is a fundamental conviction at the basis of Calvin's theology.

Myriam Yardeni has grasped this point well:

> In Calvin's writings there is no more just and painful example than the Jewish people to illustrate the fall of all human beings and the fallibility of the whole human race after the original sin. This was the people he [God] loved first of all but who proved to be grossly and criminally ungrateful. But—and here we must look for the deep roots of Calvin's attitude toward the Jews—in this they resemble all human beings. Genuine Christians, if they are not careful, will share the same fate as the Jews.[32]

---

28. Ibid., II.10.2. Cf. Clavairoly, "Calvin et les Juifs," 540–41.
29. Calvin, *Évangile de Jean*, 112. Cf. Clavairoly, "Calvin et les Juifs," 539.
30. Quoted in Blocher, "Fondements," 64.
31. Calvin, *Leçons de M. J. Calvin sur le Livre des Prophéties de Daniel*, 24. Cf. Yardeni, *Huguenots et Juifs*, 39.
32. Yardeni, *Huguenots et Juifs*, 39.

Calvin exonerates the Jews from a crime supposedly more heinous than those committed by other people. To quote Yardeni again, he "completely upsets people's way of thinking about and behaving toward the Jews."[33] She adds,

> the roots of this shift can be found in Calvin's deep conviction that since the Fall all sinners are equal. From this point of view, for the first time after many centuries Jews retrieve their status as human beings. More than this: this new perspective displays the relativity of evil. The Jews are no longer at the bottom of Calvin's hierarchy.[34]

BEZA

The Reformers were conscious that the necessary reforms would take more than a single lifetime and that they had started a movement which their successors would need to pursue, hence their slogan *ecclesia reformata semper reformanda*. On the issue of the responsibility for Christ's death, it was Theodore Beza, the greatest theologian of French Calvinism after Calvin, who proved to be the most philo-Semite by initiating an even more profound shift. In a series of over forty sermons he analyzed the circumstances of and reasons for Jesus' death. In the past this had been a dangerous subject for Jews, which had stirred waves of hatred against them. But Beza did not preach *against* the Jews but *to* Christians, who are no less guilty than the Jews. For Beza it was not the Jews who crucified Christ, but all humanity: "We" are the guilty ones![35]

Yardeni is eloquent in her comment:

> Following in Calvin's footsteps, Beza keeps returning to the theme of human wickedness and the corruption of all human beings. From this perspective he emphasizes less the harshness of divine punishment of the Jews, but rather its tragic aspects. The Jews are of course not exempt of all responsibility. Beza refers to their malice and hypocrisy. And more than once he underlines the preponderant guilt of their teachers.
>
> Beza's attitude marks a turning point, for he stresses the relativity of the crimes and the Jews' guilt. He is probably alone

---

33. Ibid., 42.
34. Ibid., 43.
35. de Bèze, *Sermons* 13–14. Cf. Yardeni, *Huguenots et Juifs*, 54–55.

among his contemporaries to say unequivocally that the Jews did not crucify Jesus.[36]

DIVINE ELECTION

Calvin links the doctrine of universal human sin indissolubly to the doctrine of election, the effect of God's sovereign grace. The doctrine of election is an essential feature of his theology. God chooses whom he wills and rejects whom he wills. The Jews have been chosen by God totally gratuitously, not because they were better than any others but because of God's sovereign liberty. This kind of election cannot be called into question. And if God has today chosen the Protestants to be elect too, this is not on account of their merits but it is God's sovereign mercy. Yardeni summarizes this as "Election is in God's hands."[37]

There can be terrible consequences for anyone who proves unfaithful to the covenant of election, one of which is divine punishment. God chastises because he loves, just as a father punishes his children. God's punishment of his disobedient children leads not to perdition but to salvation.

This doctrine of God's electing goodness is the starting point for Calvin's view of the Jewish people. God chastized the Jews for their incredulity and hardness of heart and this chastisement took the form of exile. The punishment was so severe that from a human point of view one might have expected that as a result of the exile and persecutions the Jews would have ceased to be a people. But what is extraordinary, says Calvin, is that not only have the Jews, against all expectations, not disappeared, but they have been preserved beyond what one might have imagined. The Reformer sees this as evidence that God still has a plan for the people of Israel.[38] Despite their situation of unbelief and rebellion this people remains through its "faithful remnant"[39] a beneficiary of the prophetic promises of eschatological salvation. In other words, if God chastizes this people it is in order to lead them to repentance, so that they will regain their heritage in the end times. It is significant that Calvin firmly believed the Jews would return to the right way.[40]

36. Yardeni, *Huguenots et Juifs*, 55–57.
37. Ibid., 43.
38. The survival of the Jewish people through the centuries can only be interpreted as a living and visible sign of God's faithful love toward them. See Rempp, *Israël*, 94–95.
39. On the notion of the "faithful remnant," cf. ibid. 55–58.
40. Yardeni, *Huguenots et Juifs*, 42.

This eschatological hope for the Jewish people was also essential to the faith of Calvin's successors, both in the "Desert" in France and in the "Refuge."[41] In his remarkable book *Juifs et Protestants en France*, Patrick Cabanel gives examples of this kind of Protestant philo-Semitism:

> In Rotterdam Pierre Jurieu asked himself how the Gospel promise of the Jews' turning to God at the end of the age could be fulfilled if Christians had already massacred them beforehand. This theologian drew the practical conclusion of demanding civil tolerance for Jews.[42]

In his *Avertissement aux Juifs* (*Warning to the Jews*) on the advent of the Messiah published in 1607, Duplessis-Mornay (1549–1623) addresses himself with unusual tenderness to the Jews whose long night had not been visited by the Messiah. The millennial resonance does not deviate from the hope of a collective conversion but addresses the Jews just as other people. One meets the same expectation of conversion as in Jurieu, expressed with genuine sympathy for the Jews. When the Messiah's rule is established it will also be the reign of the Jews.[43]

If God's election cannot be called into question, it is implicitly also irrevocable. In his commentary on Romans, Calvin himself comments as follows on 11:1:

> It might seem from what he [Paul] has said previously about the Jews' blindness and obstinacy that this implied that Christ at his coming had transferred God's promises elsewhere, the Jews being dismissed from any hope of salvation. He therefore now anticipates this objection and moderates what he had said previously about the rejection of the Jews, so that no one should come to imagine that the covenant made with Abraham had been abolished or that God had so consigned it to oblivion that the Jews today are as foreign to his kingdom as were the heathen

---

41. The "Desert" refers to the time after the revocation of the Edict of Nantes in 1685 when the French Protestants, also denoted Huguenots, held their services in secret. The "Refuge" means territories and cities in which Huguenots sought refuge after Protestants had been outlawed by this revocation.

42. Calvin too made himself an advocate of the Jews with the authorities, saying: "It is time to stop persecuting the Jews." By so doing he became the father of modernity in the positive sense of the word. Yardeni, *Huguenots et Juifs*, 52, notes that according to Pierre Viret (1511–71) "it is not up to men to persecute the Jews, just as it is not up to men to persecute believers of whatever religion. In the numerous passages which he devotes to political and civil tolerance, Viret always includes the Jews."

43. Cabanel, *Juifs et Protestants*, 27–28.

> before Christ came. He denies this, as indeed he will go on to demonstrate that this is false.
>
> Paul establishes the principle that since adoption is free and founded in God and not in humans, it remains firm and inviolable whatever unbelief may ensue on the part of human beings. This is the difficulty we have to resolve so as not to imagine that God's truth and election depend on human dignity.[44]

On this Yardeni writes: "Calvin considers and believes that the collective election has passed from the Jews to the Gentiles, yet God has never refuted his first choice."[45] And she notes Calvin's relative sympathy for the Jews in contrast to the Roman Catholics:

> The picture changes if one places Calvin's bitter and violent anti-Jewish invective in a larger framework, namely that of all enemies of true religion. In this context Jews and Roman Catholics, for example, are in the same boat, but it has to be admitted that the Jews emerge in a better light from all comparisons between them and Roman Catholics, being less foolish and superstitious.
>
> Jews would never have committed such aberrations as [the real presence in and sacrifice of] the Mass. In all areas of comparison, Jews prove less corrupt than Roman Catholics. Even at the nadir of their fall from grace, the time of Jesus, they still continued to study and comment on the Holy Scriptures.
>
> In the polemic context the stupidity and malice of the Jews is seen to be diminished in comparison with Roman Catholic vices. Jews appear therefore in a new light, from which it can be concluded they are not the worst of sinners.[46]

Calvin was also the first to express compassion with the persecution of the Jews. He saw a parallel with the plight of the Protestants, as both communities were objects of the same hatred on the part of the Roman Catholic Church. For the Reformer this implies that when the Protestants are emancipated from the Roman "yoke," the Jews should be too. Yardeni comments: "When Calvin speaks of the suffering of the Jews and the humiliations undergone after their return from Babylon, it is difficult not to see his total identification with them."[47]

---

44. Calvin, *Épître aux Romains*, 258, 260. Cf. Clavairoly, "Calvin et les Juifs," 538-39.
45. Yardeni, *Huguenots et Juifs*, 38.
46. Ibid., 36-38.
47. Ibid., 40.

CONCLUSION

Yardeni concludes her chapter on "Calvin, the Jews, and Judaism"[48] as follows:

> On Calvin's scale of values the Jews no longer occupy the bottom rung, a relativization which, combined with the conviction that the whole of humanity is infected by original sin and that God alone knows who are his elect, opens the way for a process which will eventually alter the attitude towards Jews and Judaism.[49]

Calvin was certainly no philo-Semite but his theology and attitude inaugurated a new era in the Christian attitude towards the Jewish people and opened the door for the Christian philo-Semite movement.

The solidarity in suffering between the two communities noted by Yardeni underscores the similarities between the Jewish and Protestant communities in France.[50] The explanation for this lies in particular in the shared appreciation of the same book (the Bible), the common history of persecution and exile,[51] and identical concerns for the society in which they lived.[52] This is why one could speak of a "shared book and shared misfortune." These "elective affinities," to use Cabanel's expression, between the two minorities sometimes at the margin, sometimes at the heart of French history, represent a situation which is unique in Europe.

The prejudice of numerous historians, in particular Jewish Israelis, that one cannot be a Christian without at the same time being an anti-Semite, and that the roots of anti-Semitism are to be found at the very heart of Christianity,[53] can now be countered by the testimony that it is possible to be a Christian without being anti-Semitic and that anti-Semitism is not a congenital Christian disorder. The French Protestantism which descended from Calvin demonstrates this so clearly that Jean-Marc Thobois can write:

---

48. Ibid., 27–43.

49. Ibid., 43.

50. See on this point Yardeni, *Huguenots et Juifs*; Cabanel, *Juifs et Protestants*; Thobois, *Calvin et les Juifs*; and also "La spécificité des relations entre Juifs et protestants en France" (Specific relations between Jews and Protestants in France), in Rempp, *Israël*, 119–22.

51. For example, programs and Inquisition including the expulsion from Spain for the one group, the St. Bartholomew massacre of 1572, the revocation of the Edict of Nantes in 1685, and the clandestine church in the "Desert" for the other group.

52. Equal rights for all—in principle—including Protestants (in 1789) and Jews (several years later), secularity and separation of Church and State in 1905.

53. See Blocher's refutation of this thesis in "Theological Reflections."

"A particularity of French Protestantism which sets it apart from all other Christian movements is that it can assert that antisemitism, hatred of Israel, is not a Christian fatality."[54]

BIBLIOGRAPHY

Bèze, Théodore de. *Sermons sur l'histoire de la passion et sepulture de nostre Seigneur Jésus Christ descrite par les quatre Évangélistes.* N.p. [Geneva]: Jean le Preux, 1598.

Blocher, Henri. "Theological Reflections on Anti-Semitism." *Mishkan* 66 (2011) 35–57.

Blocher, Henri. "Les fondements bibliques de la confession de foi." ["The Biblical Foundations of the Confession of Faith"]. *La revue réformée* 23, no. 2 (1972) 62–68.

Cabanel, Patrick. *Juifs et Protestants en France, Les affinités électives XVIe–XXIe siècle* [*Jews and Protestants in France. Elective Affinities 16th—21st century*]. La Flèche: Fayard, 2004.

Calvin, Jean. *Ad questiones et objecta Judaei. Réponses aux questions et objection d'un certain Juif* [*Replies to Questions and Objections of a Certain Jew*]. Translated and edited by Marc Faessler. Geneva: Labor et Fides, 2010.

———. *Épîtres aux Thessaloniciens, à Timothée et Philémon* [Thessalonians, Timothy, and Philemon]. Aix-en-Provence: Kerygma, 1991.

———. *Épître aux Romains* [Romans]. Aix-en-Provence: Kerygma, 1978.

———. *Évangile de Jean* [John's Gospel]. Aix-en-Provence: Kerygma, 1978.

———. *Institution de la religion chrétienne.* 4 vols. Geneva: Labor et Fides, 1955–58.

———. *Leçons de M. J. Calvin sur le Livre des Prophéties de Daniel. Recueillies fidèlement par Jean Budé et Charles de Jonviller.* Geneva, 1559.

Clavairoly, François. "Calvin et les Juifs" ["Calvin and the Jews"]. *Sens* 351 (2010) 534–46.

Dowdey, David. *Jewish-Christian Relations in Eighteenth-Century Germany: Textual Studies on German Archival Holdings, 1729–1742.* New York: Mellen, 2006.

Kaennel, Lucie. *Luther était-il antisémite?* [*Was Luther Anti-Semitic?*]. Geneva: Labor et Fides, 1997.

Lecat, Jean-Philippe. "L'idée de croisade selon saint Bernard de Clairvaux" ["Bernard of Claivaux's Concept of Crusade"]. *Grandes signatures* 1 (2008) 60–71.

Leplay, Michel. *Les églises protestantes et les Juifs face à l'antisémitisme au vingtième siècle* [*Protestant Churches and the Jews Facing the Antisemitism of the Twentieth Century*]. Lyon: Olivétan, 2006.

Lienhard, Marc. *Martin Luther. Un temps, une vie, un message* [*Martin Luther. His Times, His Life, His Message*]. Paris: Le Centurion, 1983.

Luther, Martin. *Commentary on the Magnificat* (1521). In *Œuvres* (Works). Geneva: Labor et Fides, 1957–.

———. *Dass Jesus Christus ein geborener Jude sei.* In *Martin Luthers Werke: Kritische Gesammtausgabe* (WA), 11:307–36. Weimar: Böhlau, 1900.

Rempp, Jean-Paul. *Israël, peuple, foi et terre* [*Israel, People, Faith, and Land*]. Charols, France: Excelsis, 2010.

Thobois, Jean-Marc. "Calvin et les Juifs" ["Calvin and the Jews"]. *Keren Israël* 80 (2009) 16–22.

---

54. Thobois, "Calvin et les Juifs," 22.

Yardeni, Myriam. *Huguenots et Juifs* [*Huguenots and Jews*]. Paris: Honoré Champion, 2008.

10

The Reformation and the Challenge of Islam

Thomas Schirrmacher

INTRODUCTION

I once was talking to a Patriarch from the Middle East about a series of lectures he wanted evangelical scholars to offer to his bishops and priests. Exaggerating somewhat, he said about oriental Christians:

> We hate Muslims, but do not really know much about Muslim theology and the different schools of Muslim thoughts. You know much about these things and have many good arguments against Islam in detail, and yet you love Muslims. We would like to learn both from you, apologetic skills and your mission of love.

At first sight, this modern-day evangelical mindset does not seem to owe much to the time of the Reformation and the harsh language with which the first "Protestants" spoke about Muslims. Yet I believe that the Reformers can help us if we dig below their unacceptable polemic and, for example, rediscover Luther's arguments against the crusades.

The Reformation took place at the peak of the extension of the Ottoman Empire. Sultan Suleiman the Magnificent (ruled 1520–66) conquered Beograd in 1521, Rhodes and Cyprus in 1522, and the Hungarian city of Mohács in 1526; in 1529, his troops beleaguered Vienna. (The Ottoman Empire reached its largest extension in 1683, and it tried to conquer Vienna a second time in that year—again in vain.) In 1532, Suleiman started a second large campaign against the Habsburgers and in 1541–43 conquered Budapest and large parts of Hungary. In 1547, a peace treaty ended any attempts to get those areas back from Suleiman.

In Luther's time people did not speak about "Islam" or "Muslims," but they called them "Turks," or with still older terms "Saracens," "Mahometists," or else, and Islam was called "the Turkish faith." After the fall of Constantinople in 1453, the Ottoman Empire was ruled from "Istanbul," which served as a perennial reminder to Europe that the crusades of more than four centuries earlier had failed.

This brief chapter will not provide a detailed overview over the extensive research of recent times into the Reformers' views about Islam, the perception of Islam in the sixteenth century as a whole, or the complicated history of the Ottoman conquests and their final defeat at Vienna. It is still debated if Luther and Calvin (to restrict ourselves to the two most famous names) could have known more about Islam and could have obtained more accurate information, and whether or not they did enough to obtain it. I for one doubt that they would have had any chance to get unbiased information or would have been able to realize its trustworthiness over the rumors that were around.[1]

It is easy to list the failures and the things we do not want to copy when it comes to the Reformers and Islam. Apart from the many wrong evaluations caused by ignorance, there is their drastic language, which even exceeded the drastic language they used against the Catholics and especially the pope.[2] We only can agree with the (non-evangelical) evaluation of the Protestant Church in Germany: "A transfer of the Reformation's positions and demarcations against Islam into the present is not easily possible and we have to do it with very much diligence."[3]

---

1. Beeler, "John Calvin on Islam," thinks that Calvin did not even read the Koran. On the other side Lee, "Calvin on Islam," 1, argues that even Calvin honored the "reverence" of Muslims in his commentary on Deuteronomy 4:8, even though immediately comparing him with the "Papists" in this.

2. Ehmann, *Luther, Türken und Islam*, 190, 403.

3. "Reformation und Islam." That the authors ask later in the text how we can talk about the "sola Christus" without offending Muslims and others, goes too far from an evangelical perspective.

Nonetheless, I think that there is much to learn about Islam from the Reformers for today if one is willing to search patiently. This is because the challenges of relating to Islam are similar in the sixteenth and the twenty-first century. This chapter will focus on what can we learn from the Reformation concerning Islam. Based on the study by the Catholic author Johannes Kritzl on Luther and Islam—especially the Turkish wars—and on the large research project on Luther and Islam by Johannes Ehmann,[4] I will first introduce three theses.

THE NEED TO STUDY THE ORIGINAL SOURCES

The first thesis is that when we study Islam, we need to study the original sources in their original languages to gain trustworthy and truthful information.

In sixteenth-century Europe there was no reliable information on Islam available. Luther was well aware that even the translations of the Koran were not good and he used qualifications such as "a really badly done translation" („doch seer übel verdolmetscht").[5] He supported the printing of a new translation of the Koran into Latin by Theodor Bibliander and even wrote the foreword for the 1543 edition[6]—judging from our times in a very nasty tone. Luther also wanted to translate this Latin Koran into German, but later gave up this idea and instead translated and edited (or better, rewrote) a German translation of one of the better books on Islam from the Middle Ages.[7]

Luther was also aware that the Muslim doctrine that the Koran cannot be translated from the Arab original was the major reason why good translations by Muslims were not available.[8] For him this doctrine itself proved Islam to be wrong—understandable for one who wanted the Bible to be translated into everyday language and into any language spoken anywhere.

---

4. Kritzl, "*Adversus turcas*." Ehmann, *Luther, Türken und Islam*; both books published in German only.

5. Kritzl, "*Adversus turcas*," 56. See more examples in Ehmann, *Luther, Türken und Islam*, 319.

6. Luther, WA 53:569–72.

7. Luther, "Verlegung des Alcoran Bruder."

8. Kritzl, "*Adversus turcas*," 55.

TWO FURTHER THESES

The second thesis is that self-criticism and repentance of Christians should come first. Any arguing with or against Muslim positions should be done in a spirit of humility.[9] Kritzl shows how Luther radically called for "self-criticism," which "theologically framed was called repentance" ("Buße").[10] He saw Islam as "our God's rod of wrath."[11]

The third thesis is that, in the midst of it all, Luther saw the need for peaceful mission and witness by simple Christians. He therefore wrote a missionary handbook for Christians in Ottoman prisons, and he heavily criticized the pope for engaging in calls for crusades, while not sending peaceful missionaries to the Turkish world.[12]

CRUSADES AND WARS

Luther clearly saw a problem that still exists today: Islam generally does not separate, or even know a distinction between, "church" and "state." Such as separation is basic to Christianity and to the Old Testament. (Even if the Catholic side had a different view on the relationship between pope and emperor, at least both existed separate from each other at that time.) For Luther the central problem was that "this vexed devil does not stop to cook and brew the two kingdoms into each another."[13] The debate between Christianity and Islam was complicated, as it is once again today, because religious questions were intermingled with questions of politics, war, military campaigns, physical persecution of Christians, and the fear of people for their life.

The original reaction of Christianity to the Islamic expansion had been the crusades, but Luther and the other Reformers were absolutely opposed to the idea of crusades because they meant a complete mingling of church and state.[14] Luther criticized the emperor for his religious tone against Islam and he criticized the pope for getting involved in wars against the Turks at all. This went so far that the accusation that Luther would leave Europe

---

9. In the spirit of 2 Chr 7:14.
10. Ibid., 45.
11. Ibid., 24; see further examples on 24–28.
12. Ibid., 80. Ehmann, *Luther, Türken und Islam*, discusses the peaceful mission theology of Luther over against the idea of crusades in depth.
13. Kritzl, "*Adversus turcas*," 21–22.
14. Ehmann, *Luther, Türken und Islam*, 232–36, 277.

defenseless to the Turks became one of the most successful arguments against him, e.g. in the 1520 papal bull which excommunicated him.[15]

Yet this accusation was not true because Luther was very much in favor of combining the European armies against the Turks. Yet he was also convinced that those wars had to be merely acts of self-defense (a "Notkrieg"[16]), that they should not attempt to conquer Muslim areas, and that they should be led by the emperor as the secular head of the state—that is to say, they should not be religious crusades.[17] The emperor should not call such wars Christian wars, and the pope and the church should keep out of those wars altogether and rather repent. In this respect, Luther agreed with his contemporaries Erasmus of Rotterdam, Theophrastus Paracelsus, and others.[18]

This issue had already come up in his Ninety-five theses, and frequently later as well, because the crusades were financed by indulgences. The pope even claimed that a fight against indulgences would be a fight in favor of the Turks.[19] Luther's anti-crusade position was also central in his important treatise on war of 1526, „Ob Kriegsleute auch in seligem Stande sein können"[20] ("Whether soldiers can be in a state of grace"), in which he claims that the war against the Turks is a war like any others and should be dealt with as such.[21]

Luther had some hope that Islam would one day be overcome by the gospel and he quoted Daniel 7:24-25 in this respect. But he lacked the certainty and optimism of Calvin, who was convinced that, although Islam was somehow related to the Antichrist, it would be overcome by the gospel in the future. Calvin thought that Old Testament prophecies concerning Egypt converting to the God of Israel predicted that Muslims would convert to Christianity.[22]

EIGHT EXAMPLES OF REFORMATION VERSUS MUSLIM VIEWS

The remainder of this chapter gives examples of how central messages and Biblical themes emphasized by the Reformers are relevant today for seeing

15. Cf. ibid., 212-15.
16. Kritzl, "Adversus turcas," 38.
17. See the good description from the sources in Kritzl, "Adversus turcas," 28-43.
18. Ibid., 39.
19. See the examples in Ehmann, *Luther, Türken und Islam*, 204-9.
20. Luther, WA 19:623-62.
21. Ehmann, *Luther, Türken und Islam*, 259-60.
22. See the examples in Lee, "Calvin on Islam."

the deep differences between the Christian and the Muslim faith, both in their major forms.[23]

Submission or Trust with Lament and Doubt?

In Islam, doubts and laments before God and his revelation are excluded and are understood as direct attacks on God. The Koran is not familiar with, and does not contain, any laments directed towards God. It considers doubts about God and about basic Islamic teachings as unacceptable, supposing that they do not arise in true believers. For a Muslim, laments and doubts can never be part of a conversation with God, because that would call his dignity and position as creator and lord into question. To question Allah's goodness and his mercy for even a short time would be a demonstration of ingratitude and unbelief. Humankind is not entitled to accuse the omnipotent creator and lord of the world, to call him to account, or to question his actions.

Since humankind always remains God's servant and submissive subject, the sole possible stance is that of humbly accepting the will of Allah in revelation and in actual history.

> The Koran forbids that people are so moved by their own needs that they call God to account: "He cannot be questioned concerning what He does and they shall be questioned" (Sura 21:22–23). There is no room here for voices of consternation about the disorder in the world and the suffering of the righteous, least of all for the theodicy problem of how God allows certain things to happen or even brings them about. Such appeals face the claim that everything created is absolutely perfect: ". . . you see no incongruity in the creation of the Beneficent God; then look again, can you see any disorder? Then turn back the eye again and again; your look shall come back to you confused while it is fatigued" (Sura 67:3b–4).[24]

On the other hand, the Bible includes complete books containing doubts and laments (Lamentations, Jeremiah, Job, cf. the Psalms of lament). It encourages believers to turn to God with their laments and doubts, to suffer through them, and to overcome them in relationship with God. Doubts and laments are often central themes and they are a normal component of a living relationship with God. Jeremiah's laments (Lamentations; Jer

---

23. I have taken these examples from my *Koran and Bible*, but reordered and reworked them.

24. Zirker, *Koran*, 165.

11–20) do not show a prophet who triumphs over evil, but rather a struggling person who has his deepest experiences of God through his doubts. The same applies to the prophet Elijah's depression. In Job, God is not glibly proclaimed as the highest and most beautiful; rather, after endless dialogues God remains the creator and friend to whom one can also hold on during suffering and confusion. The Psalms of lament have been a shaping factor in Judaism and for Christianity up to the present time (e.g., Pss 3, 5, 6, 13, 44, 74, 77, and 79). The Psalmists call to God in a manner that alternates between energetic imperatives and insistent questioning:

> Awake, O Lord! Why do you sleep? Rouse yourself! Do not reject us forever. Why do you hide your face and forget our misery and oppression? . . . Rise up and help us; redeem us because of your unfailing love. (Ps 44: 23–24, 26)[25]

Faith as Submission or as a Relationship?

In the Koran, faith (Arabic *iman*) is humble devotion to God and submission (*islam*) to his will. Submission means that humans avoid what Allah calls evil and do what he calls good, especially following the five pillars of Islam. Faith is above all the recognition of the lordship and omnipotence of God, and it requires belief in the judgment, the angels, the Holy Scriptures, and the prophets (Sura 2:177). But faith is not limited to a theoretical "accepting something as true" with respect to certain truths; rather, it has consequences, namely doing good and avoiding evil (Sura 3:110). The believer is to ." . . convey good news to those who believe and do good deeds . . ." (Sura 2:25), to follow the five pillars of Islam, to live this life responsibly before God, and to configure it in light of the knowledge of the sure coming of the future life.

The confession of faith (*shahada*), which is the first of the five pillars of Islam, reads: "I testify that there is no god but God, and I testify that Mohammed is his prophet," and is always said in Arabic.[26] This places the uniqueness of God (*tauhid*) in the center, as well as the sending of Mohammed as the Prophet of God who announces this uniqueness. The confession is said several times daily in ritual prayer and it plays a definitive role in the practice of faith for all men and women beyond puberty. A non–Muslim

---

25. Ibid.

26. Shiites add as praise for the fourth Khalif Ali (nephew and son-in-law of Mohammed): "And Ali is the friend of God."

irreversibly crosses over to Islam by saying the confession in the presence of two witnesses or before an iman or a qadi.

Central to the Bible is the conviction that faith (Hebrew *emuna*, Greek *pistis*, Latin *fides*) is a reaction to God's "faithfulness," a trust in God, and the expression of a personal relationship with God. This is the case even when this relationship includes a recognition of certain doctrines and it is assumed that the one who believes in God also wants to do his will. Trust in God is also specifically necessary due to the fact that believers often do not do the will of God. Faith is a mutual relationship of trust, and for God's faithfulness the same word is used. Faith thus has both an active and a passive meaning: it is both fidelity towards a person or a promise one has made, and trust in the promises another person makes. The people of God who throughout history devoted their lives to God in unwavering trust and obedience teach us what faith is (Heb 11).

Already in the Old Testament faith is not only a mere recognition of tenets or an external consent to a law. Rather, it is a deep and ultimate trust in the faithfulness and credibility of God and loving obedience to his will. The New Testament rejects a mere "accepting as true:" "You believe that there is one God. Good! Even the demons believe that—and shudder" (Jas 2:19). In the New Testament the terms "belief" and "to believe" are used almost 500 times. The basic assertion is that belief in God and belief in redemption as achieved by Jesus Christ are necessary to obtain eternal life. The first Christians named themselves "believers" or "the believing" (Acts 2:44). In the letters of Paul, belief is set over against one's own works as a means of redemption (e.g. Rom 3:20–22). Belief is a gift of God, for which a person can ask and should ask, because it is impossible to acquire belief by means of one's own energy. It is for this reason that believers pray: "I do believe; help me overcome my unbelief!" (Mark 9:24b).

According to the Bible, the good works of a person are a consequence of belief, not its foundation: ". . . faith by itself, if it is not accompanied by action, is dead" (Jas 2:17). The Bible also calls this "bearing fruit" ("Those who abide in me and I in them bear much fruit . . ." John 15:5 NRSV) and establishes this with the example of Jesus: "Whoever claims to live in him must walk as Jesus did" (1 John 2:6).

Is God Bound by His Promises?

The Koran proclaims a God who is so absolute, sovereign, and independent that he never can, or wants to, commit himself with respect to people. God's promises always carry the qualification that he could decide differently and no one can prevent him, since otherwise he would be subject to human judgment. As the omnipotent one, God is always free and sovereign in his decisions. This principle applies especially to God's decision with respect to the last judgment. To be able to foretell here and now what will occur would limit God's freedom and omnipotence, and to stipulate his decision, which is not humankind's position.

Allah is indeed identified as the gracious and merciful one, as the forgiving and magnanimous one, but with regard to forgiveness believing Muslims will only have final assurance after death: ". . . But not (so) the Lord of the worlds; Who created me, then He has shown me the way . . . And He who will cause me to die, then give me life; And who, I hope, will forgive me my mistakes on the day of judgment" (Sura 26:77-82).

The Koran identifies God as cunning: "He is the one who is best at devising tricks . . ." (Sura 13:33) or translated otherwise, "He is full of treachery" (Rudi Paret). "And when those who disbelieved devised plans against you that they might confine you or slay you or drive you away; and they devised plans and Allah too had arranged a plan; and Allah is the best of planners," or otherwise translated "Allah schemes. He can do it best" (Sura 8:30). Several Muslim commentators say that these verses refer only to deception vis-à-vis unbelievers, but other commentators argue that they have to do with everyone, since God cannot be limited nor nailed down. That is why the Koran indeed knows many vows, but it knows none in which God would obligate himself to humans, for that would place God and humans on the same level.[27]

The Bible proclaims a God who as Lord and creator is absolute, sovereign, and independent. No one could resist him if he changed his plans and did not keep his promises. His sovereignty comes to bear precisely in the fact that no one can prevent him from putting his plans, promises, and vows into action and holding to them.

However, the Lord binds himself to his own word and swears by himself. He is faithful and absolutely trustworthy. The Lord's reliability, trustworthiness, and truth are his most prominent characteristics (e.g., Exod 34:6; Ps 117:2). He is the "God of truth" (Isa 65:16), who is absolutely trustworthy. Whatever God has promised, "he is faithful in all he does" (Ps 33:4b). The trust (belief) that relates to this truthfulness of God is not accidentally, along with love, the most frequently used and most important description of the relationship between humans and God. He has once and for all committed himself to save and redeem his creatures, and he has

---

27. Also according to Kandil, "Schwüre," 46-47, cf. 51-57, regarding all vows in the Koran.

covenanted (Gen 13:1–3; Exod 20:1–3) to demonstrate his grace towards them and to save them from sin and death (Jonah 4:2). God confirmed the covenant of salvation with an oath by his own name (Heb 5–6), "since there was no one greater for him to swear by" (Heb 6:13). It is no wonder that the signs of the covenant (sacraments), with which the beginning of the covenant (baptism) and the continual covenant renewal (Lord's Supper) in the "New Covenant" (1 Cor 11:25) are celebrated, are the external identifying features of the Christian church.

Some 82 times the Bible reports that God swears by his own name (e.g., Gen 22:16; Exod 32:13; Isa 45:23; Jer 22:5, 44:26, 49:13; Amos 4:2, 6:8; Rom 14:11). Forty additional times he makes a covenant and provides humanity with the steadfast assurance of his nature and action. The unsworn message that Nineveh would be destroyed in 40 days (Jonah 3:4) was true, but it left open the possibility of a reversal. An oath, on the other hand, makes a promise firm and irrevocable, underlining its irreversibility (Heb 6:16–18). No one in the Old and New Testaments swears more frequently than the God of truth, due to the fact that he thereby makes his promises irrevocable and binds himself with regard to the future.

The portrayal of the Lord with two complementary sides is a distinct characteristic of his revelation in Judaism and Christianity. On the one hand, God is absolutely sovereign; on the other hand, within the framework of a covenant with humanity, he binds himself and places obligations upon himself, allowing himself to be evaluated. In this way, God graciously takes the initiative, so that his sovereign freedom leads to a trustworthy covenant with his people. This is clearly and classically seen at the beginning of the Ten Commandments: "I am the Lord your God, who brought you out of Egypt, out of the land of slavery. You shall . . ." (Exod 20:2–3a). God first frees Israel, then he calls the people to obey—in that order.

It is no accident that God's absolute trustworthiness also finds expression in the fact that he has given his revelation a final, written form. In it he commits himself with the gospel. And it is no accident that he outdoes himself by sending his Son, Jesus Christ, to become a man. The certainty that God reveals himself as a covenantal God, and as a God who freely commits himself in love—without humankind being able to force him—also demonstrates why in the Bible particular promises and texts are repeatedly presented as completely credible (Ps 119:43, 160; 1 Thess 2:13; John 17:17).

Can God be Tested?

The Koran has no notion of God's trustworthiness being tested. Very often it reports that Allah tests humankind in order to see who holds to him (e.g., Sura 67:2), but no creature is entitled to test the creator or to call him to account. Again, God "cannot be questioned concerning what He does and they shall be questioned" (Sura 21:23).

In the Bible the emphasis on the trustworthiness of God leads to situations in which God tests people, but also to the reverse situations, in which believers are invited to test God (Mal 3:10), to argue with him (Isa 1:18 NRSV, 41:1, 43:26), and to assess whether he truly keeps his word. God places commitments upon himself, he reveals himself, and he has given his word—all these things mean that he himself becomes the standard against which he can be measured.

If believers do not understand God, they should not suppress their questions but rather discuss and experience them with God. In the end God indeed shows himself to be trustworthy, but not due to the fact that questions and probing were prohibited. Rather, it is due to the fact that he proves himself to be actually and really trustworthy according to the standards which he himself provides.

As we saw above, the Lord allows himself to be intensely accused in laments and imprecatory psalms when it seems as if he has not kept his promises. Repeatedly the question arises how there can be so much misery and suffering in the world when there is a good and loving God (e.g., Ps 73; Job; Lamentations). However, suffering is only a problem if one assumes that there is a standard against which God can be judged, namely his own love and goodness. Paul can even ask: "Is God unjust?" (Rom 9:14), and he indeed answers the question negatively (Rom 9:15-26), but it is distinctive that this question is raised and discussed in the Bible.

Is the Trinity Polytheism?

The Koran maintains that the Christian teaching that Jesus is not only a prophet and teacher, but God himself, as well as the closely related teaching about the Trinity, is polytheism. It thus denies that Christianity is a monotheistic religion. "The most important concept in Islam, and the source of all its other principles and approaches, is the unity of God (*Tauhid*). Monotheism is most purely depicted in Islam."[28] Although the Koran differentiates between actual idolaters, who are to be rejected and fought, and the

---

28. Way to Allah Team, "Was ist Islam."

adherents of the better religions (Christians and Jews), these better religions are given a status subordinate to Islam. Often idolaters and Christians are mentioned together (e.g., Sura 98:1, 6).

The Trinity is sharply rejected:

> Certainly they disbelieve who say: Surely Allah is the third (person) of the three; and there is no god but the one God, and if they desist not from what they say, a painful chastisement shall befall those among them who disbelieve . . . The Messiah, son of Marium is but an apostle (Sura 5:73, 75).

> O followers of the Book! do not exceed the limits in your religion, and do not speak (lies) against Allah, but (speak) the truth; the Messiah, Isa son of Marium is only an apostle of Allah and His Word which He communicated to Marium and a spirit from Him; . . . say not, Three. Desist, it is better for you; Allah is only one God; far be it from His glory that He should have a son. . . (Sura 4:171–72).

The Westminster Confession of 1648 summarizes the Bible's teaching in the following words:

> In the unity of the Godhead there are three persons with one essence, one power, and one eternity—God the Father, God the Son, and God the Holy Spirit. The Father is born of no one nor is the Father derived from anyone; the Son is born eternally from the Father; the Holy Spirit proceeds eternally from[29] the Father and the Son.

The teaching, drawn from the Bible, that God is triune was formulated at the Council of Nicea (AD 325). Together with the teaching that Jesus is truly man and truly God, formulated at the Council of Chalcedon (AD 451), it counts as the decisive ideas that have always united the various Christian denominations. Neither of these was ever disputed during the Reformation. However, the Trinity has never been understood as something that was devised by councils, but as something taught in the New Testament. The confessions merely complemented, summarized and put into words what was taught in the New Testament. For instance, the instruction to baptize believers mentions the single "name," which is "the name of the Father and of the Son and of the Holy Spirit" (Matt 28:19). In Galatians 4:6 one reads:

---

29. The suffix "from the Son" (*filioque*) was added later and is historically justifiably rejected by orthodox churches.

"Because you are sons, God (the Father) sent the Spirit (Holy Spirit) of his Son (Jesus) into our hearts, the Spirit who calls out, 'Abba, Father.'"[30]

Any rapprochement between the great monotheistic religions will only be possible if the teaching of the Trinity and the associated teaching of the divinity of Jesus are removed from Christian theology and mission. The German word for Trinity, *Dreieinigkeit* (Three-one-ness), shows that the teaching of the Trinity stands over against two other views of God. In the German word the *ein* (from *eins*, or one) excludes polytheism, and the *drei* (three) likewise stands over against "monistic monotheism" (an only-one-God-belief).

The teaching of the Trinity has a different meaning in Christianity than it would have in other religions. The Bible states that "God is love" (1 John 4:8, 16) and the love between Father, Son, and Spirit is the starting point of all thinking about love (John 17:24). Love means to speak, to decide, and to act for the benefit of another, so it always includes at least two agents. In "monistic monotheism," love is impossible because love can only be practiced when God has a counterpart. According to Trinitarian monotheism, the persons of the Trinity have loved each other since eternity, long before a counterpart was created. The persons of the Trinity love each other, speak with each other, and act for each other.

Since humankind is made in the image of God, the eternal community of love in God is the standard and starting point for community among humans. People speak with each other because God speaks with others. People should work for each other, because God himself works and exists for others.

Sin Against People or Above All Against God?

In the Koran, sin is a wrong action against oneself but not against God. Adam and his wife sin in paradise, but they confess their sin and Allah once again shows them the straight path (Sura 2:37), since they sinned in such a way that they said, "We have been unjust to ourselves" (Sura 7:23). About the sin of ungratefulness of the Israelites the Koran says: "And We made the clouds to give shade over you and We sent to you manna and quails: Eat of the good things that We have given you; and they did not do Us (God) any harm, but they made their own souls suffer the loss" (Sura 2:57). Correspondingly, death is not a consequence of sin (Sura 2:35–39).

Sin in the Bible is in the final instance always directed against God himself. In the famous song of repentance, Psalm 51, King David acknowledges

---

30. See also 2 Cor 13:14 and Rev 1:4–5.

murder and adultery (committed with a woman, against another man, 2 Sam 11–12) as follows: "Against *you*, you only, have I sinned and done what is evil in your sight" (Ps 51:4a). The Old Testament frequently compares the relationship between God and Israel to a marriage, and Israel's falling away from God to adultery. God is angered by human sin and at the same time aggrieved: "Yet they rebelled and grieved his Holy Spirit" (Isa 63:10; cf. Eph 4:30). In his holy anger Jesus was also always distressed (Mark 3:5 and John 11:33).

Sin as Isolated Act or as Foundational Rupture?

In the Koran, human sin is always an individual act, which can be overcome by leaving it behind from that point onwards. There is no original sin, and there is no notion that only God could help in overcoming sin. Adam's "fall" (Sura 2:36) has no consequences for the rest of humanity and Islam has no notion of a "fall of mankind" or "original sin." As the Koran says, "No bearer of burden shall bear the burden of another" (Sura 39:7). Thus there is no necessity for deliverance from original sin. When humans forget God's commands, stray from them, or obey the "whispers" of Satan—who is an egregious "enemy" of humankind (Sura 35:6)—they indeed commit a sinful act. However, they are not basically lost as a result, nor are they fallen or separated from God. When they remember God's commandments and take refuge in God, they are in the position to do good again. Full of grace and mercy, God again turns to the individual. As Abdoldjavad Falaturi writes:

> According to the Koran, mankind by his created nature is geared towards God. He is not burdened with sinfulness. Adam's sin was forgiven by his contrition. This model is valid for everyone. In Islam the act of deliverance is replaced by divine mercy.[31]

Evil is not found within people or in their nature; it is only a temptation that comes to people from the outside:

> At first sight, the view of humanity found in the Koran appears above all to be marked by character weakness. Yet in principle it is through and through optimistic and positive. This is due to the notion that in the final instance weaknesses are interpreted as unbelief.[32]

---

31. Falaturi in *WDR*, *Koran*, 11.
32. Nagel, *Koran*, 253.

This view has obvious consequences for the questions of superiority and self-criticism.

The Bible views sin not primarily as an individual act, a wicked deed, but rather in its aggregate as the breaking of a covenant between God and humankind. It is also a mark of humanity's infidelity toward God (esp. Rom 1:18–32). Humans are unable to free themselves from sin without God's help. Deliverance from sin is not so much deliverance from a particular act, but from the sinfulness of human nature and from enmity towards God.

The teaching of original sin is unique to Christianity.[33] It says not only that individuals sin, but also that humankind is already marked by sin prior to the moment when an individual commits his or her first sin. This inherited state of being outside of God's grace was unleashed by the fall of the first humans, Adam and Eve (Gen 3). This fact necessitates collective salvation by the new Adam, Jesus Christ. Though their concrete, personal transgression, each person confirms that there is original sin, although he or she does not cause it. Evil resides within people themselves, as Jesus says:

> For it is from within, from the human heart, that evil intentions come: fornication, theft, murder, adultery, avarice, wickedness, deceit, licentiousness, envy, slander, pride, folly. All these evil things come from within, and they defile a person. (Mark 7:21–23 NRSV)

Humankind is basically not in the position "to not sin," since they are "sold" to sin (Rom 7:14–15). Paul declares, "For what I do is not the good I want to do; no, the evil I do not want to do—this I keep on doing" (Rom 7:19).

Human beings remain under the curse of sin and will always repeatedly do evil until they accept that they cannot really improve themselves. They must see and accept that Jesus' death on the cross occurred as atonement for their sins. Only then does the Holy Spirit take up residence in them, and the sinners can withstand sin. If they nevertheless sin—and this happens again and again in the life of Christians—and ask for forgiveness of their sins, they experience forgiveness and new fellowship with their creator (1 John 1:9).

Superiority or Self-Criticism?

The Koran differentiates between two types of people. There are those who submit to Allah with the prophets and for that reason will triumph in every

---

33. With few exceptions, Christian confessions are basically consistent with regard to the teaching of original sin. However, they differ considerably on the question of the extent to which original sin affected humankind.

aspect. And there are the unbelievers who do not submit to God and for that reason are doomed. The Koran serves above all to substantiate and proclaim the supremacy of God, his revelation, his prophet Mohammed, and the believers. When the Koran is directed against people, it is not directed against believers but rather against others. Self-criticism would mean that the supremacy of truth was called into question. The "preeminence"[34] of the Koran and the "victory"[35] of Islam (Sura 110:1) are regarded as the inevitable consequence of the truth. Islam does not seek to discourage believers via self-criticism. In its understanding of sin, human beings are always considered as basically capable of doing good.

Above all else, the Bible intends to substantiate and proclaim God's mercy for a world that lives in enmity with him; it likewise intends to substantiate and proclaim God's mercy toward his people, insofar as they have turned from him. When the Bible turns against people, it does this above all against the believers: the Jews in the Old Testament and the followers of Jesus in the New Testament. This self-criticism goes so far that unbelievers or pagans are sometimes held up as role models for believers. The Bible is not very useful when it comes to celebrating the spiritual condition of Christians or Jews! In fact, revelation often critically turns against God's people and frequently calls the true situation what it is.

The Old Testament proclaims monotheism, but it also reveals how difficult it was to achieve this among the Jews. David's adultery and murder do not weaken the Psalms; rather, they provide the occasion for the most important psalm of repentance in the Old Testament and in the history of the church (Ps 51, discussed above). Not only David, but Moses and Paul were also murderers. It is not from writings which oppose the Scriptures that we find out about Peter's failings, including his idea that Jesus' sufferings were senseless, his statement shortly before the crucifixion in which he guaranteed to never deny Jesus (Matt 26:33–35), and the incident when he had to be sharply criticized by Paul (Gal 2). Rather, the sins of biblical characters are recorded in the Bible itself. The New Testament reports both that the early church developed a social program very early (Acts 6), that the wealthy members of the church often let the poor in the church go hungry (1 Cor 11:21–22), and that they did not pay wages on time (Jas 5:4). Complete books of the Old Testament are dedicated to ruthlessly revealing the conditions in Israel (e.g., Amos and Micah) and complete books of the New

---

34. This is the title of the chapter on the meaning of the Koran in Guellouz, *Koran*, 77.

35. See the many evidences in the Koran presented in Hofmann, *Koran*, 511.

Testament such as 1 Corinthians expose the upsetting situation in Christian churches.

It is neither the pagan nations in the Old Testament nor the Romans and the Greeks in the New Testament whose atrocities and misguided notions are central. Rather, it is the errors of the alleged or actual people of God. In the church in Corinth, Paul discovered a form of incest "of a kind that does not occur even among pagans" (1 Cor 5:1b). All too often God has to call on an outsider in order to bring his people back to their senses. In no religion do the followers get such a bad report as in the Bible. The teaching that Jews and Christians are sinners and are capable of the worst is graphically illustrated. And Paul admonishes Christians not to think of themselves as any better than the Jewish people: "Do not be arrogant, but be afraid" (Rom 11:17–22).

Self-criticism belongs to the essence of being a Christian. To become a Christian includes seeing oneself as a sinner, not to identify the sins of others. Christians are not better, they only "have it better." According to Luther, being a Christian means that one beggar tells another where there is something to eat.[36] Paul writes for instance: "For I am the least of the apostles and do not even deserve to be called an apostle, because I persecuted the church of God. But by the grace of God I am what I am . . ." (1 Cor 15:9–10a).

The relentless and honest self-analysis of biblical Christianity has shaped its later history. Christian historians, not Muslim historians, have worked through the crusades, and no religion has admitted its errors so clearly as Christianity. It is no coincidence that critical historiography arose in the Christian West and was able to include the churches.

Self-criticism is deeply rooted in the center of the Christian message—the good news of forgiveness. An early consequence of turning away from God was that humans began to look for guilt in others (Gen 3:11–13). Jesus condemns the words of the Pharisee: "God, I thank you that I am not like other men . . .," and he praises the words of the tax collector: "God, have mercy on me, a sinner" (Luke 18:10–14). In the Bible, faith begins with the recognition of one's own shortcomings. In the Judeo-Christian world self-criticism counts as a virtue: it is a sign of strength and not an admission of weakness. To the contrary, in Islam a critique of its own history is unthinkable, a blasphemy which would pull away the foundation from under revelation. It would be an insult to the prophet. No wonder that until today countries shaped by Islam have neither freedom of speech nor debate in freely elected parliaments.[37]

---

36. Luther, WA 17/2:101.
37. Cf. Stein, *Moses und die Offenbarung*, 47.

BIBLIOGRAPHY

Beeler, Katharina. "John Calvin on Islam." 2015. https://theologyandthecity.com/2015/01/02/john-calvin-on-islam/.

Ehmann, Johannes. *Luther, Türken und Islam: Eine Untersuchung zum Türken- und Islambild Martin Luthers (1515-1546)*. Quellen und Forschungen zur Reformationsgeschichte 80. 2nd ed. Gütersloh: Gütersloher, 2015.

Falaturi, Abdoldjavad. *Der Koran: Ein fremdes Heiligtum entdecken*. Edited by WDR [= Westdeutscher Rundfunk]. Cologne: WDR, 1994.

Guellouz, Azzedine. *Der Koran*. Bergisch Gladbach: Bastei-Lübbe, 1998.

Hofmann, Murad, ed. *Der Koran*. Kreuzlingen: Hugendubel, 2007.

Kandil, Lamya. "Schwüre in den mekkanischen Suren." In *The Koran as Text*, edited by Stefan Wild, 41-58. Leiden: Brill, 1996.

Kritzl, Johannes. *"Adversus turcas et turcarum Deum": Beurteilungskriterien des Türkenkriegs und des Islam in den Werken Martin Luthers*. Disputationes religionum orbis Sectio O. Bonn: Verlag für Kultur und Wissenschaft, 2008.

Lee, Francis Nigel. "Calvin on Islam" 2000. http://www.historicism.net/readingmaterials/CalvIslam.pdf.

Luther, Martin. *Fastenpostille*. 1525. WA 17/2:3-247. http://www.maartenluther.com/weimarausgabe.html.

———. *Ob Kriegsleute auch in seligem Stande sein können*. 1526. WA 19:623-62. http://www.maartenluther.com/weimarausgabe.html.

———. *Verlegung des Alcoran Bruder Richardi, Prediger Ordens. Verdeutscht und herausgegeben von M. Luther*. 1542. WA 53:272-396. http://www.maartenluther.com/weimarausgabe.html.

———. "Vorrede zu Theodor Biblianders Koranausgabe." *Schriften 1542/43*. WA 53: 569-72. http://www.maartenluther.com/weimarausgabe.html.

Nagel, Tilman. *Der Koran, Einführung—Texte—Erläuterungen*. Munich: Beck, 1998.

"Reformation und Islam: Ein Impulspapier der Konferenz für Islamfragen der Evangelischen Kirche in Deutschland (EKD)." 2016. https://www.ekd.de/EKD-Texte/105303.html.

Schirrmacher, Thomas. *The Koran and the Bible*. World of Theology 7. Bonn: Verlag für Kultur und Wissenschaft, 2013.

Stein, Hannes. *Moses und die Offenbarung der Demokratie*. Berlin: Rowohlt, 1998.

Way to Allah Team. "Was ist Islam." www.way-to-allah.com/islam_zum_kennenlernen/was_ist_islam.html.

Zirker, Hans. *Der Koran*. 2nd ed. Darmstadt: Primus, 2007.

11

Theologia Crucis[1] and the Persecuted Church

Frank-Ole Thoresen

A few years ago I served as a missionary among the Somali population on the Horn of Africa.[2] The Somalis are close to a hundred percent Muslim and persecution of those turning to Christianity is commonplace. In such areas, denominational and theological differences among mission agencies, as well as new believers, tend to become less accentuated. It was in this context that an experienced missionary colleague from a Baptist background drew my attention to the theme at hand. He argued that Lutheran theology has a lot to offer for our Somali Christian friends who face stark persecution. From his perspective it was not simply a matter of a single theological position or statement; it was rather the general Lutheran theological understanding of a "hidden God," as opposed to external Christian success and glory, and an emphasis on how this perspective permeates Lutheran theology as such.

Since then I have often pondered his observation. Is there a deeper perspective in Lutheran theology that could be of particular gain to the persecuted church, regardless of time and place?

---

1. I will use the Latin term *theologia crucis* and the English term "theology of the cross" interchangeably.

2. I wrote my PhD thesis on the persecuted church on the Horn of Africa; see Thoresen, *Reconciled Community*.

In this chapter I will discuss the Lutheran aspect of the "theology of the cross" and ask what possible implications this perspective may have for a relevant and coherent theology of persecution.

THEOLOGIA CRUCIS

Martin Luther's theology of the cross was neglected for generations, and, according to Alister E. McGrath, it was not really restored to its importance until after World War II. From that time onwards it has once more played a significant theological role for many scholars.[3]

Luther initially employed the term *theologia crucis* in the Heidelberg Disputation of 1518.[4] In this disputation, Luther develops the argument that it is a mistake to depend upon the works of humans, and that this is based on a fundamental theological fallacy concerning the power of the will. God's judgement is therefore on such works. Thesis 18 of the disputation then concludes with anguish: "It is certain that man must utterly despair of his own ability before he is prepared to receive the grace of Christ."[5]

This discussion leads to Luther's conclusion that there is a theological divide between "the theologian of glory" and "the theologian of the cross," which he deals with in theses 19–24.[6] The theologian of glory is anyone who will rely on works rather than on the suffering and cross of Christ. Such a person should not really be called a theologian at all. There is a logical coherence between the theology of the cross and the fact that the true church will face suffering and persecution. Luther claims that a theology of glory always seeks to gain some sort of merit.[7] The fundamental theological conviction that there must be a way to glory that can be obtained through free will and good deeds is always close at hand. "He deserves to be called a theologian, however, who comprehends the visible and manifest things of God seen through suffering and the cross."[8] Human good works, the law, and

---

3. McGrath, *Luther's Theology of the Cross*, 202. At the beginning of the twentieth century it was common to argue that the theology of the cross represented a "pre-Reformation" theology, imprinted by the experiences of the monk. Westhelle, *Transfiguring Luther*, 116.

4. McGrath, however, argues that "Luther's theological breakthrough—which we date in 1515—contains within itself the germs of the theology of the cross." McGrath, *Luther's Theology of the Cross*, 230.

5. LW 31:51.

6. Forde, *Being a Theologian of the Cross*, 70.

7. LW 31:53.

8. LW 31:52. McGrath strongly criticizes the employment of the term "manifest things of God" in this translation, as it loses the significance of the hiddenness of God's

human reasoning are all opposed to the cross of Christ and his suffering. A theology that becomes intellectual speculation and abstract reasoning, rather than true "experience" of Christ's suffering, loses the fundamental understanding of the cross as paradigmatic for Christian theology.[9]

According to Luther, it is only through the cross that we can know God, and the one who does not know God, hidden in suffering, does not know God at all.[10] God is therefore paradoxically at the same time both revealed and hidden, on the cross (*Deus revelatus et Deus absconditus*). Humans are only granted "a glimpse of God's back."[11] The revelation of God on the cross is, therefore, only "an *indirect* revelation of God—but a genuine revelation nonetheless."[12]

According to Walter von Loewenich, the principle of *theologia crucis* permeates Luther's entire theology, and therefore every basic theological standpoint must be interpreted in this perspective.[13] Likewise, Robert A. Kelly emphasizes that "the theology of the cross is an epistemological and structural principle of Luther's total theology."[14] Both theologians argue that in Luther's perspective cross and suffering represent the permanent mark of any true theology. Luther thus claims that being a theologian of the cross is a way of living, and that the cross accordingly plays a fundamental role in the life of every Christian.[15] The true comprehension of Christ's suffering is to take part in his tribulations. This means on the one hand, to understand and accept that it is my sins that torment Christ on the cross[16] and on the other hand to accept that contemporary Christians can expect nothing less than what Christ and the forefathers of faith have endured. Jon Sobrino defines this state of affairs as an analogous relation between the cross and the "crucified people" of God.[17] The cross, therefore, represents a paradigm not only for individual believers, but for the collective fate of the church.

In the following, we will pursue this perspective further and discuss what such an approach to the suffering of Christ may imply for persecution theology, as well as for the contemporary persecuted church.

---

revelation. McGrath, *Luther's Theology of the Cross*, 204.

9. Ibid., 206.
10. Forde, *Being a Theologian of the Cross*, 86.
11. McGrath, *Luther's Theology of the Cross*, 203.
12. Ibid., 204.
13. Loewenich, *Luther's Theology of the Cross*, 167.
14. Kelly, "The Suffering Church," 3.
15. Forde, *Being a Theologian of the Cross*, 4.
16. LW 42:9.
17. Sobrino, *Jesus the Liberator*, 235.

THE SUFFERING OF THE CHURCH AS A LOGICAL CONSEQUENCE OF THE THEOLOGY OF THE CROSS[18]

According to Luther, the basic understanding in a theology of glory is that human works are good, whereas suffering is evil. Therefore, God must be distanced from suffering. The good God can only be involved in what is experienced as good. Luther contends that this theology represents a simplistic image of God and he questions whether it can find any room for God's involvement in the cross at all. A theology of the cross claims that the will is bound and must be set free. We see in Christ's death on the cross our own death and so we learn how to die. We are dust into which God breathes life. Obviously, contemporary Christians can expect nothing less than what Christ and the forefathers of faith have endured;[19] but the hope is born in his followers that those who die with him shall also live with him.

Luther thus sees everything from the perspective of the cross and interprets things in its light. The cross becomes the story of each believer. We are not minor gods but human beings of flesh and blood, imprinted by sin. We therefore have to partake in the cross in order to "die" from our perverted flesh; that is the only way to glory.[20] Accordingly, the persecution and suffering of the global church is a logical consequence of partaking in the story of the cross. The world cannot accept the Word of God and it will always attack it, one way or another. The church should therefore expect to face persecution when it preaches the Gospel purely.[21] Since this is the case, the church is spiritually better off when it faces persecution than when it experiences prosperity. Wealth, power, and peace are the greatest dangers to the church, since they weaken the church in the long run. Such a situation may, according to Luther, be "a sure sign that the pure teaching of the Word has been taken away."[22] There is, so to speak, a logical coherence between the sufferings of Christ and the sufferings of the church. The consequence of this reasoning is further developed in Luther's argument concerning the different signs of the true church.

---

18. I have earlier argued that the Pauline literature considers persecution to be a logical consequence of godly living; see Thoresen, *Reconciled Community*, 169–71.

19. Ibid., 171–73.

20. Forde, *Being a Theologian of the Cross*, 9–14.

21. Kelly, "The Suffering Church," 8.

22. LW 27:43; also quoted by Kelly, "The Suffering Church," 6; see also LW 27:343–44.

THE SEVENTH SIGN OF THE TRUE CHURCH

Luther's doctrine of the church is well known. It was first and foremost centered on the community of saints. His emphasis was not on a gathering of people, but on a gathering of faith, namely the community of those who have faith and the Holy Spirit in their hearts.[23] He was also ambiguous towards terms such as *Kirche*, which he feared was too focused on external institutions.[24] He concludes that since faith is an internal gift of grace, no single institutional church can claim to be the true church. Furthermore, since faith is internal, the true church is to some extent "hidden." The true church is not apparent to the eyes of the external world. There are, however, certain signs by which the presence of the hidden church can be detected, and Luther mentions seven such signs in "On the Councils and the Church."[25] The most important of these signs is 1) the preaching of the Word of God. "Now, wherever you hear or see this word preached, believed, professed, and lived, do not doubt that the true *ecclesia sancta catholica* . . . must be there."[26] The other signs are 2) baptism, 3) Holy Communion, 4) the office of the keys, 5) consecration, and call to public offices of the Word, sacraments, and keys. The sixth sign is public worship. Finally, Luther argues that the seventh such sign is that,

> the holy Christian people are externally recognized by the holy possession of the sacred cross. They must endure every misfortune and persecution, all kinds of trials and evil from the devil, the world, and the flesh (as the Lord's Prayer indicates) by inward sadness, timidity, fear, outward poverty, contempt, illness, and weakness, in order to become like their head, Christ.[27]

In Luther's approach, suffering and persecution are not necessarily a misfortune that may become the church, but they are a "possession whereby the Holy Spirit not only sanctifies his people, but also blesses them."[28] As long as such suffering is solely because of Christ, it both entails and causes sanctification. As such, the suffering and persecution of the church signify clearly that the true church is present. Persecution is thus not an anomaly for the church but should rather be an anticipated effect of belonging to the community of saints. It may even be taken to be a "hallmark of legitimacy"

---

23. LW 41:143–46.
24. Kelly, "The Suffering Church," 4–5.
25. LW 41:148–66.
26. Ibid., 41:150.
27. Ibid., 41:164–65.
28. Ibid., 41:165.

for the church.[29] Hence, the deepest problem of the church is not persecution but the church's external success.[30] The persecuted church at present is part of an uninterrupted community of suffering disciples, which started with the birth of the church. In this perspective, the situation of the persecuted church represents a degree of historical and theological continuity. Further, since there is an aspect of spiritual growth and sanctification inherent to suffering and persecution, the persecuted church is, in one sense, in a better situation than, e.g., the contemporary church of the West.

This line of argumentation, however, raises an important question. Does Luther imply that every local church around the globe should at all times face persecution in order to be a true church? He gives us an indication of how he considers the interrelation between the church and persecution in his commentary to Galatians 5:11:

> Here someone may say: "Christians must be quite insane if they expose themselves to dangers voluntarily. For all they accomplish with their preaching is to gain for themselves the anger and hatred of the world and to create stumbling blocks. And that, as the saying goes, is laboring in vain and simply looking for trouble." "This fact," says Paul, "does not offend or bother us at all; it only makes us courageous and optimistic about the success and growth of the church, which flourishes and grows under persecution. . . . On the other hand, when the cross and the raging of tyrants and heretics have been removed, and the stumbling blocks have come to an end, and when the devil "guards his own palace, and his goods are in peace" (Luke 11:21), this is a sure sign that the pure teaching of the Word has been taken away."[31]

Luther, thus, presupposes that the pure teaching of the Word of God will necessarily create anger and hatred in the world. He is further convinced that such anger and hatred will lead to dangers, and presumably also physical persecution. His conclusion is therefore that the church grows under persecution, as long as the Word is preached, and that peace in the world necessarily equals a situation where the church has ceased to preach the pure Word of God. This argument reflects, at least to some extent, the Reformation context of sixteenth-century Germany. At present, many churches in contexts of persecution obviously experience a similar situation, and in such contexts Luther's argument may still apply. In other contexts, however,

---

29. Kelly, "The Suffering Church," 5–6.
30. Thoresen, *Reconciled Community*, 181.
31. LW 27:43

Luther's logic presumably falls short. In situations where physical persecution is not commonplace, churches may naturally preach the Word of God freely. Nonetheless, Luther's argument may still carry weight to the extent that the Word of God, when preached purely, may at all times be expected to generate a degree of opposition. The term "persecution" is then employed in a wider sense, to include various negative reactions, such as ridicule and social marginalization, rather than in the narrow sense of more serious physical or psychological maltreatment.[32]

Further, Luther's argument that the church grows and flourishes under persecution mirrors the ancient and often quoted declaration of Tertullian, "[a]s often you mow us down, the more numerous do we become; the blood of the Christians is the seed."[33] On various occasions, scholars have confirmed a correlation between persecution and church growth.[34] Paul R. House, for instance, argues convincingly that the willingness of the first Christians to sacrifice their lives and comfort was a strong message to their immediate successors, and accordingly that it may also have an equivalent effect on the contemporary church.[35] Nevertheless, although the church has often grown during times of tribulation, I believe the claim that persecution more or less as a rule furthers church growth lacks firm support both theologically and in the witness of church history.[36]

"WHY MUST WE ALWAYS SUFFER?"

A few years back, I participated in a mission conference where the main theme was how to reach Muslims in Scandinavia with the Gospel. One of the participants was a young man from Somalia who had become a Christian some years previously. During this conference, the young man was informed that a former Somali friend had recently been killed for his faith, on the Horn of Africa. I still remember this young man's cry as he learned of this tragic event. As tears were running down his cheeks, he gave voice to a

---

32. I have argued elsewhere that there are good reasons for maintaining a narrow definition of persecution. Thoresen, *Reconciled Community*, 132–33. This does not exclude the understanding that discipleship implies "carrying crosses" of various sorts. Bonhoeffer, *Cost of Discipleship*, 98–99.

33. Bettenson, *The Early Christian Fathers*, 166.

34. See, e.g., House, "Suffering and the Purpose of Acts," 326: "Clearly suffering is a major force in the Gospel's expansion. It is a rare thing for the Way to spread without it." The whole section from pages 321 to 326 deals with this theme. Similarly also Marshall, *Acts of the Apostles*, 152, and Peterson, *Acts of the Apostles*, 275.

35. House, "Suffering and the Purpose of Acts," 330.

36. Thoresen, *Reconciled Community*, 165–68.

feeling of pain and despair. "Why must we Somali Christians always suffer? Why must we always be killed, persecuted, and tormented? What have we done wrong? Why can't we just be left alone?"

There is obviously a lesson to be learned from this story. On the one hand, this young man gives voice to the feeling of disheartenment and sorrow that we all experience when we learn of the suffering and persecution of our Christian brothers and sisters. And, as Thomas Schirrmacher has emphasized, the pain of the persecuted church should concern us all.[37] On the other hand, his cry gives voice to a very natural and human perception, namely, that there must be some sort of correlation between wrongdoings and suffering. We seek to avoid suffering with all our efforts. Suffering is painful and the human mind, more or less consciously, considers it to be evil. There must thus be a reason for suffering which originates from our wrongdoings. From Luther's perspective such reasoning is, in the deepest sense, influenced by a theology of glory. As natural and understandable as it may be in a human perception, it still carries theological flaws. It gives voice to the innate anticipation that God's blessings should entail a degree of material or external success, rather than simply the church's spiritual growth. When suffering befalls us, they must therefore be the result of our wrongdoings.

Luther emphasized that suffering is not necessarily evil. Although it is painful, it is only through suffering and the cross that the sinner can see God and come to know God. "This is clear: He who does not know Christ does not know God hidden in suffering." And further, "God can be found only in suffering and the cross."[38] There is thus more to suffering than reaches the eye. The late German missiologist, Peter Beyerhaus, argued that the global church should not narrowly consider persecution, martyrdom, and sufferings in a pathetic category. Persecution and martyrdom unite the church with Christ and the apostles in an intimate fellowship.[39] He thus maintains that persecution may include an element of blessing, since those who are suffering, in a spiritual manner, partake in the sufferings of Christ and the apostles. And, further, that the global church potentially also may partake in the sufferings of Christ through identifying with the persecuted believers. When we embrace their witness and experiences, and let their story become ours, an element of spiritual blessing may also befall the larger community of believers.

37. Schirrmacher, *Persecution of Christians*.
38. LW 31:53.
39. With reference to Phil 1:29, "For it has been granted to you that for the sake of Christ you should not only believe in him but also suffer for his sake, engaged in the same conflict you saw and now hear to be mine." Beyerhaus, *God's Kingdom*, 170.

TO PARTAKE IN THE SUFFERINGS OF CHRIST IS PLEASING TO GOD[40]

> Since we know then that it is God's good pleasure that we should suffer, and that God's glory is manifested in our suffering, better than in any other way, and since we are the kind of people who cannot hold on to the Word and our faith without suffering, and moreover since we have the noble previous promise that the cross which God sends to us is not a bad thing, but rather an utterly precious and noble holy thing, why should we not be bold to suffer?[41]

The Saturday before Easter 1530, Luther preached at Coburg on the theme of cross and suffering. Here, he identifies four main reasons for the sufferings of those who confess Christ. First, the Lord wants his people to be conformed to the image of his dear Son. Secondly, the devil hates the Word of God and the believers; through his vicious attacks we can learn that God is the stronger one, and our only shield and comfort. Thirdly, suffering counteracts what unfortunately is often experienced, namely that God's people become sleepy and secure. Hence, our cross keeps us at the cross of Christ, and it is only through tribulations that we can learn to depend upon God's promises. Lastly, Luther teaches that because Christ himself suffered and has "touched" the sufferings of the Christians with his own suffering, the suffering of believers has become "utterly holy."[42] Consequently, Luther did not see persecution and suffering for the sake of Christ as something from which believers should shy away. It is, so to speak, God's pleasure that we should suffer, and it is a gift of grace that inherently carries the effect that God may keep and sanctify his children through these sufferings:

> But when you are condemned, cursed, reviled, slandered, and plagued because of Christ, you are sanctified. It mortifies the old Adam and teaches him patience, humility, gentleness, praise and thanks, and good cheer in suffering. That is what it means to be sanctified by the Holy Spirit and to be renewed to a new life in Christ.[43]

---

40. I have elsewhere argued that in Luke and Acts there is an interrelation between persecution and discipleship, and that the life and suffering of Christ have a paradigmatic function, worthy of imitation. Thoresen, *Reconciled Community*, 171–73.
41. LW 51:208.
42. LW 51:206–8.
43. LW 41:165.

When God accepts that his church faces suffering and persecution, he may employ this to a joyful end. He makes sure that his children are kept and depend upon his comfort alone. A further consequence of Luther's argument is the sanctification and purification not only of the individual believer, but of the community of believers. Since Christians are sanctified by suffering, those who hold on to the Word of God will presumably have a stronger conviction. They are determined and, so to speak, willing to pay the cost of discipleship.[44]

It is, however, important to understand that in Luther's perspective, although God in a certain manner takes pleasure in our sufferings, it is not part of God's "proper work," but rather of his "alien work." According to Luther, God's alien work has the function of furthering his proper work in the long run, and accordingly, what may be experienced as painful and hurting may further his larger objective, and it is therefore not necessarily evil in the eyes of the Lord:

> It is as if he were saying: "Although He is the God of life and salvation and this is His proper work, yet, in order to accomplish this, He kills and destroys. These works are alien to Him, but through them He accomplishes His proper work. For He kills our will that His may be established in us. He subdues the flesh and its lusts that the spirit and its desires may come to life."[45]

It is therefore pleasing to God that his children partake in the sufferings of Christ, and to suffer for Christ's sake inherently carries a holy objective. The destiny of Christ on earth was focused on dying and rising, and the destiny of every disciple is, so to speak, to imitate Christ in suffering—but also in glory.[46]

Luther thus claims that suffering, in a fallen world, carries a promise of hope in a larger, eschatological, perspective.

PERSECUTION AS TESTIMONY

During my study of the persecuted church among Somalis in the Horn of Africa, one of my informants whom I will call Nuur shared an extensive testimony of how his local community perceived him as a Christian Somali. Among the things he emphasized was a degree of respect he often met from the Muslim community because of his willingness to endure persecution:

---

44. Thoresen, *Reconciled Community*, 107–14.
45. LW 14:335, quoted in Forde, *On Being a Theologian of the Cross*, 88.
46. Norlander, "Theology of Martyrdom," 61.

> [B]ut when you are living among your own people like in [name of place] now, every day I meet Somalis. Day to day, I meet them. You know what they tell me? "[Nuur] you are a good man. You do not run away when you are persecuted." Of course I have gone, but finally I came. You don't run away, that is one thing. . . . One thing is that you should never encourage believers to run. You should encourage them to stay . . . to stay in their locality. . . . So, I think we shall encourage . . . I have stayed among my people. I am happy. My aim is to continue and to press hard. We do our part, and God will do his part.[47]

Persecution and suffering for the sake of the Word of God is a powerful testimony to those outside the church. When Nuur was being persecuted but accepted to face the persecution and refused to give up his faith, friends and relatives considered his boldness as something to be respected and appreciated. The church may thus experience a degree of "success" and growth in such times. Nuur, consequently, focused on perseverance in the face of tribulations. He wanted to continue "to press hard," to stay, and witness, despite the dangers he faced.

Leonardo Boff has argued that the total willingness to sacrifice one's life points to something which is of higher value than even life itself. Martyrdom and persecution are therefore a testimony to the relative value of everything besides the Christian faith and they show that the Christian faith constitutes a greater good.[48] Luther argues, similarly, that unwillingness to compromise on "the pure teaching of the Word" represents a strong testimony with regard to the integrity of the church and the Gospel. The main principle in both cases is the concept of personal sacrifice for a higher good, and thus a willingness to endure suffering. As we have seen, Luther's argument regarding persecution and the seventh sign of the true church underscores that the contemporary church facing persecution and suffering is in continuity with the Christian church from the earliest times, and that "the pure teaching of the Word" has not been compromised. It may be their "hallmark of legitimacy."

In the present, however, this line of argumentation may be challenged. Religious persecution is not exclusively the experience of Christians, and even religious groups who are generally non-violent now face maltreatment because of their convictions. The persecution of Ahmadi Muslims in Pakistan and the Yazidi community in Iraq may be taken as examples.

---

47. Thoresen, *Reconciled Community*, 160. Nuur is not the informant's real name, but a pseudonym employed in order to protect friends and relatives. Sadly, Nuur was later shot and killed, presumably because of his Christian faith.

48. Boff, "Martyrdom," 15–16.

The question is whether the indiscriminate persecution of various religious groups invalidates Luther's argument of persecution being a "hallmark of legitimacy." Are the faiths of various persecuted groups more legitimate simply because they are being persecuted? Although the world at large may not necessarily accept that the willingness to suffer for the Word represents a "hallmark of legitimacy" of the Christian message per se, it may at least be a testimony to the genuineness of the faith and conviction of those believers who accept unjust suffering. This also corresponds to what Nuur experienced. The genuineness of the faith and convictions of individual believers may generate respect, and consequently also stir interest in the message and the testimony of that believer.

"BE PERSECUTED OR SURRENDER CHRIST?"

Luther never glorifies suffering and persecution, but at times he nevertheless comes close to arguing in such a way that the gravity of persecution may be somewhat reduced and belittled. In his last sermon in Eisleben in 1546 he says, for instance, that God will make persecution "so sweet for you that you easily would be able to bear it,"[49] and further that persecution "will not be heavy for you, but light and easy to bear."[50] At other times, the reader may question whether he rejects the possibility of fleeing from persecution. He states, for instance, that the one who avoids persecution surrenders Christ and denies Christ.[51] Luther's chosen terminology when discussing persecution is, thus, often radical and not very nuanced.

Most often, however, Luther argues his case with a particular objective. His aim is to strengthen and comfort those who face persecution or fear for persecution. He also says that the kind of suffering he and his followers are facing is not something they have chosen and that they would gladly be rid of it if it were possible.[52] Nevertheless, the impression remains that Luther argues rather consistently that persecution and suffering for the sake of Christ are to be expected and should not be shied away from.[53] As such,

49. LW 51:391.

50. LW 51:392. Beyerhaus argues in a similar manner as he states that God "imparts to them a degree of sustaining grace which surpasses all blessings we receive through the means of grace under normal conditions." Beyerhaus, *God's Kingdom*, 171.

51. LW 21:45; and similarly ibid., 51:199.

52. LW 51:198.

53. Luther was often coherent and systematic in his theological reasoning. It could be argued, however, that he was inclined to be more pragmatic when it came to practical application. Following his excommunication by Pope Leo X in 1521, for instance, he went incognito and stayed at the Wartburg under the protection of Frederick III.

there is consistency between Luther's argument of the seventh sign of the true church and the understanding that suffering is a logical consequence of the sufferings of Christ.

Although I agree with Luther in his main theological reasoning concerning suffering and persecution, I question whether he may be too bold in some of his claims. The New Testament repeatedly mentions Christians who were fleeing from persecution, without any criticism. According to Matthew 10:23, Jesus even urged his followers to flee when facing persecution. Further, Acts, in several passages, describes how both Paul and the early Christians ran from persecution.[54] We may therefore identify parallel lines of reasoning in the Scriptures. On the one hand, persecution and martyrdom are integral features of the church; on the other hand, running from persecution may be justified. In real-life situations the choice of strategy should therefore be left to the suffering community and the suffering individual.[55]

CONCLUSION

Luther's "theology of the cross" had important implications for his basic theological understanding. This theological approach also gave a theological basis to his approach to the suffering and persecution experienced by the contemporary church. Luther considered suffering and persecution as part of the church's foundation. According to a "theology of the cross," Christ suffered and the church should always be ready to suffer in the same manner.[56] In this sense, Luther's theology corresponds to Dietrich Bonhoeffer's pointed argument that "Christ is only Christ as the suffering and rejected One, and in the same way, the disciple is only a disciple as suffering and rejected, as crucified with Christ."[57] By means of this emphasis on "the theology of the cross" Luther establishes a framework for the suffering church at present, in which they also may interpret their life stories.

Luther identifies a deeper theological perspective to persecution and suffering. The suffering of the church did not only represent a spiritual or "sacramental" relation to the suffering of Christ, but the cross also has a paradigmatic function to all theology. Luther claims not only that Christians should be willing to face persecution, but states that persecution is a sign of the presence of the true church. The church should face persecution when

54. See, e.g., Acts 14:4–7 and similarly 8:1–4.
55. Thoresen, *Reconciled Community*, 175–76.
56. John 15:20.
57. Bonhoeffer, *Cost of Discipleship*, 96.

preaching the pure Word of God. Further, it may very well be God who is cleansing and sanctifying his church through tribulations, and suffering is therefore not something to fear or run away from. The church is better off when facing persecution than when experiencing external success.

Luther was always a bold speaker and in some of his arguments he goes further than most later theologians have been willing to go. Nevertheless, his basic approach to this theme has a lot to offer also to a contemporary theology of persecution, and through remembrance of a historical past, imprinted by suffering and persecution the present church may also be empowered to persevere in future trials.

BIBLIOGRAPHY

Bauckham, Richard. *The Theology of the Book of Revelation*. New York: Cambridge University Press, 1993.

Bettenson, Henry, ed. *The Early Christian Fathers: A Selection from the Writings of the Fathers from St. Clement of Rome to St. Athanasius*. 11th ed. New York: Oxford University Press, 1991.

Beyerhaus, Peter J. *God's Kingdom and the Utopian Error: Discerning the Biblical Kingdom of God from Its Political Counterfeits*. Wheaton, IL: Crossway, 1992.

Boff, Leonardo. "Martyrdom: An Attempt at Systematic Reflection." In *Martyrdom Today*, edited by Johannes-Baptist Metz and Edward Schillebeeckx, 12–17. Edinburgh: T. & T. Clark, 1983.

Bonhoeffer, Dietrich. *The Cost of Discipleship*. Translated by R. H. Fuller. Rev. ed. New York: Macmillan, 1963.

Conzelmann, Hans. *The Theology of St. Luke*. New York: Harper & Row, 1961.

Forde, Gerhard O. *On Being a Theologian of the Cross. Reflections on Luther's Heidelberg Disputation, 1518*. Grand Rapids: Eerdmans, 1997.

House, Paul R. "Suffering and the Purpose of Acts." *Journal of the Evangelical Theological Society* 33 (1990) 317–30.

Jongeneel, Jan A. B. "Do Christian Witness and Mission Provoke Persecution?" In *Freedom of Belief and Christian Mission*, edited by Hans Aage Gravaas et al., 430–43. Oxford: Regnum, 2015.

Jørgensen, Knud. "Christians in a Minority Situation." In *Freedom of Belief and Christian Mission*, edited by Hans Aage Gravaas et al., 114–26. Oxford: Regnum, 2015.

Kadai, Heino O. "Luther's Theology of the Cross." *Concordia Theological Quarterly* 63 (1999) 169–204.

Kelly, Robert A. "The Suffering Church: A Study of Luther's *Theologia Crucis*." *Concordia Theological Quarterly* 50 (1986) 3–18.

Loewenich, Walter von. *Luther's Theology of the Cross*. Minneapolis: Augsburg, 1976.

Longenecker, Richard N., ed. *Patterns of Discipleship in the New Testament*. Grand Rapids: Eerdmans, 1996.

Luther's Works: American Edition [LW]. 82 vols. Edited by Jaroslav Pelikan et al. Philadelphia: Fortress; Saint Louis: Concordia, 1955–2013.

Marius, Richard. *Martin Luther: The Christian Between God and Death.* London: Harvard University Press, 1999.
Marshall, I. Howard. *The Acts of the Apostles: An Introduction and Commentary.* Tyndale New Testament Commentaries. Grand Rapids: Eerdmans, 1980.
McGrath, Alister E. *Luther's Theology of the Cross: Martin Luther's Theological Breakthrough.* Oxford: Wiley-Blackwell, 2011.
Moltmann, Jürgen, *The Crucified God: The Cross of Christ as the Foundation and Criticism of Christian Theology.* London: SCM, 1979.
Ngien, Dennis. *The Suffering of God according to Martin Luther's "Theologia Crucis."* New York: Lang, 1995.
Norlander, Agne. "A Theology of Martyrdom." In *Freedom of Belief and Christian Mission,* edited by Hans Aage Gravaas et al., 58–66. Oxford: Regnum, 2015.
Penner, Glenn M. *In the Shadow of the Cross: A Biblical Theology of Persecution and Discipleship.* Bartlesville, OK: Living Sacrifice, 2004.
Peterson, David G. *The Acts of the Apostles.* Pillar New Testament Commentary. Grand Rapids: Eerdmans, 2009.
Prenter, Regin. *Luther's Theology of the Cross.* Philadelphia: Fortress, 1959.
Sauer, Christof. "Christian Solidarity in the Face of Discrimination and Persecution." In *Freedom of Belief and Christian Mission,* edited by Hans Aage Gravaas et al., 452–64. Oxford: Regnum, 2015.
Sauer, Christof, and Dwi Maria Handayani. "A Doxological Framework for Interpreting Discrimination, Persecution and Martyrdom." In *Freedom of Belief and Christian Mission,* edited by Hans Aage Gravaas et al., 47–57. Oxford: Regnum, 2015.
Schirrmacher, Thomas. *The Persecution of Christians Concerns Us All: Towards a Theology of Martyrdom. 70 Biblical-Theological Theses written for the German Evangelical Alliance and its Religious Liberty Commission.* Edited by Geoff Tunnicliffe and Thomas Schirrmacher. WEA Global Issues 5. Bonn: Culture and Science, 2008.
Sobrino, Jon. *Jesus the Liberator. A Historical-Theological View.* Maryknoll, NY: Orbis, 1999.
Thoresen, Frank-Ole. *A Reconciled Community of Suffering Disciples: Aspects of a Contextual Somali Ecclesiology.* New York: Lang, 2014.
———. "In the Midst of Umma on the Internet: Religious Profession and Witness in a Globalized Era." In *The Church Going Global: Mission and Globalization,* ed. Tormod Engelsviken et al., 151–62. Oxford: Regnum, 2011.
Tiénou, Tite. "The Missionary Witness of the Persecuted and the Martyrs." In *Freedom of Belief and Christian Mission,* edited by Hans Aage Gravaas et al., 444–51. Oxford: Regnum, 2015
Ton, Josef. *Suffering, Martyrdom and Rewards in Heaven.* 2nd ed. Lanham, MD: Romanian Missionary Society, 2000.
Westhelle, Vítor. *Transfiguring Luther: The Planetary Promise of Luther's Theology.* Eugene OR: Wipf and Stock, 2016.

12

Freedom of Conscience, Reformation, and the Advent of Secularism

Paul Wells

INTRODUCTION

Unfettered freedom of conscience seems like the height of our aspirations for civilized humanity. But does it bear out in reality? C. S. Lewis, in *The Voyage of the Dawn Treader,* tells of a Dark Island, the Island Where Dreams Come True, a fabled desired destination, but there is an unexpected sting in the tale. The island's powers bring to life dreams that make you afraid of going back to sleep, as its visitors' nightmares come true. Those trapped on the island are driven to distraction by terror. One such unfortunate, Lord Rhoop, implores the travelers, "Mercy! Mercy! Even if you are only one more dream, have mercy. Take me on board. Take me, even if you strike me dead. But in the name of all mercies do not fade away and leave me in this horrible land."[1]

Lewis's allegory feels like the world we inhabit. Setting sail from the Christian liberty of the New Testament and arriving in the hoped-for utopia of the twenty-first century, we land on a desert island of so-called freedoms, some of which resemble the worst forms of oppression or moral turpitude,

1. Lewis, *Voyage of the Dawn Treader,* 139.

nightmares come true. Escaping from this one-dimensional prison seems impossible. Freedom of conscience, a fabulous dream, has become servility to sterile self-absorption. It has slowly and grindingly mutated over the last five centuries into something our ancestors would have found difficult to imagine. Conscience was superseded by free-thinking, by consciousness, then by the expressive individualism that I will call self-conscience, conscience dominated by the dictates of the individual, a responsibility to my-self and her desires alone. This last state makes for the moral misery and moral blindness that afflicts us today.[2]

These interpretations of freedom of conscience do not replace each other temporally, but seem to exist together alongside each other at present. Competition between them leads to the complex "cultural wars" and alignments, as they jockey for legal predominance.

This is the story we have to tell.

A FINE BUT ELUSIVE BUTTERFLY

A central issue at the time of the Reformation was freedom of conscience and that is what many people retain—Protestantism is the religion of freedom of conscience. Who can forget the words of Luther before Emperor Charles V at the Diet of Worms in April 1521 that ring across the years? Interrogated by Eck and requested to answer "without horns" and repudiate his books, Luther rejoined in German:

> Since Your Majesty and your lordships desire a simple reply, I will answer without horns and without teeth. Unless I am convicted by Scripture and plain reason (I do not accept the authority of popes and councils, for they have contradicted each other), my conscience is captive to the Word of God. I cannot and I will not recant anything, for to go against conscience is neither safe nor right.

The earliest printed version of these words added "Here I stand, I cannot do otherwise," before concluding with "God help me. Amen." There is, however, no indication of this finale in the transcripts of the Diet, although Roland Bainton suggested in his classic work on Luther that perhaps the witnesses were too moved at the time to record them, and no doubt confusion ensued as Luther left the scene.[3]

---

2. Bauman and Donskis, *Moral Blindness*, 17–49.
3. Bainton, *Here I Stand*, 185–86.

So what is meant by a conscience captive to the Word of God? In spite of the enigmatic nature of the expression, there is no doubt that for Luther a conscience captive to God's Word was one that is truly free, and free from all other authorities.

Freedom of conscience, however, is like a fine but elusive butterfly—difficult to net. Everyone knows what it is, or thinks they do. As part of the democratic mindset it has pride of place in the baggage of human rights campaigners, closely followed by its siblings, freedom of speech and action. However, in spite of the instant intuitive reaction on hearing the word, if you ask almost anyone what it means, they flounder. This is part of Dark Island deception. Should you look up the definitive cultural history on the subject, you will be surprised that it is still to be written.[4] You might fall back on John Bagnell Bury's century-old classic, or Karl Popper's defense of open societies, but even they do not contain a good definition of freedom of conscience.[5] So what does it mean?

Article 9 of the European convention on Human Rights entitled "Freedom of thought, conscience and religion" establishes the right, but strangely without defining what it is:

> 1. Everyone has the right to freedom of thought, conscience and religion; this right includes freedom to change his religion or belief and freedom, either alone or in community with others and in public or private, to manifest his religion or belief, in worship, teaching, practice and observance.
>
> 2. Freedom to manifest one's religion or beliefs shall be subject only to such limitations as are prescribed by law and are necessary in a democratic society in the interests of public safety, for the protection of public order, health or morals, or for the protection of the rights and freedoms of others.[6]

---

4. Two difficulties were encountered in researching this subject. Firstly, the periodization of historical research (supercessionist history) imprisons its flow, and makes the thematic development of ideas over several centuries difficult to trace. Secondly, although freedom of conscience seems ideologically self-evident in the modern West, to my knowledge no histories of its development exist from the time of the Reformation to the present, and only scant references in the standard histories or works on secularization. A limited exception is Lecler, "Liberté de conscience," 370–406.

5. Bury, *History of the Freedom of Thought*; Popper, *Open Society*.

6. Murdoch, *Freedom of Thought*, 4.

To complicate matters, the Siamese twins freedom of conscience and tolerance are often confused, given that it is difficult to speak of one without the other.[7]

Each of the issues involved in the relationship between freedom of conscience, Reformation and secularism is multilayered and complex. The profusion of ideas in the Reformation and following it, the multiplicity of theories and systems, the complexity of situations in both state and church, invite suspicion of simplistic or reductionist appropriations of the past. The danger is praising those who correspond to our ideal, demeaning those who do not, and forgetting the labyrinth of issues they wrestled with in their day. Three forms of complexity can be indicated initially.

COMPLEXITIES

Firstly, there is the realm of definition. Freedom of conscience, like freedom itself, is not a univocal notion; it means different things in different contexts, and this will be the primary focus of this chapter.[8] Its meaning is often taken to be a feature of Western or European culture, related to three core values that have come to the forefront since the Reformation, namely individual freedom and responsibility, objectivity or reason, and the sense of history and progress. These are assumed to be modern European values. However, in our hyper-secular context it is often forgotten that they owe their appearance in a certain measure to the influence of Christianity. Joseph Boot goes as far as to affirm that freedom of conscience and speech has flourished *only* in Christian dominated societies.[9]

However, a further comment is in order. Christians believed they were responsible to God to show care and compassion for others. Henri Blocher quotes Jürgen Habermas, saying that Christianity is the ultimate foundation of liberty, conscience, human rights, and democracy, which are all marks of Western civilization.[10] Conscience as such functions as part of a world-view in the context of an understanding of God, creation, and creatureliness. Freedom of conscience is not semantically neutral, its meaning and its reli-

---

7. In the previous generation Joseph Lecler wrote a fine *Histoire de la tolérance au siècle de la Réforme*. Cf. also Murray, *Problem of Religious Freedom*.

8. Pinckaers, *Sources of Christian Ethics*, 327–78, considers that the notion of freedom itself is not uniform in its expressions and distinguishes the freedom of indifference that produces individualism and the freedom of excellence leading to love of truth and goodness.

9. Boot, *Mission of God*, 313.

10. Blocher comments on these aspects in "Le contexte européen de notre théologie," 9–10, quoting Jürgen Habermas, *Time of Transitions* (New York: Polity, 2006).

gious function mutates as world-view shifts. Today it seems to have become a function of individualistic freedom in general, and when the conscience motif slips away self-conscience is the outcome.

Secondly, Reformation is a very broad term, and how it impacted Western culture is debatable. When speaking about what the Reformation achieved for freedom of conscience, the magisterial Reformers, Luther, Melanchthon, and Calvin are my primary focus, not because the radical Reformation is unimportant, but for reasons of commodity. History rarely validates a clear relationship between one simple cause and the resulting situation. Outcomes are more often the result of multiple factors, including meanders, changes of direction, rapids, and unexpected waterfalls. However, time flows on, as rivers flow to the sea, and to ignore the continuities in the historical process removes meaningfulness from the big picture. So "the Western world today is an extraordinary complex, tangled product of rejections, retentions and transformations of medieval Western Christianity, in which the Reformation era constitutes the critical watershed."[11]

There are many interpretations of the movement initiated by the Reformation and its later developments, including its consequences for human freedoms, and three of these can be mentioned here.[12] Firstly, Charles Taylor, in his monumental work, *A Secular Age*, while recognizing the centrality of the Reformation, subsumes it under broad reformism as "an engine of disenchantment" which "attempts to re-order whole societies."[13] It has become fashionable, in this perspective, and to avoid hagiographic inflation, to attach the adjective "unintended" to the supposed consequences of the Reformation.[14] This is no doubt justifiable with regard to freedom of conscience and human rights. The modern concept of freedom of thought is not patently biblical, nor did it appear on the radar of the sixteenth-century Reformers. It was present only germinally in the first stirrings of secularization in the time of the Enlightenment, before becoming the accepted wisdom of modernism in the West.

Another take on the movement began by Luther sees it as inevitably connected to the rise of modern secularism and freedoms, considered either in a positive or a negative sense. Liberal Protestantism has on occasion implied a quasi-causal relation of progression from the Reformation to the

---

11. Gregory, *Unintended Reformation*, 2.

12. We are not talking about the "tragic necessity of the Reformation" (Pelikan, *Riddle of Roman Catholicism*) debate here.

13. Taylor, *Secular Age*, 77–80.

14. Ibid., 146–58.

modern spirit, linking the spirit of the Reformation to modernism.[15] In this line of argument, justification by faith is often seen as metamorphosing into modern liberties. A positive relationship is established between the thought of the Reformers and the advent of Enlightenment humanism, taking opposing forces, such as the contributions of Castellion, Coornheert, and the radical Reformation, into the broad scope of reforming movements. Hugh Trevor-Roper, for example, argues for the link between the Reformation and Enlightenment: without Calvin there would have been no Voltaire:

> The virtue of Calvinism, in respect of the Enlightenment, may perhaps be reduced to this. As a suit of armour it proved serviceable in battle, and though more uncomfortable to wear, proved easier to discard than the archaic, ornamentally encrusted chain-mail which protected, but also stifled the philosophers of the rival Church.[16]

Perhaps Abraham Kuyper was drawn in this direction as well, for quite different reasons, in spite of his trenchant criticism of the French Revolution, in that he considered the Reformation in relation to modern freedoms, the separation of church and state under the umbrella of the overarching Kingdom, and secularization in the light of sphere sovereignty.[17] The Reformation contributed positively to modern liberties such as freedom of speech and the democratic process.

Classic Roman Catholicism, on the other hand, particularly in former generations, saw the Reformation negatively as being responsible for the ills of modernism, and tended to draw a line linking the Reformation to the Enlightenment, the French Revolution, and modern secularism. The seeds of rebellion, sown in the sixteenth century, were reaped in the Enlightenment from the seventeenth to the nineteenth century, and we are still suffering the effects of that harvest today.[18]

Finally, a certain agnosticism appears legitimate concerning the engendering of modernity by the Reformation. Luther, Calvin, and their peers were people of their time, just as much as we are of ours. Progress, equality, and freedom, including freedom of conscience, were not high on their

---

15. Cf. Troeltsch, *Protestantism and Progress*; Tillich, *Protestant Era*.

16. Trevor-Roper, *Crisis of the Seventeenth Century*, 217–18, chap. 4 on "The Religious Origins of the Enlightenment."

17. Kuyper, *Lectures*, 78–109. On Kuyper and the French Revolution see the articles by James Bratt and Mark Elliott in Eglinton and Harinck, *Neo-Calvinism*.

18. More recent Catholic interpretations moderate this point of view, sometimes linking what is perceived to be negative aspects of the Reformation to theological liberalism. Cf. Bouyer, *Spirit and Forms of Protestantism*.

agenda and the danger of anachronism and of apology is ever present in the interpretation and reconstruction of their contribution. Kuyper, not always praised for his broad-mindedness, is frank enough to say of the Servetus affair, "I not only deplore that one stake, but I unconditionally disapprove of it."[19] When the Reformers spoke about the liberty of the Christian or freedom of conscience what is currently meant by it today, the free-thinking self-conscience, was nowhere in their sights. This is the view I have reached. Direct links, either positive or negative, are tenuous at best, and "unintended consequences" are speculative construals, and have questionable feasibility.

Thirdly, the question of secularism. Secularization theory *à la* Steve Bruce, right or wrong, need not concern us here.[20] Secularization maps "the decline of the social significance of religion" and has many diverse facets.[21] Secularism we take not to be a theory, but the resultant situation, the situation in the West today, which is by no stretch of imagination global. It is well defined by Charles Taylor as the secular age:

> . . . one in which the eclipse of all goals beyond human flourishing becomes conceivable . . . within the range of an imaginable life for masses of people. This is the crucial link between secularity and self-sufficing humanism.[22]

What is the crux of secularism? Answering this question, Larry Siedentop surprisingly sees it as Christianity's gift to the world, its "central egalitarian moral insight":

> It is the belief in an underlying moral equality of humans (that) implies that there is a sphere in which each should be free to make his or her own decisions, a sphere of conscience and free action. That belief is summarised in the central value of classical liberalism: the commitment to "equal liberty." Is this indifference or non-belief? Not at all. It rests on at the firm belief that to be human means being a rational and moral agent, a free chooser with responsibility for one's actions. It puts a premium on conscience rather than the "blind" following of rules. It joins rights with duties to others.[23]

---

19. Ibid., 100.
20. Bruce, *Secularization*, 1–23; cf. Taylor, "Why We Need a Radical Redefinition," 34–59.
21. Wilson, *Religion in Sociological Perspective*, 149.
22. Taylor, *Secular Age*, 19–20; on secularization theory, see 427–36.
23. Siedentop, *Inventing the Individual*, 361.

This optimistic definition of secularism probably ruffles the feathers of Christians and agnostic secularists alike. However, it is interesting that the emphasis here falls on secularism as a complex mode of social governance that encourages the moral equality of free individuals and freedom of conscience, including in religion. As a result of a new moral ordering, secularism is the disenchantment of the world, opening the door to an integral humanism, nature replacing the divine presence, with an accent on discipline and responsibility.[24]

This all seems so plausible, and yet . . . Are the "free choosers" following self-conscience rather than the rule of Christian conscience on a trajectory to freedom? This description of humanity and conscience is lightyears away from the Christian conscience of the Reformers, who probably would have considered it a recipe for disaster, as Christian ideas are secularized and made to function in a way that is contrary to their original intention.

Allow me a final comment about secularism as an outcome. It is sometimes overlooked that the real bite of secularism is not in the realm of ideas but in the realm of law. The process of secularization happens at different speeds on different levels. The order is first philosophical, then sociological, and finally juridical. Secularization is initially a disenchantment with ideas, limited to the free-thinking élite, long before it touches base with the masses. It is conceptual before it is social. Ideas take a while to trickle down in a social sense and change the world-view of the majority. In the end the new ethos impacts the legal sphere, and laws are changed because the majority view has changed. Then the boomerang comes back, and what is legal becomes generally accepted as being right and beneficent. In this development, the truths of Christianity which were widely accepted, albeit implicitly, until the second half of the last century, become a minority position under attack. This happens very rapidly once the legal stage is passed, and is the present experience of many Christians in the West in the realm of personal ethics and lifestyle.[25] Changes in belief lead to changes in law and in political power.[26] Religious conviction, whether Christianity, Islam, humanism, or atheism, is always the power behind the throne.

---

24. Maclure and Taylor, *Secularism and Freedom of Conscience*, 3–4.

25. Berman, *Law and Revolution*, 2:16–17. Berman describes the process: the western legal tradition was founded on Christian belief in a God-given law. Until 1914 "it continued to be widely believed in the West that the ultimate source of authentic positive law are divine law, especially the Ten Commandments, natural law discovered by reason and conscience, and historical tradition expressed in sources such as Magna Carta." A century later, two world wars and the Soviet revolution intervening, this consensus has vanished.

26. Ibid., 380, contrasting his conclusions with Marxian and Weberian theory.

FREEDOM OF CONSCIENCE

The theme of conscience was intensively cultivated in the theology of the Middle Ages. Abelard, Bonaventure, and Thomas Aquinas, together with others such as Alexander of Hales, debated the *scintilla conscientiae*, the light of nature turning humans away from evil to good, and the rights of erroneous conscience.[27] These discussions prepared the way for conscience to come to the forefront in the theology of the Reformers, but differently, as a practical issue, before becoming a prime concern for the Puritans who, like their predecessors, were faced with the problem of the freedom of conscience in the face of hostile authorities.[28] It was not conscience as a natural faculty, "the mind of man passing moral judgments," that primarily concerned them, but restriction of conscience and its rights.

In these often complex discussions, conscience was far from being seen as an autonomous moral capacity. In the Reformers' case, it was not even considered a natural capacity, but was seen in relation to sin's accusation and grace's pardon. The Reformers recovered something of the light of the New Testament use of *syneidesis*, the good as it witnesses to rightness in terms of God's law, a consciousness of being in a right relation with God.[29] So

> the conscience is not an organ separate from the heart with which men believe. The conscience expresses the richness of life in communion with God and the prospect of salvation, which resonates into the deepest regions of man's heart and life, and so leads to a godly boldness.[30]

Some Puritans, who were more influenced by Thomas Aquinas than their continental predecessors, conceived of conscience "as a rational faculty,

---

27. Philosophical theories of conscience are often categorized as moral knowledge, motivation, and reflection theories, which are not mutually exclusive. Christian theories of conscience distinguish *synderesis* (Jerome), the source of moral knowledge, from conscience as a volitional response to moral knowledge (Bonaventure), and for others it is the application of moral knowledge to action (Thomas Aquinas). We leave aside the scholastic discussions about *synderesis*, the nature of the drive to moral good in humankind. See on this Chalmers, *Conscience in Context*, 78–151; and Kirk, *Conscience*, 179–81.

28. Among the Puritans who wrote treatises on conscience the names of William Perkins, William Ames, Samuel Rutherford, Thomas Goodwin, John Owen, and Richard Baxter can be retained among the many writings on this subject. Roger Williams and John Cotton also debated the subject in New England. Cf. Beeke and Jones, *Puritan Theology*, chap. 56.

29. Pierce, *Conscience*.

30. Berkouwer, *Man*, 173.

a power of moral self-knowledge and judgment, dealing with questions of right and wrong, duty and dessert, and dealing with them authoritatively as God's voice." Referring to the form of the word *con-scientia,* joint knowledge or knowledge with, they considered that "the judgments of conscience express the deepest and truest self-knowledge that a man ever has—the knowledge of himself as God knows him."[31]

The ultimate question about freedom of conscience is whether conscience is autonomous or theonomous. The apostle Paul makes the mind and its renewal the lynch-pin for Christian living: "Do not conform any longer to the pattern of this world, but be transformed by the renewing of your mind" (Rom 12:2). New birth brings into spiritual standing with the living God and it never happens without a change of mind. The mind is an agent in ongoing transformation via a biblically-informed conscience.

This is standard fare, but sometimes the fact that God, as a spiritual living being has a mind, a divine and infinite intelligence, characterized by holiness, light, infinite wisdom, and knowledge is insufficiently accented (Ps 94:8–11). God is the ultimate criterion of all truth, and he made humans in his image with some of the attributes and complexities of his divine mind. In spite of the infinite difference, humans have a mind that can think thoughts about God, distinguish truth and error, make decisions that are right or wrong, and communicate with God in prayer. Conscience is active in all these workings of the human mind as a quality truth control. God also controls events in this world because he mysteriously acts via human minds and their workings, whether it be the mind of Adam, Pharaoh, Nebuchadnezzar, the enemies of Jesus, or Saul when he persecuted the church.

As the creator of the human mind, God is the ultimate reference point for its functioning; this determines the nature of the human relationship with God and freedom of conscience before him. Since the mind is created, its capacities for action, including freedom of conscience, are related to the Lordship of God, in three complementary ways:

- God is the *normative* perspective of conscience as God governs human thought through his revelation, both natural and special;
- the factual situation in which human knowledge develops provides a *situational* perspective in which the conscience operates;
- personal experiences under the rule of conscience before God constitute the *existential* aspect of a relationship with God who is present with us and within us by his Spirit.[32]

---

31. Packer, *Among God's Giants*, 142, 140–60.
32. I am using categories developed by Frame, *Systematic Theology*, 32–33.

- Freedom of conscience is therefore the flowering of the mind *coram Deo* in terms of God's revelation in norms, by acting on objective facts, and through human subjectivity.

The writings of Paul and, in particular, the important passage in Romans 2:12–16, are of capital importance in discussions of the workings of conscience. Paul speaks of God's righteous judgment of humans who are outside the pale of biblical special revelation. Verse 14, following from verse 12, states that the Gentiles, although deprived of the special revelation of the written law, know the law of God another way. They are "a law for themselves" having "the requirements of the law written on their hearts" (verse 15). They spontaneously do the "things required by the law" (verse 14). The expression "requirement of the law" (*to ergon tou nomou*) indicates that pagans perform concrete actions which are in accordance with God's law, without the benefit of special revelation. They do what Moses prescribed, motivated by another form of revelation than that which the Jews received: "not a different law . . . but the same law brought to bear upon them by a different method of revelation."[33] The requirements of the law are written on what is deepest and most determinative in the pagans' moral and spiritual being. This itself is not conscience, but it is the material with which conscience works in its witness, and an indication that conscience is the moral discrimination establishing unity in human thought and action. Conscience presupposes a response to God's revelation, even in the case of those who have no access to special revelation. Thus, freedom of conscience can only function correctly when it stands in a relation of freedom to God.

The Preacher found out from his enquiry into the human condition that "God made mankind upright, but men have gone in search of many schemes"; wisdom is to "fear God and do his commandments as the whole duty of man." (Eccl 7:29; 12:13) This conclusion presents humanity as created, integrally fallen, and human responsibility to keep God's law. In the creation conscience is initially characterized by true freedom and the call to responsible action: "whatever among men originates directly from creation is possessed of all the data for its development, in human nature as such."[34] Humans are sovereign under God to exercise responsibility in thought, word, and deed, according to the dictates of good conscience with love for God and the neighbor. True liberty rests on and in obedience to God; rights and responsibilities flow from it and express the sovereign freedom of conscience that defines the individual: "the sovereignty of conscience is the

---

33. Murray, *Romans*, 75; Wells, "Dieu et la conscience," 17–24.
34. Kuyper, *Lectures*, 91.

palladium of all personal liberty, in this sense conscience is never subject to man but always and ever to God Almighty."[35]

Nevertheless, sin works with fatal efficiency. Sin is a revolution in the conscience, an unfree conscience rebellious against God's norms. It perverts the facts and it is captive to the service of self. As a result, humans become dysfunctional with regard to God and suffer from a self-accusing conscience. Human culture as it unfolds is a mixture of created greatness and degraded fallenness, a projection of the reality of human nature on the social world. This presents the regressive framework in which fallen conscience operates. So conscience is either created in its original state, fallen, or in the process of restoration, striving "to take captive every thought to make it obedient to Christ." (2 Cor 10:5) The spirit of the Reformation is not to oppose freedom and authority. The Reformation

> by preaching and practicing absolute submission to God's will, obedience to men in obedience to God, and resistance to man's law insofar as it disagreed with God's law, and by insisting on personal responsibility and independence, prepared the way for freedom of conscience and the right of free enquiry.[36]

Freedom of conscience is not semantically neutral because it is not culturally neutral; it functions in the context of a world-view which is crystallized out of deep heart commitments.[37] Freedom flourishes in the shadow of fundamental commitment, whether it be faith in the living God or something else. Beliefs, ideas, values, and the culture they produce, including its morality and laws, are not neutral, but together express a world-view. Freedom of conscience, like freedom itself, even if almost impossible to portray, will be defined in terms of a precise world-view, over against other perspectives. This is what makes the fundamental difference between freedom of conscience in the Reformers' world-view and in humanism—where is becomes free-thinking under the assumption of neutrality—or in late modernity, where it mutates yet again.

Finally, a further legitimate question about freedom of conscience is unavoidable: is it not simply a pleonasm, redundant in terms of meaning? Does freedom of conscience exist at all? Some scholars express doubts about whether conscience is ever "free." An individual's conscience *per se* is self-witness reactive to a form of commitment, expressed in terms of recognized norms, whether they be Christian, Islamic, free-thinking, postmodern, or

---

35. Ibid., 107.

36. Groen van Prinsterer, *Christian Political Action*, 93.

37. Worldview is defined here as "the set of presuppositions which we hold about the basic makeup of our world." Sire, *Universe Next Door*, 18.

whatever. In practice, a conscience that does not benefit from biblical revelation is stimulated by the realities of general revelation, supplemented by common grace. Non-Christians, including the multitudes living under the sway of other faiths and of atheism, have the input which the apostle Paul accorded to the pagans in Romans 2. Conscience by the norms of natural religion will be good, bad, or dead, according to the New Testament categories.[38] So God has not left himself without witness and nor does their conscience. Freedom of conscience never exists apart from such structures; indifferent freedom of conscience is an illusion.

Conscience is therefore always bound by different forms of belief in the context of a person's world-view, and concrete expressions of freedom of conscience stand against each other. The one that has majority status in a given society will be the one that prevails. Then it behoves the majority in that society to be generous in spirit, respecting the freedom of conscience of the minority and showing tolerance. This was extremely difficult for our ancestors to do; Christianity has been guilty of forms of intolerance which range from inquisition to censorship of the press.[39] Today it is far from evident that political correctness will be any more tolerant of Christian belief than Christians have been to others in the past. This illustrates the fact that more often than not, when most people talk about freedom of conscience they are in fact confusing it with tolerance. Is freedom of conscience not rather like Luther's freedom of the will, something that flatters to deceive, but is never detached from factors that condition it?

THE REFORMATION

Writing to a certain André Dudith in 1570, Theodore Beza replied to a question about freedom of conscience: "Do we say that freedom of conscience is permissible? Not in the least, it is a diabolical dogma if it is thought to be the liberty to worship God simply as one wishes."[40] No doubt for Beza, as for Calvin, liberty of conscience was even more reprehensible when it argued in favor of libertarian attitudes along the lines of Rabelais. This negative attitude to freedom is certainly offensive to us, but it illustrates something in Calvin's successor which Olivier Millet also discerns in Calvin himself:

---

38. 1 Tim 1:3–5, 8, 18–20; Titus 1:15–16; Heb 9:9, 14; 10:22; 13:18; 1 Pet 3:16; 1 Cor 4:3–4; 2 Cor 1:12.

39. One of the freedoms championed by Puritanism was freedom of press, as in John Milton's 1644 tract *Areopagitica . . . or the Liberty of Unlicenc'd Printing*.

40. Théodore de Bèze, *Correspondance de Théodore de Bèze*, I, 179, quoted in Guggisberg et al., *Liberté*, 1.

> . . . liberty of conscience in the modern sense is avoided or rejected, at the point at which Calvin seems to establish the right of the individual conscience to judge the validity of all laws by his doctrine of conscience as a witness to natural law.[41]

Why is this the case? It is so because freedom of conscience is not the same as free-thinking and tolerance. Whether for Luther, Calvin, or the Puritans, the conscience is personal and is either alive to the gospel and the Word of God or not.

This description puts the problem of the Reformation in a nutshell. It concerns the believer's conscience and its rights before God, which are primary. The conscience is sovereign, but it exists in a broader context of revelation, natural law, and public order. The challenge arises when faithful believers finds themselves in opposition to the establishment. What then is to be done? Conscience must be followed over against the authority whether of church or state, when public conformity to biblical truth is absent there. The Reformers' ideal was that public order *ought to* recognize God's truth and establish it, or at least to seek for concord in society. When this is not the case, then the rights of conscience take priority for the individual who is called to be faithful to God, and they must be respected by the powers that be. So the Reformers' standpoint was not freedom of conscience as we know it, but freedom of the biblical conscience, and at best non-infringement on its rights, when this is not the majority view in society. The practical way to achieve this was *cuius regio, eius religio* ("whose realm, his religion"), meaning that the religion of the ruler was to be the religion of those ruled. At the Peace of Augsburg in 1555, which ended a period of armed conflict between Roman Catholic and Protestant forces in the Holy Roman Empire, the rulers of the German-speaking states and Emperor Charles V agreed to accept this principle.

LUTHER

> From the scholasticism of the Middle Ages Luther inherited a notion of conscience which made it secondary to the judgment of reason (*synderesis*).[42] He diverged from his predecessors in teaching that conscience is not the skill of applying the rational principles of natural law and knowledge, but it is the religious root of humanity, the bearer of their relationship with

---

41. Millet, "Le thème de la conscience libre chez Calvin," in ibid., 32.
42. Lohse, "Conscience and Authority," 59.

God, which shapes the exercise of the faculties. Thus Luther subordinated reason to conscience and conscience to faith. As Harold Berman says, conscience, in Lutheran theology, is derived directly from faith; it not only applies the principles of divine and natural law to concrete situations, but also is a source and an embodiment of our understanding of those principles.[43]

Luther believed that the Ten Commandments were a summary of natural law, accessible to pagans and Christians alike, which applied not only to citizens directly and personally, but also positively through the civil ruler and the law. They are divinely ordained for the earthly realm alone, not for the heavenly, and therefore obedience to them cannot lead to God. Knowledge of God depends on faith alone, as the normative principle, Scripture being the formal principle. Moreover, in Luther's view to those outside the gospel and faith, natural law is hidden by false teaching and also by the wiles of Satan.[44]

So there are two kinds of conscience, related to the law and the gospel. Luther described conscience as a capacity for judging good and evil, more a power to receive instruction than a power of autonomous self-legislation.[45] As part of humanity's fallen condition, conscience itself cannot lead to God by any form of natural obedience, and it can only be bound by the Word of God. Divine and natural law, as well as any positive laws derived from them, serve to make people aware of their outward duty in the civil sense, and their inward inability before God, because salvation depends on grace, not on the works of the law. A conscience imprisoned by the pope, by unjust laws, by sin, and superstition is a wrong conscience. It is the witness of conscience to itself which is made on the basis of outward things, the works of the law, and leads directly to a false idea of God and an erroneous theology of glory.

The theology of the cross, on the other hand, contradicts what is apparent and natural, and leads to God by what is invisible to the natural eye, through the suffering of the cross. The gospel of the cross brings "the great fire of the love of God for us, whereby the heart and conscience become happy, secure and content."[46] This puts the "lone voice" of conscience, freed by the gospel and Scripture, above all earthly powers. "Where a man's conscience remains fallen, Luther wrote, his reason will also inevitably be

---

43. Berman, *Law and Revolution*, 2:75. I am following Berman's presentation here, 73–77. Cf. Lecler, *Histoire de la tolérance*, 161–67.

44. Zachman, *Assurance of Faith*, 25–28.

45. Ibid., 28.

46. Luther, "A Brief Instruction on What to Look for and Expect in the Gospels" (1521) in Lull, *Luther's Theological Writings*, 106.

darkened, distorted, and deficient," but where redeemed "his rational apprehensions will also be enhanced."[47] Moreover, "nature wants to be certain before she believes, grace believes before she perceives."[48]

MELANCHTHON

Philip Melanchthon, the "teacher of Germany," took up Luther's insights as to the corruption of human nature and the limitations of reason, and with it the distortion of the law of nature. If the Ten Commandments are the ultimate source and summary of natural law, and a model for positive law enacted by rulers, human reason can discern divine and natural law only when guided by faith.[49] Human traditions and laws are not finally binding, because only God is the ultimate lawgiver. Melanchthon states:

> They can be tolerated only insofar as the conscience remains untroubled by them: "We ought to obey God rather than men" (Acts 5:29). Therefore when traditions obscure faith, when they are an occasion for sin, they should be violated. . . . But those who have had the freedom of their consciences stolen from them through traditions become slaves of men. For just as Christian freedom is freedom of the conscience, so also the slavery of Christians is the slavery of their conscience.[50]

True freedom of conscience is the "freedom of the conscience that understands by faith that its sin has been forgiven" and "nothing obligates the conscience except God's Law (*ius divinum*)."[51]

CALVIN

Much has been made of the differences between Luther and Calvin, including regarding their teaching on conscience. Randall Zachman, in his work on the two Reformers, *The Assurance of Faith,* deals with many of these problems. In the realm of conscience Calvin looks for certainty in God's sight in the good conscience of the believer's true obedience, whereas Luther insisted on an assurance of conscience based on the testimony of

---

47. Quoted by Berman, *Law and Revolution,* 2:75.
48. Quoted by Zachman, *Assurance of Faith,* 19.
49. Berman, *Law and Revolution,* 2:78–80.
50. Melanchthon, *Commonplaces,* 178.
51. Ibid., 327, 388.

forgiveness of sins spoken by the Word of God in the gospel.[52] Zachman concludes that in spite of different accents certainty of conscience for both Reformers lies in the grace of God revealed to the conscience by the external witness of the Word and the internal witness of the Spirit. A good conscience does not tell us about God's grace, but about the sincerity of our response. "The testimony of the good conscience builds on the foundation of God's witness to us in the gospel and cannot replace that foundation."[53] Both Luther and Calvin were more aware of hypocritical attitudes of the conscience than of those to do with tolerance. Luther was more concerned with good works as the motor of hypocrisy, whereas Calvin was troubled by practical non-conformity to one's outward profession.

Calvin deals with Christian freedom in chapter 14 of the French 1541 edition of the *Institutes* and expanded his discussion in the 1559 version. In both, he presents three parts of Christian freedom. Firstly, conscience rises above the law's righteousness to seek assurance of justification before God. Secondly, following one of the themes in Luther's treatise *On Christian Freedom* (1520), conscience is free from the constraints and practices of the law to be obedient to the will of God. Finally, following Melanchthon's *Loci*, comes freedom of conscience in things indifferent, customs or traditions not demanded by Scripture.[54] In the 1559 edition Calvin expands the conclusion on conscience and the two kingdoms: "there are in man two worlds, over which different kings and different laws have authority." Because Christians have their consciences set free in God's sight, they remain subject to outward human laws for conscience's sake. Conscience is "a certain mean between God and man" and if works concern humans in the civil sphere, conscience regards God.[55] This together with the doctrine of the two kingdoms, inspired by Luther, indicates that for Calvin, freedom of conscience is primarily a spiritual reality, being free to obey God's Word in all areas of life. It is the solitary witness of the law of God, and Calvin can say "My conscience is subjected to the observance of this law, though there were not another man in the world."[56] The moral law of God expressed in human conscience is above all human laws, and is therefore a judge of validity and equity in the realm of positive, religious, moral, and political law. Nor can conscience ever be invoked against God's law in natural or biblical revela-

---

52. Zachman, *Assurance of Faith*, 1–5.

53. Ibid., 6. Zachman takes this to be different from the practical syllogism that came later with Beza, because of an inconsistency that both Reformers overlooked, 6–7.

54. Melanchthon's *Commonplaces* deal with this in a section on scandals, 392–95.

55. Calvin, *Institutes* III.xix.15–16.

56. Ibid., III.xix.16.

tion. As Olivier Millet concludes, by empowering the Christian in the realm of liberty, Calvin gave people control over their lives and, by his doctrine of conscience, unintentionally prepared the way for future resistance.[57]

In conclusion, in the light of the teaching of Jesus and Paul, why is there so little room for tolerance in the magisterial Reformers? Obviously their background, past precedents, and the practices of the times resulted in an atrophy that is hardly excusable today. Joseph Lecler indicates that Luther follows Chrysostom and Jerome in his early works, saying that heretics should not by torn up and burned, like the weeds in Jesus' parable of the harvest, and that he was hostile to the use of force or inquisition against unbelief.[58] But that was soon to change. The problem was Caesaropapism, the incapacity to conceive of another form of belief existing alongside the sole authorized one in a national state. Calvin and those who followed him were inconsistent, because, as Kuyper stated,

> by praising aloud liberty of conscience Calvinism has in principle abandoned every absolute characteristic of the visible Church... Only the system of a free Church in a free State, may be honored from a Calvinistic standpoint.

He added "Rome perceived how liberty of conscience must loosen the foundations of the unity of the visible Church, and therefore she opposed it."[59] The Reformation advocated the principle of freedom of conscience, but lacked the experience and maturity to put it into practice in the social sphere.

THE ADVENT OF SECULARISM

In his analysis of Plato's sociology in *The Open Society and Its Enemies*, Karl Popper makes two comments that are typical of secularism:

> If you accept the "Christian" ethics of equality and toleration and freedom of conscience only because of its claim to rest upon divine authority, then you build on a weak basis; for it has been only too often claimed that inequality is willed by God, and that we must not be tolerant with unbelievers... The doctrine of the autonomy of ethics is independent of the problem of religion,

---

57. Millet, "Conscience libre," 36–37.
58. Lecler, *Histoire de la tolérance*, 164–67.
59. Kuyper, *Lectures*, 102, 106.

but compatible with, and perhaps even necessary for, any religion that respects the individual conscience.[60]

The secular attitude and its notion of freedom of conscience are constructed on this basis. Three factors sustain comment:

- Human thought and actions, including freedom of conscience, are autonomous and reasonable, or objective; religion must be built on the basis of autonomy as an expression of human subjectivity, not on any divine reality out there;
- Popper does not demonstrate why it is assumed to be weak to build freedom of conscience on divine authority, particularly if we are talking of the living, all-controlling God of the Bible;
- Finally, have the autonomous ethics of Marxism or National Socialism done any better in being tolerant with "unbelievers," given their vicious assaults on human liberty? Intolerance is a trans-ideological feature of human sin.

Popper is typical of secularist attitudes, whatever their multifarious forms. He has no idea that religion (in this case Christianity) is not reducible to a subjective human projection, a feeble understanding of God, and no recognition of the depth and length of human sinfulness. These three constants of humanist secularism have characterized human-centered culture in various ways since the Enlightenment. Relativism and naturalism follow in their slipstream. They also make it impossible for humanists to understand where fundamentalist terrorists are coming from. Humanists just don't have a handle on the nature of religious commitment.

Secularism arose indirectly out of the magisterial Reformers' failure to deal squarely and biblically with freedom of conscience and tolerance, other than by claiming liberty for Protestant worship. One of the earliest civil expressions of tolerance was the Edict of Nantes, signed by king Henry IV of France in 1598, which put an end to the bloody religious conflict between Roman Catholics and Protestants that had plagued France for thirty years.[61] Those who penned the document held the view current at the time, that it was wrong to coerce free individuals against their conscience in the worship of God, which was seen as sacred and to be respected.

---

60. Popper, *Open Society*, 1:55.

61. Edward Langerac defines tolerance as "the enduring of something disagreeable. Thus it is not indifference toward things that do not matter and it is not broad-minded celebration of differences. It involves a decision to forgo using powers of coercion." Quoted by Carson, *Intolerance*, 87.

Arguments in favor of freedom of conscience and tolerance were advanced following the lead of the humanists of the time, often by the opponents of the Reformers. Obviously the polemic on heresy which followed the Servetus affair (Sebastien Castellion against Calvin and Beza) occupies an important place in the history of tolerance. Fundamentally, the critics of the Reformers pointed out the false zeal of pursuing heretics, its eschatological impatience, the wrong use of earthly powers in a spiritual disagreement, and dubious exegesis of the Old Testament. Lecler also notices a doctrinal indifference in the critics which is more accented than what one finds in Erasmus, for example.[62] A tendency in this direction, which precedes the spirit of the Enlightenment, is illustrated by Dirck Coornhert's imaginary *Synod on Freedom of Conscience,* which follows the lead of Castellion.[63] Coornhert was hardly a rationalist, but he was much influenced by the tradition of Christian humanism of his time, the dignity of humanity, and the golden rule, and he tended to relativize objective truth.

In the century following the Reformation, religious minorities in the European countries refused to be silenced or crushed, following the example of the Huguenots.[64] Liberties were won not by concessions to skepticism, but out of religious conviction and resistance. In England freedom of conscience had its advocates, such as John Milton's *Areopagitica* (1644) and John Locke's *Letter on Tolerance* (1689), neither of which defended freedom of public worship for Roman Catholics, as well as the writings of the Puritan independents, Henry Jacob, John Robinson, John Goodwin, John Owen, and in New England, Roger Williams. The opposing position was ably represented by the presbyterian Samuel Rutherford who penned *A free disputation against pretended liberty of conscience* (1649).[65] These debates on freedom of conscience were often conducted in the context of discussions about the relation of state and church, Erastianism, and disestablishment, and they culminated in the settlement of the Glorious Revolution of 1688.[66]

62. Lecler, *Histoire de la tolérance,* 322–31. See also Guggisberg, "Haïr ou instruire les hérétiques? La notion d'hérétique chez Sébastien Castellion et sa situation dans l'exil bâlois." In Guggisberg et al., *Liberté,* 65–81. Zweig's *The Right to Heresy* gives a lively if tendentious and dated account, in which Zweig's invective against Calvin is a fair match for the Reformer.

63. Coornhert, *Synod on the Freedom*; Lecler, *Histoire de la tolérance,* 628–40.

64. Cf. Bonney and Trim, *Persecution.*

65. Helm, "Rutherford," 57–74.

66. Carson, *Intolerance,* 104–12. "The point to observe in these debates between, on the one hand, Williams, Owen, and Milton, and, on the other, Rutherford, is that tolerance and intolerance were being debated in the framework of larger issues about the common good, about the nature of truth and authority, about the relationship between church and state." 108.

On the continent, an outstanding advocate of freedom of conscience was Pierre Bayle.[67] Contrary to Locke, Bayle sought to establish tolerance on the basis of freedom of conscience. An orthodox Calvinist, and author of a four-volume philosophical dictionary, Bayle dared to go against the current orthodoxy and to criticize Augustine's interpretation of Luke 14:23 and the intolerance of Calvin and Beza in a treatise entitled *Philosophical commentary on the words of Jesus Christ: "Constrain them to enter"* (1686). To establish his position, Bayle drew on Thomas Aquinas's argument on the rights of the erroneous conscience: even if the conscience errs in judgment its ultimate conviction (the *dictamen*) must be respected, because the erring conscience acquires the same formal right in error as the right conscience does in truthfulness.[68] By putting the two forms of conscience on the same level, Bayle theoretically established the right to error, implying a parity of orthodoxy and heresy, and logically accepting the social legitimacy of papists and atheists. Heretics, according to Bayle, are to be instructed in the truth and respected if they continue to be unreceptive. Heresy acquires civil rights, and therefore is to be tolerated, a position that did not gladden the hearts of the Reformed orthodox, particularly Bayle's colleague Pierre Jurieu.[69]

Bayle marks a watershed in the pre-Enlightenment discussions of conscience and tolerance. After him the emphasis shifted from freedom of conscience, a moral issue, to epistemological freedom of thought. Coercion of ideas became unthinkable in the realm of private opinion, demonstration by reason became crucial, including in so far as religious truths are concerned. Tolerance was recognized as a positive political and moral attitude in the public sphere, the external realm of power where negotiation between parties goes on.[70] "This dualism," says Carson, "this fundamental contrast between the objective public sphere and the subjective private sphere, has become one of the foundations of many contemporary notions of religious toleration and religious liberty."[71]

---

67. Mario Turchetti, "La liberté de conscience et l'autorité du magistrat au lendemain de la Révocation," in Guggisberg et al., *Liberté*, 289–367; Labrousse, *Pierre Bayle*.

68. Thomas Aquinas, *Summa Theologiae* II.19.1-6, 196–97; Lecler, *Histoire de la tolérance*, 117–26. Cf. Johnstone, "Conscience and Error," 163–74.

69. Turchetti, "Liberté de conscience," 308–30. Jacques Saurin, using a distinction from William Ames, criticized Bayle for confusing the absolute and hypothetical obligations of conscience, 328.

70. Bernard Cottret, "La tolérance et la liberté de conscience à l'épreuve (1685–1688)." In Guggisberg et al., *Liberté*, 269–76.

71. Carson, *Intolerance*, 111. Carson is particularly commenting here on the dualism of Descartes and Locke.

EVALUATION

The advent of secularism is marked by what Charles Taylor calls a shift in the understanding of what "fullness" is considered to be. It involves a change "that did not happen overnight" from "a condition in which our highest spiritual and moral aspirations point us inescapably to God (and) make no sense without God, to one in which they can be related to a host of different sources, and frequently are referred to sources which deny God."[72] It is a 180° change of direction from what Taylor calls "enchantment," the situation in which God was seen as directly present in the world, implicated in society, an active force, to the new sense of self and its place in the cosmos, which is no longer "porous" but becomes "buffered." However, "it took more than disenchantment to produce the buffered self; it was also necessary to have confidence in our own powers of moral ordering."[73] That is what secularism is all about, human power and confidence to get on with things by themselves.

The arrival of secularism marks a movement from a society in which the collective life-experience was belief in God as the default position to one in which the presumption of unbelief liberates the individual from the tutelage of God.[74] This involves a deep change in the notion of conscience and freedom of conscience, away from *con-science,* knowing with the witness of God and before God, an outward reference which defines fullness in terms of right and wrong, good and evil, and which also implies a shared social faith. The focus of freedom of conscience shifts to an inner reference, freedom of thought, experiencing the good, feeling that it is right, an "inside" life-reference which is individual and private. Conscience becomes autonomous: "the self-sufficiency of the individual over social responsibilities was exalted to a sacred creed."[75] Today we are at the end of the line of secularization that began at the Enlightenment, which has "run its course and excluded transcendence, (and) left us with meagre crumbs of relativism, subjectivism, political pluralism, and a concomitant return to esoteric pagan spirituality that is successfully merging itself with humanistic 'science.'"[76]

---

72. Taylor, *Secular Age*, 26, 28.

73. Ibid., 27; Taylor is against "substraction" theories of secularization, which only tell half the story. Secularism is not a loss of something, but gaining a new sense of human "flourishing," a long, complex, and multi-layered process.

74. Bosch, *Transforming Mission*, 267–68.

75. Ibid., 267.

76. Boot, *Mission of God*, 445.

The movement to autonomy progressively replaced references to the Christian faith in God with faith in human personhood. Subsequent developments tended to accentuate either human rational abilities or alternatively, human feelings and experiences. Deism, the religion of the Enlightenment, substituted a belief in designer reason and the supremacy of public order for the Bible and divine law.[77] This was not a replacement of faith and superstition by reason and science, says Taylor, but a moral distaste for a God who is an agent in history, a stance that was not based on facts but "flows from an interpretative grid."[78] Its attractive feature is that it fosters the illusion that "the agent is free, unconstrained by authority." However, this is not freedom in the place of authority, but the introduction of a new form of authority, that of a self-imposed law in the context of what is taken to be reasonable. Freedom of conscience is bound by what is reasonable in an impersonal natural order. Taylor comments on the current that had Deism at its fountainhead:

> Modernity, as the era of freedom, can be seen to be congruent with our relating ourselves to an impersonal law, not to the goals which arise out of a personal relation. All these forms of impersonal order: the natural, the political, and the ethical can be made to speak together against orthodox Christianity, in its understanding of God as personal agent. There is a certain idea of human dignity . . . which seems incombinable with Christian faith.[79]

Freedom of conscience in this context becomes a freedom disengaged from God, free thought in the context of a "buffered" self, with control over human destiny, reason generating truth, and dignity attained by the self. In this context, which Taylor calls the Modern Moral Order, humans become a new personal god for themselves, in an impersonal order.[80] As Julien de La Mettrie said in his *L'homme machine (Man as a Machine)* published anonymously in 1748: "Deaf to all other voices, tranquil mortals (as atheists) would follow only the spontaneous dictates of their own being, the only commands . . . which can lead us to happiness."[81]

Deism is a halfway house to unbelief, because it is irreligious practical atheism and it "deactivates God."[82] Human autonomy and conscience strand

77. Berman, *Law and Revolution*, 2:17.
78. Taylor, *Secular Age*, 270–75.
79. Ibid., 283.
80. Ibid., 293.
81. De la Mettrie, quoted by McGrath, *Twilight of Atheism*, 33.
82. Bavinck, *Reformed Dogmatics*, 2:603.

the human subject alone in the universe, in an impersonal natural order, which is the frontier for human thought and action. In this mechanical world, human self-conscience is comparable to light in the natural world; the contents of the human agent's mental world are self-luminous. Put humorously, conscience is simply reason lecturing in sabbatical mode.[83] Emmanuel Kant, as an heir of the autonomous mind of the Enlightenment, is well portrayed by novelist Iris Murdoch (1919–1990), commenting on his *Groundwork of the Metaphysic of Morals* (1785):

> How recognizable, how familiar to us is the man so beautifully portrayed in the *Grundlegung (Groundwork)*, who confronted even with Christ turns away to consider the judgement of his own conscience and to hear the voice of his own reason. . . this man is with us still, free, independent, lonely, powerful, rational, responsible, brave, the hero of so many novels and books of moral philosophy.[84]

Is it not telling that Murdoch equates *conscience* with the "voice of his own *reason*"? Although her punditry is more poetical than philosophical, she hits the nail on the head by presenting conscience as a duty to oneself, the process of self-examination and evaluation which is distinct from the faculty of moral judgment.

Autonomous reason leads to a reduction of conscience to the individual subject and its self-consciousness. Rather than procuring a transcendent liberty of conscience, as in Christianity, reason hedges conscience in by the possible, in terms which are either subjective or objective, personal or scientific. On the one hand it promotes the utilitarian "greatest happiness principle" of liberalism. Freedom of conscience is the first article of the liberal creed of a John Stuart Mill, a free expression necessary to the well-being of humankind: "liberty of thought and feeling, absolute freedom of opinion and sentiment on all subjects, practical or speculative, scientific, moral, or theological."[85] Limits are set solely by "the moral rules which forbid mankind to hurt one another" and provide protection from being harmed by others.[86] The ultimate sanction of utilitarian morality is not duty and conscience but, with further progress, the social inclination of humankind.

---

83. Ryle, *Concept of Mind*, 141, 288. Skeptical about "the ghost in the machine," Ryle states critically: "The mind can 'see' or 'look at' its own operations in the 'light' given off by themselves." And he concludes, "The myth of consciousness is a piece of para-optics."

84. Murdoch, *Sovereignty of the Good*, 80, quoted by Taylor, *Sources of the Self*, 84.

85. John Stuart Mill, *On Liberty*, quoted by O'Rourke, *John Stuart Mill*, 77, 162.

86. Ibid., 111, 118.

On the other hand there is the "scientific" approach inspired by Hegel, in which the good is a social virtue based on historicist moral theory:

> the true principles of morality, or rather of social virtue (are) in opposition to false morality; the History of the World occupies a higher ground than that morality which is personal in character—the conscience of individuals, their particular will and mode of action . . .[87]

For Marxism conscience is class-conditioned, and true conscience is scientific historical awareness: Marx famously affirmed that "it is not the consciousness of men that determines their existence but their social existence that determines their consciousness."[88] Freud subsequently applied rational causality to individual psychological development, thus transforming conscience into the socially interiorized superego.

The reductions of rationalism are juxtaposed, without abandoning autonomy, by the freeing of conscience in mystery, which liberates imagination from constraints. The usual suspect is Jean-Jacques Rousseau. He argues that whereas arid reason stifles the inner voice of the good and the true, nature is a reservoir of authenticity, of pristine innocent desire and love of the good. "Everything is good coming from the Author of things, but everything is debased in man's hands" is the opening sentence of Book I of Rousseau's treatise on education, *Emile* (1762). Humans suffer loss when reason intervenes to make us lose contact with the original impulses of conscience, which are good and innocent. Conscience speaks the unadulterated language of nature to us, but it is stifled by social conditioning. In *The Profession of Faith of a Savoyard Vicar*, we hear Rousseau on conscience:

> Conscience! Conscience! Divine instinct, immortal and heavenly voice; sure guide for an ignorant and limited being, yet intelligent and free; infallible judge of good and evil, which makes man like God, you make the excellence of his nature and the morality of his actions . . .[89]

Rousseau was not a primitivist, as Charles Taylor points out. He defined freedom and morality in terms of one another, which implied listening to

---

87. Hegel, *The Philosophy of Law*, §345, quoted by Popper, *Open Society*, 2:64.

88. Marx, Preface to *A Contribution to the Critique of Political Economy* (1859), 2.. Cf. Fromm, *Marx's Concept of Man*, chap. 3.

89. Jean-Jacques Rousseau, *The Profession of Faith of a Savoyard Vicar*, in *Emile* IV (1762), quoted in Taylor, *Sources of the Self*, 358.

the inner voice: "true sentiments define what is the good; since the *élan* of nature in me is the good, it is this which has to be consulted to discover it."[90]

There is, however, another perspective to take into consideration. The Romantic movement bore witness to a shift of perception in its view of the nature in which humanity participated, from the designer *cosmos* of Galileo and Newton, fixed and bounded, to an evolving *universe* unlimited in time and space. The mystery of all, beyond the bounds of rationality, opened up new depths to explore. Conscience became unbounded and freedom was found in unfettered imagination. As Taylor says of the innerness of Romanticism: "The rediscovery of what I really am within is made possible by the resonance I feel with the great current of nature outside of me. This idea of resonance is also given its sense by the dark genesis" in the abyss of space and time.[91] The turn away from Enlightenment rationalism in the nineteenth-century search for mystery did not, however, lead back to Christian transcendence but led, on the contrary, to pagan forms of pantheism and to the mystery of the oneness of all things, often poetically expressed.

Objective rational consciousness and the imagination of mystery hastened the advent of the modern secular world as they cross-pollinated each other, acting in cahoots against the Christian world-view. They fostered deeper forms of materialism and unbelief and gave new scope for imagining a world detached from belief in a personal God. Freedom of conscience was redefined as consciousness in an ongoing historical process, or consciousness of the creative possibilities of inner exploration and new self-knowledge. Both perspectives leave the primitive world of Christian revelation behind, to progress to higher planes of human flourishing. Together these attitudes set the scene for modern unbelief. The self is "buffered" against intrusions either in the historical process or by interference in the depths of nature's abyss. Any claims made to revelation can only be of private interest because they do not belong to the shared public knowledge and experience of human beings. Religious particularities and beliefs exist in the private domain. The public forum is one of autonomous shared rationality or shared feelings—neutral, self-evident, and progressive. Human beings will be happier in the search for themselves. "Miserable-sinner Christianity" is buried by the rationalists.[92] Freedom of conscience is far from freedom from sin with a God-centered world-view and a goal in the service of God and our fellow human beings. It has kafkaed into a self-consciousness of unlimited human freedom, adventure, and challenge.

90. Ibid., 359–63, 362.
91. Taylor, *Secular Age*, 344.
92. Cf. Warfield's articles on "'Miserable-Sinner Christianity,'" in *Works*, 7:113–301.

THREE NIGHTMARES

Growth may have been tortuous, but from these seeds come the fruits of Western secularism. The abyss has become a volcano, as the Romantic ethos prevailed in the exclusive self-humanism of the last fifty years. In this liquid situation, described by some as beyond post-modern, three nightmares threaten freedom of conscience, at least for what is left of it.[93]

Firstly, the sovereign secular state, an ideal which accommodates many world-views and multiculturalism through exclusive neutrality, is in crisis. In the area of the economy it is powerless over global crises, in security it is incapable of protecting its citizens against terrorism, its frontiers have become like sieves, and social media undermine respect for the political process. Politics everywhere assumes a new vocation of limited governance and social engineering. The freedom of conscience of individuals is overridden by lobby interests. The right to think and to say what one thinks is threatened. Republican or national values are often referred to, but there is no consensus over core convictions.[94] The notion of "public good" crushes opposition. No longer is the totalitarianism of the majority a threat, but the lobbying minority. When multinationals and embassies fly the rainbow flag, we see where real power lies. Freedom of conscience is in danger from manipulation.

Secondly, having mutated into free-thinking, social consciousness, and self-conscience, freedom of conscience becomes the obligation to be tolerant, even of things recently considered intolerable. All sorts of behavior demand acceptance in the name of libertarian rights and equality, but those who demand tolerance seldom recognize the right of objection of conscience to their life-style or ideologies. Donald Carson distinguishes between old and new tolerance.[95] Toleration in the context of present social pluralism is freedom for everything that does not claim to be exclusively true or right. As nothing is true in a context of moral relativism, tolerance no longer functions in terms of ethical considerations, but only in terms of all things being equally acceptable. Those who disagree with the preferences of others find themselves classed as intolerant fundamentalists, racists, bigots, or fascists, and are exposed to inquisitorial intolerance by those who claim to be victimized. Christianophobia is on the rise.[96] It is difficult to

---

93. Bauman and Bordini, *State of Crisis*, 76–87, claim that the postmodern period ran from 1970 to around 2000, but no longer exists. Cf. Carson, *Intolerance*, 129–32.

94. Maclure and Taylor, *Secularism and Freedom of Conscience*, 11–12.

95. Carson, *Intolerance*, 28–29, 133, 167–68.

96. Yancey, *Hostile Environment*, gives ample documentation. Cf. George, *Conscience*.

debate anything serenely. Buzz words become argument-stoppers and occlude real moral dilemmas.[97] Freedom of conscience is under attack from the law of lawlessness.

Finally, hyper-individualism is paradoxically collective suffocation. When individual human flourishing is feelgoodism, all that matters is "how does it feel?" Facts are superfluous and what counts is what flips the emotional switch. In the "culture of authenticity" individuals have the inalienable right to make what they want of themselves, with virtual bling as the norm. Status is determined by stuff, the stuff one consumes, the stuff one does with one's body, the stuff that is awesome. Social status is my stuff in the eye of the beholder, preferably designer stuff. The sideways look at others confirms that one is stuff correct, but a hard look in the mirror would show that we have been stuffed by the ridicule of it all. Conscience has disappeared into self-conscience according to the gospel of stuff, enslaved by materialism to a zombyesque existence in the kingdom of whatever.[98] The flourishing of emotivism is the end point of moral decay—at least for the time being—and the failure of Enlightenment rationality.[99]

The hypermodern digital age brings the suppression of historical consciousness, with a feeling of rootlessness and aimlessness. The past, and God as a thing of the past, have become an arcane irrelevance to what is going on in the here and now. Historicity is limited to the immediate "breaking news," stranding us in the present, out of touch with the past, the world we have lost because there is no contact with it. All this deeply impacts the freedom of conscience in a way that often escapes our notice. No longer accountable to time-tested institutions, to moral virtues recognized since time began, to social values (with the demise of the Marxian proletariat), to national identity with globalization and globetrotting, the human conscience is subjected to the pressures of subjectivism and superficial self-promotion. An invasive moral blindness has as its counterpart the absence of compassion in progressive liberal societies.[100]

CONCLUSION

The volcano of postmodernism is emitting a lot of ash, but how long can it go on before it blows its core or becomes extinct? Equally menacing is another fact: "the apostasy of Christianity is exposing the entire West to the

---

97. Taylor, *Secular Age,* 473–504.
98. Gregory, *Unintended Reformation,* 377.
99. MacIntyre, *After Virtue,* 8–10, 37–38.
100. Bauman and Donskis, *Moral Blindness,* 94–130.

risk of a grave cultural and political crisis, and perhaps even to a collapse of civilization."[101]

Cuban novelist Leonardo Padura recounts in his book on the assassination of Trotsky how, in 1934, the Bolshevik revolutionary Nikolai Bukharin wrote in *Izvestia* about

> the illegality of any type of dissidence within the Soviet Union, while at the same time repeating Stalin's motto that opposition only leads to counter-revolution, and exemplified it as the degradation of degenerate fascists.[102]

Do not the nightmares of political correctness embroil us in a new Stalinism today? Religious freedom and conscience, the rule of law, church, and family liberties are increasingly violated by state snoopers, by the lobbies of victim-minorities and by media trolling.

From a Christian perspective, world-view is shaped by the idea that the best times in the history of humanity are those that come closest to the spiritual blessings of Pentecost, when God shed forth on his people the grace of his new and final covenant, and with those blessings, life, freedom, and hope for the nations. However, no historical *kairos* is utopia, the hoped-for future, because Christ's Kingdom is not of this world. (John 18:36) The spiritual reign of Christ, which will ultimately be established at the *parousia*, is the teleological point to which all history flows. Between the times history is a kaleidoscope of developing patterns. Sometimes, we are nearer the *parousia* in a purely temporal perspective, but we are further from it in a spiritual sense, because we are further from the Spirit of Pentecost and the apostolic message. The revival of the Reformation was both nearer and further from the *parousia* than we are today. However, seeds sown by the reforming Fathers contribute to the growth of history that leads God's people inevitably to the coming of Christ.

Assurance of the teleological finality of history will condition our evaluation of progress in both freedom of conscience and secularism. What the *Zeitgeist* sees as progressive, we will at times consider regressive. Christ's people are for no compromises of conscience with the spirit of the age, because there is no truth greater than that of the Lord Jesus: "you will know the truth, and the truth will set you free." (John 8:32)

---

101. Pera, *Call Ourselves Christians*, 62.
102. Padura, *Man Who Loved*, 140.

BIBLIOGRAPHY

Aquinas, Thomas. *Summa Theologiae: A Concise Translation*. Translated by Timothy McDermott. London: Methuen, 1989.
Bainton, Roland H. *Here I Stand: A Life of Martin Luther*. New York: Abingdon, 1950.
Bauman, Zygmunt, and Leonidas Donskis. *Moral Blindness: The Loss of Sensitivity in Liquid Modernity*. Cambridge: Polity, 2013.
Bauman, Zygmunt, and Carlo Bordini. *State of Crisis*. Cambridge: Polity, 2014.
Bavinck, Herman. *Reformed Dogmatics*. Vol. 2. Grand Rapids: Baker Academic, 2004.
Beeke, Joel R., and Mark Jones. *A Puritan Theology: Doctrine for Life*. Grand Rapids: Reformation Heritage, 2012.
Berkouwer, G. C. *Man: The Image of God*. Grand Rapids: Eerdmans, 1962.
Berman, Harold J. *Law and Revolution*. Vol. 2, *The Impact of the Protestant Reformations on the Western Legal Traditions*. Cambridge, MA: Harvard University Press, 2003.
Blocher, Henri. "Le contexte européen de notre théologie." *Hokhma* 98 (2010) 9–10.
Bonney, Richard, and D. J. B. Trim, eds. *Persecution and Pluralism: Calvinists and Religious Minorities in Early Modern Europe, 1550–1700*. Frankfurt: Lang, 2006.
Boot, Joseph. *The Mission of God: A Manifesto of Hope*. St Catherines, ON: Freedom, 2014.
Bosch, David. *Transforming Mission: Paradigm Shifts in Theology of Mission*. New York: Orbis, 1998.
Bouyer, Louis. *The Spirit and Forms of Protestantism*. London: Collins, 1956.
Bury, John B. *A History of the Freedom of Thought*. New York: Holt, 1913.
Bruce, Steve. *Secularization: In Defense of an Unfashionable Theory*. Oxford: Oxford University Press, 2011.
Calvin, John. *Institutes of the Christian Religion*. London: SCM, 1960.
Carson, Donald A. *The Intolerance of Tolerance*. Grand Rapids: Eerdmans, 2012.
Chalmers, Stuart P. *Conscience in Context: Historical and Existential Perspectives*. Bern: Lang, 2014.
Coornhert, Dirck V. *Synod on the Freedom of Conscience: A Thorough Examination during the Gathering Held in the Year 1582 in the City of Freetown*. Translated by Gerrit Voogt. Amsterdam: Amsterdam University Press, 2008.
Cottret, Bernard. "La tolérance et la liberté de conscience à l'épreuve (1685–1688)." In *La liberté de conscience: XVIe–XVIIe siècles*, by Hans R. Guggisberg et al., 269–76. Geneva: Droz, 1991.
Eglinton, James, and George Harinck. *Neo-Calvinism and the French Revolution*. London: Bloomsbury T. & T. Clark, 2014.
Frame, John M. *Systematic Theology*. Phillipsburg, NJ: Presbyterian and Reformed, 2013.
Fromm, Erich. *Marx's Concept of Man*. New York: Ungar, 1961.
George, Robert P. *Conscience and Its Enemies: Confronting the Dogmas of Liberal Secularism*. 2nd ed. Wilmington, DE: ISI, 2016.
Gregory, Brad S. *The Unintended Reformation: How a Religious Revolution Secularized Society*. Cambridge, MA: Belknap, 2012.
Groen van Prinsterer, Guillaume. *Christian Political Action in an Age of Revolution*. Translated by Colin Wright. Aalten, Netherlands: Wordbridge, 2015.
Guggisberg, Hans R., et al. *La liberté de conscience: XVIe–XVIIe siècles*. Geneva: Droz, 1991.

Helm, Paul. "Rutherford and the Limits of Toleration." In *Tolerance and Truth: The Spirit of the Age or the Spirit of God?*, edited by Angus Morrison, 57–74. Edinburgh: Rutherford House, 2007.
Johnstone, Brian V. "Conscience and Error." In *Conscience*, edited by Charles E. Curran, 163–74. New York: Paulist, 2004.
Kirk, Kenneth E. *Conscience and Its Problems*. London: Longmans, Green, 1936.
Kuyper, Abraham. *Lectures on Calvinism*. 1931. Repr., Grand Rapids: Eerdmans, 1961.
Labrousse, Elisabeth. *Pierre Bayle*. 2 vols. The Hague: Nijhoff, 1963.
Lecler, Joseph. *Histoire de la tolérance au siècle de la Réforme*. Paris: Editions Montaigne, 1955. ET, *Toleration and the Reformation*. London: Longmans, Green, 1960.
———. "Liberté de conscience, origines et sens divers de l'expression." *Recherches de Science Religieuse* 45 (1966) 370–406.
Lewis, C. S. *The Voyage of the Dawn Treader*. 1952. Repr., London: Grafton, 2002.
Lohse, Bernhard. "Conscience and Authority in Luther." In *Luther and the Dawn of the Modern Era*, edited by Heiko Oberman, 158–83. Leiden: Brill, 1974.
Lull, Timothy F., ed. *Martin Luther's Basic Theological Writings*. Minneapolis: Fortress, 1989.
MacIntyre, Alasdair. *After Virtue: A Study in Moral Theory*. London: Duckworth, 1985.
Maclure, Jocelyn, and Charles Taylor. *Secularism and Freedom of Conscience*. Cambridge, MA: Harvard University Press, 2011.
Marx, Karl. Preface to *A Contribution to the Critique of Political Economy*. Moscow: Progress, 1993.
McGrath, Alister. *The Twilight of Atheism: The Rise and Fall of Disbelief in the Modern World*. London: Random House, 2004.
Melanchthon, Philip. *Commonplaces: Loci Communes*. 1521. St Louis: Concordia, 2014.
Murdoch, Iris. *The Sovereignty of the Good*. London: Routledge, 1970.
Murdoch, Jim. *Freedom of Thought, Conscience and Religion: A Guide to the Implementation of Article 9 of the European Convention of Human Rights*. Strasbourg: Council of Europe, 2007.
Murray, John. *The Epistle to Romans*. Grand Rapids: Eerdmans, 1965.
Murray, John C. *The Problem of Religious Freedom. On the Problems of Conscience and Authority concerning Church and State*. London: Chapman, 1965.
O'Rourke, K. C. *John Stuart Mill and Freedom of Expression*. London: Routledge, 2001.
Packer, James I. *Among God's Giants: The Puritan Vision of the Christian Life*. Eastbourne, UK: Kingsway, 1991.
Padura, Leonardo. *The Man Who Loved Dogs*. London: Bitter Lemon, 2013.
Pelikan, Jaroslav. *The Riddle of Roman Catholicism*. New York: Abingdon, 1959.
Pera, Marcello. *Why We Should Call Ourselves Christians: The Religious Roots of Free Societies*. New York: Encounter, 2008.
Pinckaers, Servais. *The Sources of Christian Ethics*. Edinburgh: T. & T. Clark, 2001.
Pierce, C. A. *Conscience in the New Testament*. London: SCM, 1958.
Popper, Karl. *The Open Society and its Enemies*. 2 vols. London: Routledge, 2002.
Ryle, Gilbert. *The Concept of Mind*. 1949. Repr., London: Routledge, 2009.
Siedentop, Larry. *Inventing the Individual: The Origins of Western Liberalism*. London: Penguin, 2015.
Sire, James W. *The Universe Next Door: A Basic World-view Catalog*. Downers Grove, IL: InterVarsity, 1977.
Taylor, Charles. *A Secular Age*. Cambridge, MA: Harvard University Press, 2007.

———. *Sources of the Self: The Making of Modern Identity*. Cambridge, MA: Harvard University Press, 1989.

———. "Why We Need a Radical Redefinition of Secularism." In *The Power of Religion in the Public Sphere*, edited by Eduardo Mendieta and Jonathan Vanantwerpen, 34–59. New York: Columbia University Press, 2011.

Tillich, Paul. *The Protestant Era*. Chicago: University of Chicago Press, 1957.

Turchetti, Mario. "La liberté de conscience et l'autorité du magistrat au lendemain de la Révocation." In *La liberté de conscience: XVIe–XVIIe siècles*, by Hans R. Guggisberg et al., 289–367. Geneva: Droz, 1991.

Trevor-Roper, Hugh. *The Crisis of the Seventeenth Century: Religion, the Reformation, and Social Change*. Indianapolis: Liberty Fund, 1967.

Troeltsch, Ernst. *Protestantism and Progress: A Historical Study of the Relation of Protestantism to the Modern World*. New ed. Eugene, OR: Wipf and Stock, 1999.

Warfield, Benjamin B. "'Miserable-sinner Christianity' in the Hands of the Rationalists." In *Works*, 7:113–301. 1931. Repr., Grand Rapids: Baker, 1981.

Wells, Paul. "Dieu et la conscience de l'homme." In *En tout occasion favorable ou non: Positions et propositions évangélique*. Aix-en-Provence: Kerygma, 2014.

Wilson, Bryan R. *Religion in Sociological Perspective*. Oxford: Oxford University Press, 1982.

Yancey, George. *Hostile Environment: Understanding and Responding to Anti-Christian Bias*. Downers Grove, IL: InterVarsity, 2015.

Zachman, Randall C. *The Assurance of Faith. Conscience in the Theology of Martin Luther and John Calvin*. Louisville: Westminster John Knox Press, 2005.

Zweig, Stefan. *The Right to Heresy: Castellio against Calvin*. New York: Viking, 1936.

www.ingramcontent.com/pod-product-compliance
Lightning Source LLC
Chambersburg PA
CBHW070938240426
43667CB00036B/2306